Between Centre and Locality

INSTITUTE OF LOCAL GOVERNMENT STUDIES

Approaches in Public Policy
Edited by Steve Leach and John Stewart

Local Government: The Conditions of Local Choice
John Stewart

Between Centre and Locality:
The Politics of Public Policy
Stewart Ranson, George Jones and Kieron Walsh

Between Centre and Locality

The Politics of Public Policy

Edited by

STEWART RANSON
Institute of Local Government Studies,
University of Birmingham

GEORGE JONES
London School of Economics and Political Science

and

KIERON WALSH
Institute of Local Government Studies,
University of Birmingham

For the
Institute of Local Government Studies
University of Birmingham

GEORGE ALLEN & UNWIN
London   Boston   Sydney

George Allen & Unwin (Publishers) Ltd,
40 Museum Street, London WC1A 1LU, UK

Allen & Unwin, Inc.,
9 Winchester Terrace, Winchester, Mass. 01890, USA

George Allen & Unwin (Publishers) Ltd,
Park Lane, Hemel Hempstead, Herts HP2 4TE, UK

George Allen & Unwin Australia Pty Ltd,
8 Napier Street, North Sydney, NSW 2060, Australia

First published in 1985

British Library Cataloguing in Publication Data

Between centre and locality: the politics of public policy.—(Institute of Local
Government Studies; 2)
1. Local government—Great Britain—State supervision
I. Ranson, Stewart   II. Jones, G. W. (George William)
III. Walsh, Kieron   IV. Series
354.4108'3   JS311
ISBN 0-04-352116-9

14072100

Library of Congress Cataloging in Publication Data

Main entry under title:
    Between centre and locality.
'For the Institute of Local Government Studies, University of Birmingham'
Includes bibliographies and index.
1. Local government—Great Britain. 2. Decentralization in government – Great
Britain. 3. Great Britain—Politics and government—1979–
I. Ranson, Stewart.   II. Jones George W.
III. Walsh, Kieron.   IV. University of Birmingham. Institute of Local
Government Studies.
JS3137.B44 1985   352.041   84-28425
ISBN 0-04-352116-9 (alk. paper)

Set in 10 on 11 point Times by Fotographics (Bedford) Ltd
and printed and bound in Great Britain by
Biddles Ltd, Guildford and King's Lynn

To George Hodgkinson

Mayor of Coventry 1945, the quincentenary
of the city's local charter

Contents

Preface

There is a crisis in relations between central and local government. There have been problems since at least the mid-1970s when the Layfield Committee of Inquiry explored the difficulties of financing local government and recognized that those difficulties reflected fundamental issues of control and accountability between central and local government.

The Institute of Local Government Studies has made the issue of the relations between government and the local authorities central to its research and teaching since the 1970s. John Stewart sat on the Layfield Committee from 1974 to 1976 and soon began writing about the instruments, language and organization of central and local government relationships. Research soon followed. The Institute received two major SSRC research grants to examine, on the one hand, the impact of grant characteristics upon local authority decision-making and, on the other, changing procedures of policy planning in transportation, education and the inner cities.

This volume is intended to explore the changing patterns of control between central and local government across a wide range of policy sectors. Yet as readers progress from finance through housing, education, health, police, we believe what emerges is a profound sense of the restructuring of the relations between the state and society.

We would like to thank John Stewart, as always, for his persistent challenge and support. We also thank our patient secretaries, Lorna Crane, Lynne Dixon, Diana Myers and Miss Bucher, for their skilful endeavours.

Introduction:
Understanding the Crisis

STEWART RANSON and KIERON WALSH

Relations between central and local government have been problematic since the mid-1970s and are now in crisis. A Committee of Inquiry on Local Government Finance (Layfield Committee), reporting in 1976, conceived the problem of finance as resulting from confused relations between the tiers of government. The Central Policy Review Staff (1977) made a study of the relations between central government and local authorities, while academics began to direct attention to the growing problems of intergovernmental relations. Stewart (1977) defined the dilemma of central–local relations as deriving from: uncertainty or ambiguity about respective *roles*; poor *communications*; *organizational* mismatch; and difficulties of random fragmented *instruments*. The 'mechanisms' for relating centre and locality were inappropriate and confused. The Layfield Committee concluded that 'the result of the prevailing confusion has been that few people if any know where the real responsibility rests for decisions about local government services and the money to be spent on them' (Layfield Report, 1976, p. 46). The solution, the Committee believed, was to make clearer the respective responsibilities and accountability of the centre and locality.

As the 1980s approached the terms of the discussion about the problem of central–local relations began to change. The debate shifted from issues of confusion to sharper ones of control and direction. The problems of managing the economic crisis have intensified the debate about control and the distribution of power and functions between the tiers of government. New processes and instruments of control have been introduced, and further controls are proposed which would transform fundamentally the unwritten constitutional convention of distributed power within a unitary state. By removing the historic right of local authorities to set the level of their own local tax, the centre will have finally eroded any formal independent power base: a unitary state will shift perceptibly into a centralized state (cf. Stewart, 1983; Jones and Stewart, 1983; Jones *et al.*, 1983).

The problem of central–local relations had indeed been understood by the Layfield Committee as reflecting fundamental questions of control and accountability. The Committee recognized that only a fundamental recasting of the centre–local relationship would resolve these questions and argued for a solution based upon a considerable strengthening of local accountability. The Committee, however, grasped that these problems of control and accountability themselves represented more lasting social, economic and political concerns – and that 'underlying all these were the human and social considerations which are the reasons for local government' (Layfield Report, 1976, p. xxiv). Layfield suggested the economic and social foundations of the crisis of government, although such an analysis was necessarily beyond its remit.

The discussion of the changes in intergovernmental relations in this book will illuminate much of the changing structure of political power in government and state. But consideration of the changing patterns of relations in a wide range of service and policy sectors – inner cities, social services, education and health – and over key policy issues such as race and employment reveals that fundamental beliefs and values about the role of government within the state are also being transformed. Indeed, the changing structure of power is the instrument of changed purposes for the state and thus of altered economic and social relations in society. The reworking of relations between levels of government throughout the social services is a redefining of need and welfare, of citizenship and fraternity, and of place and horizons (cf. Heald, 1983; Glennerster, 1983; Habermas, 1983).

The structuring of political power and values expressed in government has changed over time in response to the demands and circumstances of particular historical periods. For much of the postwar period political power in Britain was distributed among a number of institutions and largely decentralized and devolved to local communities as in the government of education, social services and housing. This organizing of task and power acted as a vehicle for more widely held commitments and purposes. The state through social reform could gently transform economy and society: a new world could be formed out of the remnants of the old. Employment could be generated to allow individuals to participate in the creation and sharing of wealth and thus enjoy a more independent life: services would be provided for the poor and disadvantaged, and there would be greater equality of opportunity. As Gellner (1983) recently argued, the modernizing of both economy and society has been interrelated and mediated by the state. The modern, complex division of labour demanded a more mobile, interconnected society and thus one which had to erase deep divisions of class and culture. It fell to the state to assume the creative role of forging a more integrated and more egalitarian society.

This distinctive formation was, as the Centre for Contemporary Cultural Studies (CCCS) (1978) and Heald (1983) have described, a 'social democratic' state, involving 'a commitment to full employment, a willingness to use industrial intervention, and support for the public services characteristic of the welfare state ... a conviction that beneficial state action was possible in the economic and social sphere' (Heald, 1983, p. 3). This form of the state depended upon a distinctive structuring of government, and of local government in particular. Local government played the crucial part in the structure of the social democratic state because it involved the devolution of power in society and the provision of services to enhance human welfare.

The postwar social democratic state, and the beliefs about power, economy and the development of human welfare which it embodied, now face a crisis caused by the dramatic transformation in the economy and by the changing balance of social forces and ideology in society. The Middle East war and the resulting oil crisis precipitated a recession in the Western economies more severe than anything experienced since the 1930s. Economic changes were important but were overshadowed by even more significant structural changes in employment. The revolution in the nature of work created by the new technologies seems finally to be emerging. Massey and Meegan (1982) have produced a powerful account of the mechanisms of industrial intensification, rationalization and technical innovation which explain the anatomy of job loss. The shedding of surplus labour through the restructuring of employment is already beginning to raise fundamental social and political questions about preparation for and access to work, and about dependence upon the state and thus personal identity, dignity and citizenship. These cyclical and structural changes in the economy parallel and reinforce fundamental changes in society: social trends show an ageing society, more fragmented family patterns, often reflecting the changing relations between men and women; a multi-cultural society striving for more equality of opportunity; boredom as well as anxiety and alienation; and a more politicized world as differences about ways of resolving economic and social problems become sharpened.

This book seeks to develop understanding and analysis of the current restructuring of intergovernmental relations which have now entered a new and critical phase. We shall argue that we can only fully understand the present crisis when we begin to explore more fully, as Layfield indicated, the interconnections between the mechanisms of government and the wider economic and social structure.

The organizing of political power within the state we propose will typically reflect deeper beliefs about the form that economic and social relations should take in civil society. The role that the government adopts in relation to the management of the economy will demonstrate its conception of the appropriate form of wealth production or of the ownership of property. Most significantly, the structures of government embody an understanding of citizenship, a conception of individual needs and capacities as well as the proper relationship they should have – and the contribution they can make – to the polity.

We have, as Habermas (1976) has proposed, to grasp the organizing principles which have informed the restructuring of state and society. These principles governing the organization of political power and the distribution of social values have, we argue, changed over time during the postwar period. We first describe the phases of development of the postwar British state before proceeding to analyse how the contributions of the book contribute to our understanding of the present crisis.

FORMATIONS OF THE POST-WAR STATE

Table 1   *Periodizing the Postwar State*

State formation	Centre–local relations	Economy	Society
Welfare state settlement (1943–55) 1948	Steering 'partnership'	Take-off	Paternalism
Social democratic state (1956–69) 1968	Devolved	Growth	Community participation
Corporate state (1970–8) 1976	Centralization	Downturn	Elite determination
'Liberal' (nightwatchman) state (1979–84) 1984	Hierarchies and markets	Decline	Individualism

There have been four distinctive forms of the postwar British state: the initial postwar settlement created a welfare state which by the

1960s had developed into a social democratic state. The problems of managing the economy in the 1970s and 1980s have led to the development, first, of a corporate, and then a liberal state. These forms are discussed below in terms of three dimensions: economy, society and the organizing of central–local government relations. The task of the idealizing of periods is to accentuate the distinctive interdependencies of power, values and organization within the state (see Table 1).

THE WELFARE STATE SETTLEMENT: 1943–55

Rawls's work on justice has recently revived philosophical interest in the idea of a social contract as shaping duties and rights within social institutions. It is rarely believed to be something a society would ever experience in practice. Yet the notion of a social concordat or contract was arguably enacted during and after the war, as the writings of Middlemas (1979) and Beer (1965) vividly describe.

The war effort was grounded in a concordat between the state, labour and capital. Bevin had 'asked belligerently why the working class should lend the government money for the war with no guarantee of employment or improvement after'.[1] Bullock (1960, p. 137), in his biography of the great labour leader, concluded that 'the organised working class represented by the trade unions was for the first time brought into a position of partnership in the national enterprise of war – a partnership on equal not inferior terms, as in the First World War, and one from which it has never since been dislodged as it was after 1918'. Middlemas argues that the basis of the War Cabinet's contractual thinking lay in the urgent priority of ensuring production and a supply of labour. There developed, however, as much a contract for reform as for production. The political contract for military purposes raised expectations 'that the country would be better placed after the war'. Increasingly radical expectations that the state would initiate programmes of reform and reconstruction developed. Middlemas writes:

> when more open debate began about the amelioration of poverty, unemployment and unfair distribution of wealth, it took place on the basis of two or three years' experience of state activity which had *already* profoundly changed the social relationship between classes. It was not the party which benefited, but the image of government; government which had

run fairly and efficiently ... Slowly but inevitably, the state
came to be seen as something vaster and more beneficent than
the political parties under whose temporary management it
rested, as the real guarantor of reform and reconstruction which
parties could do no more than pledge themselves to fulfil.
(Middlemas, 1979, pp. 273–4)

The springboard for such interventionist state policies would be
conceptions of economic management and planning derived from
Keynes. Fiscal policy could be used to stimulate demand and
investment as a stable basis for future employment and welfare
reform.

If Keynes provided the master economic design, then Beveridge
shaped the blueprint for the welfare state. His Reconstruction
Committee during the war laid the plans for a system of social
security, health insurance and unemployment benefit that would
ensure the relief of poverty. The pattern of social reform would
also embrace town and country planning, the provision of
educational opportunity, of housing and of social services: 'by
1944 ... there could be no ignoring the great radical swing in
public opinion, anti-fascist, libertarian, egalitarian, even utopian,
blending belief in military victory with reform, equality of
sacrifice with faith in models derived from Roosevelt's New Deal
or Russia's socialist appearance' (Middlemas, 1979, p. 290).

Robson (1976) discusses the principles that were to underlie the
new welfare state and welfare society's *universalism* of provision
with services free for all on the basis of need, which was essential if
those in receipt of benefit were not to be stigmatized and social
integration in society impaired; *equality* of opportunity to realize
ability and to achieve position and status regardless of wealth or
property; and *efficiency*, the Webbs' and the Fabian Society's
concern for administrative efficiency in the formulation of policy
and the delivery of service should underpin the welfare state.
Halsey (1978) describes as *fraternity* the ideal of social institutions
working to achieve common citizenship within a community that
shares the material conditions necessary for liberty as well as
equality. Tawney's principles should underpin the fraternal
welfare society: 'social institutions –property rights, and the
organisations of industry, and the system of public health and
education – should be planned, as far as possible, to emphasise
and strengthen, not the class differences which divide but the
common humanity which unites them' (in Halsey, 1978, p. 165).
The early concerns of the welfare state were, perhaps necessarily,
the creation of an institutional framework for economic and social

reconstruction. The stress was upon the administration and provision of services *for* members of society in need. There was, therefore, a paternalistic and centralizing cast in the initial constituting of the welfare state: the state would provide for the needs of civil society.

Such concerns and assumptions were reflected in the structuring of government in the postwar welfare state. Decision-making was concentrated at the centre. Economic controls continued after the war over wages, prices and investment policies, in order to facilitate economic growth that would lay the basis for full employment. A programme of nationalization prepared to take into public ownership those industries that would become the infrastructure of the welfare state economy. When the Conservative Party assumed office in 1951, it accepted in principle a commitment to preserve state ownership of coal, railways and the Bank, to central indicative planning and to the welfare state (cf. Middlemas, 1979, p. 418).

The balance of influence between central and local government embodied and facilitated the wider state-structuring of power and values. The centre operated tight controls over finance and policy initiatives. Martlew, in reviewing the development of financial relations between centre and locality, describes the framework of early postwar controls:

> after 1945 then long term pressure for increasing state intervention predominated, and this was reflected in the Local Government Act of 1948 which established the structure of central–local financial relations for the next ten years ... increasing use was made of specific grants. Though a large proportion of these grants were distributed according to units of service or demand, there were also many percentage grants dependent upon local spending decisions ... which were consequently subject to close central scrutiny and influence. (Martlew, 1983, p. 139)

In education, for example, there was sufficient scope for the ministry to exercise fairly detailed control over the spending decisions of individual local education authorities.

THE SOCAL DEMOCRATIC STATE

In the 1960s some of the more radical ideas of the wartime 'contract to reform' came to the fore. They were facilitated by a period of economic growth and development. Mawson (1983) and Rothwell (1982) have described the central characteristics of the economy during this period. To the mid-1960s there was growth in GDP that comprised development in both manufacturing and service sectors, and increased investment led to the generation of new employment opportunities. New industries began to emerge as inventions and innovations of the 1930s in electronics, motor vehicles, aircraft and other fields were exploited. New markets began to arise, encouraging a stress upon product change and the introduction of new products. The end of the 1960s was to become a period of consolidation for the economy. It was a period of capital intensification, industrial concentration and organizational innovation.

With full employment already achieved, indeed taken for granted, and the welfare and social security elements of the welfare state gradually being accomplished, governments felt confident in a climate of economic growth to begin expanding the services which would, they believed, attack inequalities of the class structure more directly. Class division was seen as impeding economic progress as much as it offended the commitment to a just society. It was thus a period to realize more completely T. H. Marshall's analysis that the victories of civil and political rights starting from the eighteenth century were completed by the most important principle of the social democratic state – the rights of citizenship, the sharing of a common dignity, self-respect, culture and status within the community.

Citizenship presupposes equality of opportunity and influence. The expansion of education and community government were thus central to the development of citizenship within the social democratic state. Education was the key arm of public policy-making at this time. Greatly enhanced life chances through education would, it was hoped, provide the human capital to fuel economic growth, while increased equality of opportunity would support the disadvantaged and help to undermine the constraints of class domination, so facilitating a fairer and more open society. The organizing principle of education during this period was thus upon personal development, on extending opportunity, raising expectations and broadening horizons. These were considerable advances, though still guided by a limited, meritocratic vision rather than equality of material conditions and social outcomes (cf. Halsey, 1978; CCCS, 1978).

Citizenship within a democratic state implies a sharing in the decision-taking processes of government. It implies a development of what Stewart has called community government decentralizing participation to allow greater local influence upon policy formation, decision-making and implementation:

> decentralisation is an aid to social learning about complex social problems in so far as it points to a variety of responses to differing problems . . . The aim must be to create schools, old people's homes, social work teams etc. as self-governing organisations within the parameters of the [local] authority. (Stewart, 1977a, p. 16)

During the 1960s a number of reports encouraged the involvement of local communities: the Skeffington Report on physical planning and the Seebohm Report on the personal social services, both in 1967, and the Weaver Report in 1968 on education.

This greater stress within the social democratic state upon the needs and rights of individuals and communities strengthened the role of local government within the state. Local authorities, with their potential for independent decision-making, clearly represented the devolution of power which was part of the social democratic spectrum of values. But it was as much the purposes of government in this period which determined the structuring of power as values. The commitment to education and new forms of planning community services required the locus of decision-making to be close to the point of action. Task and purposes shaped the organizational arrangements of government. The key actors in the network of government became local professionals rather than central administrators.

The social democratic state led to a period of extraordinary growth in expenditure on services. Changes to the system of central–local financial relations operated to encourage growth in expenditure. Martlew shows how in the Local Government Act 1966 the introduction of domestic rate relief was used as a mechanism for financing increased local spending. The centre also allowed interim increase orders to support the expansion of services as costs began to rise: 'thus, a conscious decision was taken to increase progressively the proportion of expenditure met from grants as the only way to meet higher local spending' (Martlew, 1983, p. 141).

Assumptions of growth, Stewart (1980, p. 15) has proposed, were deeply entrenched in the decision processes within and between central and local government: 'the allocation of the increment of growth came to be seen as the key decision'. These bids reflected aspirations for the growth of service within the public sector. Dunleavy and Rhodes (1983) have argued that such

bargaining was the 'normal' style of central–local relations during
this period. Bargaining reflected the belief of the time that the most
appropriate mode of intergovernmental relations was that of
consultation between 'partners'. Negotiations took place between
the partners within a framework of consensus about the broad
purposes of government.

THE CORPORATE STATE

The oil crisis precipitated an economic crisis in the Western
capitalist economies. The juxtaposition of inflation and declining
output produced the new dilemma of 'stagflation', where fiscal
policies designed to counter a stagnant economy reinforce the
disease of inflation. Yet, as Mawson (1983) and Rothwell (1982)
record, it was also a period of growing investment and automation.
Industrial concentration began to accelerate, while the
rationalization of processes and organizational structures grew
apace. There was a steady rise in unemployment and redundancies
caused by decline in manufacturing employment began to
increase.

Habermas (1976) has argued that the deepening economic crises
of the 1970s created 'steering problems' for the state. To maintain
control and integration the state must respond by progressively
extending its boundaries, its tentacles of political leverage into the
economic and social subsystems. Offe (1975) takes the argument
further. The state, in order to maintain its functions of system
integration, is increasingly driven to develop new forms of intervention. The minimalist role of central control of overall aggregate
resources is increasingly inadequate, and the state is constrained to
adopt a productive mode to sustain and develop the system's
economic infrastructure, progressively intervening in 'education
skills, technological change, control over raw materials, health,
transportation, housing, the structure of cities, physical environment, energy and communication services'. This extension of
steering capacity presupposes the emergence of new modes of
rational planning and new knowledge about services and policies.

The new mode of intervention calls for 'stricter controls of
objectives, outputs and outcomes by such techniques as program
budgeting, cost–benefit analysis and social indicators' (ibid.,
pp. 141–2). To ensure system maintenance and development of
infrastructures the state is driven into progressively detailed
planning and production of economic and public service
activities.

The state moves from a supportive to a directive role in the economy. Pahl (1977) and Winkler (1977) have described the processes of concentration and rationalization which take place within this corporate state. The corporate state seeks to impose four principles upon economy and society: *unity*, through the collaboration and co-operation of capital and labour; *order*, to achieve stability and discipline in industrial relations; *nationalism*, to reinforce indigenous interests; and *pragmatism* of ends and purposes, to ensure efficiency. Production replaces consumption as the important preoccupation of the state, while efficiency becomes the overriding priority above the previous social democratic goals of equality and social justice. Economic pragmatism and efficiency are best facilitated by technocratic rational planning within more disciplined, bureaucratic organizational forms.

Relations between central and local government reflected the general restructuring towards a corporate state. From the early 1970s models of rational planning (PPBS, PAR) were applied to key policy sectors to determine objectives, analyse options and programme resources for the decade ahead. Formalized central–local policy planning systems were developed in a number of sectors including transportation, inner city partnerships and housing investment programmes.

Rational planning was being harnessed to the design of enhancing central control. Martlew (1983) analyses the effective implementation of the new strategies of control within the planning of public expenditure (PESC), reorienting its operation to contract public spending and particularly that of local government: cash limits became the first instrument of control.

The political means of implementing the rational policy planning of the corporate state was co-optation and consultation of national representatives of the interests of capital, labour and local government. The Labour government of 1974 once more talked explicitly about a 'social contract' with the trade unions, while important consultative machinery was created to mediate the relations between central and local government – the Consultative Council on Local Government Finance, together with its panoply of policy sector steering groups, which collectively forecast the spending needs and limits for local authorities and their services. Dunleavy and Rhodes (1983, p. 124) analyse effectively this corporate phase of central–local relations, in which 'a few powerful outside interests are extensively co-opted into closed relations with central government, taking on a dual role representing their members to government and of controlling their members on behalf of government'. They describe the effect of this corporate government planning as facilitating a decisive shift from service-oriented concerns to interests of financial control. Local government was being co-opted by the centre to legitimate its own diminishing scale and status.

The corporate state developed to meet the exigencies of a declining economy: pragmatism and efficiency were the ends, rationalization and bureaucracy the means. Local government which had been the locus of services for the community and the needs of individuals was to be contracted to reflect financial constraints and its services, wherever possible, restructured to facilitate the regeneration of the economy.

THE 'LIBERAL' (NIGHTWATCHMAN) STATE

The beginning of the 1980s saw an international slump that generated declining profitability, the closure of factories and rundown of investment. Industrial restructuring involved intensification and rationalization of operations more than the widespread introduction of new technology, although it was growing. Unemployment began to accelerate towards 2 million and beyond, with some experts (cf. Daniels, 1979–80) commenting that official figures severely underestimated real levels of unemployment. Mawson (1983, p. 8) states that 'essentially this phase expressed the geography of deindustrialization; those regions with an important share of employment in the service sector i.e. the South East, East Anglia and the South West, fared much better'. The persistence of inflation, however, led in 1976 to the introduction of alternative strategies for managing the economy, and fiscal policy in particular. Effective financial planning required 'sound money' and targets were now established for money supply and for the public sector borrowing requirement (PSBR). 1976 was also the year in which cash limits were introduced to control the expenditure of both central and local government. The seeds of change were being sown within the corporate state.

The challenge which these ideas implied for the dominant economic paradigm of Keynesian demand management was cemented by the election of a radical Conservative government in 1979. A new economic orthodoxy of monetarism would now prevail. The strategy it proposed for controlling inflation and thus protecting investment and property values was tight control of the money supply. Inflation had also been caused supposedly by the profligate expansion of public services beyond the financial means of the state, thus burdening the public sector borrowing requirement and draining resources from profitable private sector investment. A free market would encourage more stringent and effective deployment of resources. Heald describes this most vigorous attack upon postwar welfare and social democratic assumptions:

> as part of the rolling back of the state in favour of the market some of the underlying premises of the social democratic state were challenged. There began unprecedented questioning of public provision in areas such as housing and health which have been central pillars of the welfare state. Public intervention in industry was reduced with the nationalised industries being the subject of extensive privatised schemes. The emphasis which the 1979 Conservative Government placed upon restoring the operation of the free market stands in vivid contrast to the policies of its post war Conservative predecessors. (Heald, 1983, p. 3)

The new economic perspectives reflected a new spectrum of values – of freedom rather than equality, individualism rather than community, efficiency rather than justice. It also reflected an underlying conception of the social order, a return to Victorian values of 'place', security and authority, but also to a regime of law and order, patriarchalism, and authoritarian control of social and racial deviance (cf. Samuel, 1983; Hall and Jacques, 1983; Heald, 1983). The monetarist state would withdraw from the marketplace but would exercise stronger social control. It was the return of Bentham's minimal state, which protects private property but develops prisons and the panopticon to control misfits.

This book focuses upon the transition of power and values from the corporate to the neo-liberal state. The movement is from the distribution and decentralizing of power to the concentration of power; from the planning of services to the principle of market determination; and from the rights of citizenship to the extension of consumer rights.

The contributions to the book examine the struggles between central and local government over public policy and over the instruments and institutions which shape policy. The story which unfolds is of an attempt to change the relations between central and local government but also, more fundamentally, the relations between state and society by contracting the public sector and by rewriting the terms of the postwar 'social contract'.

Many of the chapters describe the contraction of public spending and the attempt to shift ownership and control of public services to private or voluntary organizations. The chapters by Raine and Gibson analyse the cuts in local government spending, while Walsh discusses the even faster decline of public sector employment, pointing out that the focus of the cuts and redundancies – in construction, non-teaching staff, transport and refuse collection – have been manual workers whose jobs are poorly protected in law and more susceptible to privatization.

The chapters on health, social services, transportation and housing describe the policies of contracting service provision. In housing the cuts have been particularly severe: expenditure on housing was planned to drop by 48 per cent and accounted for three-quarters of all public expenditure savings between 1980 and 1984.

The cuts have been designed to complement the government's main strategy of privatizing public services. Karn describes the policy of 'privatizing the existing council stock with sales to individual owners', while Stoten notes the 'directives about privatization and contracting out of laundry and domestic services' in the health service. Flynn's chapter is devoted to analysing the 'specific commitment ... to saving money by transferring work from the allegedly inefficient direct labour organizations (DLOs) to the private construction sector which was said to be 30 per cent more efficient'. The ideological shift, argue Webb and Wistow in their chapter on the social services, has required a diminishing contribution from the state to service provision and the pursuit of values surrounding the family, private enterprise and self-help. In some areas, for example, residential care for the elderly could now, they believe, 'be left entirely to the private sector'. These changes, argue Webb and Wistow, represent a real, perhaps conclusive reversal of postwar trends in social policy. Where the ideology cannot achieve a shift in control, it redefines the purposes and principles of operation. Lomas and Skelcher, in their chapters, describe the attempts of government and the courts to constrain public transport to operate according to the principles of private sector business rather than as a public service.

The intention to roll back the frontiers of the state and to transfer as much of the public sector as possible to private ownership is a significant change. Yet there are contributions to this book which suggest that it is part of a larger restructuring of the relations between state and society. The 'social contract' settled after the war tacitly established a set of interlocking economic, social and political conditions which the state would underwrite: full employment, the alleviation of poverty, equality of opportunity and a common citizenship within the polity. By transforming an outmoded and unjust social structure, the state would become an instrument of social and political reform. Now in a world of contraction and economic restructuring the state is intervening to control and reproduce rather than to reform the social structure. Realism, place and duties now replace the earlier messages of rights and opportunities. The institutions of education and the police have become central to the new state strategy. The service which formerly had concentrated upon extending young people's horizons is now concerned to reduce them. Ranson's chapter analyses the differentiating of opportunities and expectations so as to tighten the bond between educational experiences and expectations of the labour market. If education is being restructured to become the longer-term institution of social regulation, then the police force is being given powers to strengthen its immediate control over the community. Bridges's chapter discusses the recent legislation which will 'institutionalize vastly increased legal powers for the police over the citizen . . . and enhance local autonomy of the police and extend their influence over the community at large'. Civil liberties are being curtailed, while the changes are designed to 'reinforce social discipline'.

The organization of central and local government is being restructured to reflect the new economic and social order. In order to reduce the provision of public services and to discard the old social contract the government has had to impose increasingly centralized controls upon local authorities – the key agency of service provision in the previous periods of welfare and social democracy. Raine and Gibson describe the accelerating central control over local expenditure. The government in 1980 legislated to assess *individual* local authorities' need to spend. When this failed to constrain spending sufficiently to suit the government, new mechanisms – volume targets – were introduced with heavier penalties in the form of grant loss if authorities failed to meet their targets. But targets also failed to constrain a number of Conservative as well as Labour local authorities, and the government has now moved in the Rates Bill (1984) to eliminate the last loophole – the rates – and thus ensure the complete compliance of local authorities. It would mean the termination of an historic constitutional institution – an independent local government (cf. Stewart, 1983; Jones and Stewart, 1983; Jones *et al.*, 1983).

In order to contract the public sector and to transfer activity to private control the state has increasingly centralized and concentrated its power. Yet at the same time, the state has also decentralized initiative to the consumer by encouraging the creation of markets within the public sector. Flynn unravels the chosen strategy of privatizing DLOs through competition: once forced into the market-place, the intrinsic inefficiencies of DLOs would be exposed ensuring, so it was claimed, that local authorities in future contracted out to private firms. Karn describes the encouraging of a 'market economy in housing' as tenants are persuaded to purchase their own council houses. In education schools are required to publish examination results, so that parents can judge performance before identifying a school of their choice.

The upshot of these twin strategies of centralization and decentralization, of hierarchies and markets, is to undermine the strategic planning capacity of the local authority. In housing, social services, education and the management of local workforces the capacity of local authorities to provide services in response to local needs and demands is being eroded. As Webb and Wistow comment, 'these developments do mean that local authorities are being systematically by-passed and that their ability to exercise a strategic influence over local services is declining'.

What is being eroded is the distinctive role of postwar local government. Saunders's (1981, 1982) sophisticated analysis of the 'dual state' reveals a centre preoccupied with economic and investment priorities pursued typically through rational modes of corporate planning, while the locality is devoted more to social needs and priorities which are determined through the competitive modes of local politics. Where the centre has an eye to profit accumulation, the locality looks to the relief of need and the protection of citizenship rights.

The erosion of local authority autonomy, however, makes the locality an agent of the centre. More significantly, there is increasing uniformity of function between centre and locality. As Leach and Hinings show, local authorities are being encouraged, for example, in their policy-making for the inner city, to shift their concern from social to economic priorities. As the centre transforms local government into a dependent agent of economic policy the local social services – housing, education, social services and health – are redirected to maintaining and controlling the social order. The weakness of Saunders's model is that his ideal type lacks an historical dimension: what he was idealizing was a particular historical period in the development of the postwar state.

The centre has become increasingly interventionist, changing
procedures and institutions to ensure the effectiveness of centrally
determined policy. A number of chapters in the present book,
especially those by Raine, Gibson and Flynn, suggest that the
centre is prepared to change the rules of the game as frequently as is
necessary to ensure it gets its way. The problem with pursuing a
centralist strategy in a modern complex society is that the
centralization is bound to accelerate. The complexity of the
inherited legal and financial institutions (cf. Lomas and Gibson)
together with the complexity of task (cf. Hinings and Young)
implies that if the centre is to ensure control, it must continually be
driven to change rules, simplify policy tasks and concentrate
power. It must eliminate alternative centres of choice. As Stewart
argues, the dilemma of local choice is the possibility of policy
decisions reflecting local needs rather than central demands.

The continual changing of rules and institutions creates
necessarily unstable government. It makes for arbitrary government as ministers take powers which allow them to decide upon
local issues. Yet arbitrary government is presented as the
legitimate authority of a unitary state. Britain is not, however, as
the government would have us believe, a unitary state. There is, as
Kenneth Dyson has argued in his study of the concept of the state
as it has developed in Europe, no abstract, impersonal public
power expressed in a body of public law which acts to regulate and
control the actions of each member of the system. There is the
sovereignty of Parliament, not government, but sovereignty is not
unity. Within the law as it exists at any time local authorities are
free to act. They are creatures of statute, it is true, but statute makes
them free of central government as well as subordinating them.
The government acting in Parliament may change the law to
impose greater control, as the present Conservative government
has done to a greater extent than its predecessors, but it would be
wrong to claim that, in doing so, it is re-establishing a long-lost
unity. We inherit a peculiarly stateless situation. As Dyson says,
quoting for Ernest Barker: 'the state as such does not act in
England, a multitude of individual officials each separately and
severally act. There is a bundle of individual officials, each
exercising a degree of authority under the cognizance of the
Courts, but none of them, not even the Prime Minister wielding
the authority of the state.' The maze of individuals and institutions
reflect considerable internal differentiation within the state. The
fragmentation of the state can be understood as both the intended
and unintended attempt of generations to prevent the concentration of authority within the hands of the executive and to

ensure the effective dispersal of power. Actions that produced the desired results were more likely to be the result of bargaining than authority, for there have not been the mechanisms for authoritative control by one level of the state over another.

The postwar period saw attempts by successive governments to graft on to this differentiated state the possibility of it generating social reform and reconstruction. The state could transform and modernize the social structure. The creation of a 'social contract' between the state, capital and labour would protect the differentiation of power and interests, while maintaining social cohesion and the legitimation of authority.

This book charts the accelerating retreat from this ideal since the late 1970s. Yet as we witness, finally, the emergence of the post-industrial society with its wasteland of urban decay and unemployment there is an urgent need to review the relationship between the state and society, to recreate a social compact that permits economic development which is not at the expense of welfare, opportunities and the rights of local communities and their citizens.

NOTE: INTRODUCTION

1 See *Daily Herald*, 30 March 1940; quoted in Middlemas, 1979, p. 276.

REFERENCES: INTRODUCTION

Beer, S. (1965), *Modern British Politics* (London: Faber).

Bullock, A. L. C. (1960), *The Life and Times of Ernest Bevin* (London: Hodder & Stoughton), Vol. 2.

Central Policy Review Staff (1977), *Relations between Central Government and Local Authorities* (London: HMSO).

Centre for Contemporary Cultural Studies (CCCS) (1978), *Social Democracy, Education and the Crisis*, Occasional Paper SP No. 52 (Birmingham: CCCS, University of Birmingham).

Daniels, W. W. (1980), *House of Lords Select Committee, 1979–80* (London: HMSO), Vol. II.

Dunleavy, P., and Rhodes, R. A. W. (1983), 'Beyond Whitehall', in H. Drucker (ed.), *Developments in British Politics* (London: Macmillan), pp. 106–33.

Gellner, E. (1983), *Nations and Nationalism* (Oxford: Blackwell).

Glennerster, H. (ed.) (1983), *The Future of the Welfare State* (London: Heinemann).

Habermas, J. (1983), *Theories des Kommunikativen Handelas* (Frankfurt: Suhrkamp Verlag); reviewed by J. B. Thompson, *Times Literary Supplement*, 8 April 1983.

Habermas, J. (1976), *Legitimation Crisis* (London: Heinemann).

Hall, S., and Jacques, M. (1983), *The Politics of Thatcherism* (London: Lawrence & Wishart).

Halsey, A. H. (1978), *Change in British Society* (Oxford: Opus).

Heald, D. (1983a), *Public Expenditure* (London: Martin Robertson).

Held, D. (ed.) (1983), *States and Societies* (London: Martin Robertson).

Jones, G., and Stewart, J. D. (1983), *The Case for Local Government* (London: Allen & Unwin).

Jones, G., Stewart, J. D., and Travers, T. (1983), 'Rate control: the threat to local government', *Local Government Chronicle* (December), pp. 1–20.

Layfield Report (1976), *Local Government Finance: Report of the Committee of Inquiry*, Cmnd 6453 (London: HMSO).

Martlew, C. (1983), 'The state and local government finance', *Public Administration*, vol. 61.

Mawson, J. (1983), 'Explanations for the decline of the West Midlands', Working Paper, CURS/ILGS, March, pp. 1–19.

Massey, D., and Meegan, R. (1982), *The Anatomy of Job Loss* (London: University of London Press).

Middlemas, K. (1979), *Politics in Industrial Society* (London: Deutsch).

O'Connor, J. (1973), *The Fiscal Crisis of the State* (London and New York: St Martin's Press).

Offe, C. (1975), 'The theory of the capitalist state and the problem of policy formation', in L. N. Lindberg *et al.* (eds), *Stress and Contradiction in Modern Capitalism* (Lexington, Mass.: Lexington Books), pp. 125–44.

Pahl, R. (1977), 'Collective consumption and the state in capitalist and state socialist societies', in R. Scase (ed.), *Industrial Society: Class Cleavage and Control* (London: Allen & Unwin), pp. 153–71.

Robson, W. A. (1976), *Welfare State and Welfare Society* (London: Allen & Unwin).

Rothwell, R. (1982), 'The role of technology in industrial change: implications for regional policy', *Regional Studies*, vol. 16, no. 5, pp. 361–9.

Samuel, R. (1983), 'Victorian values', *New Statesman*, 27 May.

Saunders, P. (1981), *Social Theory and the Urban Question* (London: Hutchinson).

Saunders, P. (1982), 'Why study central–local relations?', *Local Government Studies*, vol. 8, no. 2 (March–April), pp. 55–62.

Stewart, J. D. (1977a), *Central and Local Government Relations* (London: The Municipal Group).

Stewart, J. D. (1977b), 'Community government and the future of planning', *Town Planning Review*, vol. 54, no. 3 (July).

Stewart, J. D. (1980), 'From growth to standstill', in M. Wright (ed.), *Public Spending Decisions: Growth and Restraint in the 1970s* (London: Allen & Unwin), pp. 9–24.

Stewart, J. D. (1983), *Local Government: The Conditions of Local Choice* (London: Allen & Unwin).

Winkler, J. (1977), 'The corporate economy: theory and administration', in R. Scase (ed.), *Industrial Society* (London: Allen & Unwin), pp. 43–58.

PART ONE

Dilemmas of Central–Local Relations

1

Dilemmas

JOHN STEWART

THE DILEMMA OF LOCAL GOVERNMENT

The relationship between local authorities and central government is the relationship between the only elected governing institutions in our society. Each is an elected body charged with government, and with the power and the duty to make choices in the exercise of government.

These choices centre not only on the administration of many functions, and involve not simply implementation, but the making of policy. Both local authorities and central government have to make multi-valued choices, weighing in the balance the relative importance not only of means to ends, but of the ends themselves.

Such choices are given to elected institutions in our society. Election conveys, or is felt to convey, the legitimate authority to exercise such governmental choices. The right to tax is conceded only to elected authorities: for local authorities the power is limited to the rates, while central government imposes a wider range of taxes.

Elections, both for central government and for local government, mean (more so in local government than heretofore) elections fought by political parties leading to party control over government.

There is a dilemma inherent in the existence of both local government and central government – each claiming the legitimacy that comes from election; each controlled by political parties, and in some authorities by different political parties; each with a legitimate right of choice and with no guarantee that the choices made at one level will be acceptable at the other; and each having the right to tax and with no certainty that policies of high or low taxation at one level will be paralleled at the other level.

The dilemma, then, is the dilemma of difference. The existence of both central and local government means that there is a potential for different views and different policy choices. The dilemma does not arise by accident, but from the very structuring of local government. Local authorities have been constituted to make a local choice as to the level and form of services they need or wish. They have been granted a tax as a means of making that choice, and they have been made accountable for that choice. Individual local authorities will differ from one another, and can and will differ from the views of central government.

This potential for local choice that has been given to the local authorities represents a belief in local government as opposed to local administration, and in local democracy as well as central democracy. It represents a diffusion of power, it can achieve a diversity of response and can lead to a responsiveness to local problems. Or so at least its advocates would argue.

The dilemma is accentuated by the creation of two political institutions, with shared areas of concern. For in many fields in which local government has the capacity for local choice central government has an organizational concern. Great departments of state have responsibilities for transport, education, housing, town and country planning, the fire service and social services. Yet for all these functions, many of the services are actually provided by local authorities. Difference and the possibility of conflict is structured into the relationship.

Local choice is not an unconstrained choice. Local authorities make choices within a statutory framework determined by Parliament largely on the initiative of central government. The pressures on Parliament mean that that framework is, however, not easily or rapidly changed, and while it remains, it is binding on central government as well as local government. The ability to legislate through Parliament is, moreover, the means by which central government lays down the conditions for local choice.

In theory, it would be possible for central government to resolve the dilemma by so limiting the conditions of local choice that no significant differences between central government and local authorities could arise. However, this ignores the reality that the dilemma must be regarded as a chosen dilemma. Such action would resolve the dilemma by eliminating significant local choice. Differences between central and local government arise from the exercise of local choice. They are not necessarily an indication of a set of relations that is problematic. The dilemma is inherent in the very nature of local government. By constituting political institutions capable of local choice, the dilemma of difference is also constituted. Eliminate difference in the fields in which both local government and central governments are concerned, and the basis of local choice in those fields is eliminated. Central government and local authorities are caught in the chosen dilemma of their relationship.

As we have seen, the dilemma is a chosen one in so far as central government has the power through Parliament to set the conditions of local choice. Those conditions are set both in the duties laid upon local authorities and in the direct controls and influences upon the decisions of local authorities which structure the relationship between central government and local authorities and can be described as the policy instruments of central–local relations.

Some of the policy instruments are direct controls. On some decisions local authorities have to seek direct ministerial approval, as in the case of closure of schools. On other decisions, for example, certain planning decisions, appeals may be made to the minister.

In some fields as discussed in Chapters 2, 8 and 9, central government has sought to structure the relationship through policy planning systems, requiring local authorities to submit plans or programmes to central government.

Over and above the direct controls there are a wide variety of policy instruments that are influences upon local authorities: they include circulars, government reports, a White Paper on Public Expenditure and ministerial speeches. Inspectors and advisers appointed by central government add to the pattern of influence on local authorities.

The main policy instruments have been created not by local authorities, but by central government through its constitutional resources. Thus in the field of local government finance central government has developed new controls and influences. The Local Government Planning and Land Act, 1980 replaced control by loan sanction of borrowing for capital expenditure by general controls over an authority's capital expenditure, however financed. New instruments were also introduced in order to use grant as a means of increasing influence upon individual local authorities' revenue expenditure. In the period since 1980, as described in Chapter 4, the instruments have been structured and restructured.

Targets have been set not merely for the aggregate of local government expenditure, but for individual local authorities. If local authorities do not meet the targets, they are subject to penalties in the form of grant reduction. Whether or not local authorities meet those targets is a matter of local choice. The dilemma remains because local choice remains.

At present the government is proposing new policy instruments which will resolve the dilemma over local government expenditure by direct control over the rates. The dilemma will be resolved, but only at the expense of local choice because the dilemma *is* local choice.

MODELLING THE CENTRAL–LOCAL RELATIONSHIP

The set of policy instruments specify the rules of the game within which the relationship between central government and local authorities is developed. Within the rules of the game both central government and local authorities have resources they can deploy.

It may be thought that as political institutions they will deploy those resources to the limit of their capacity. Yet as we have seen, the chosen dilemma of central–local relations is a choice by central government to limit its constitutional resources. Equally local authorities have rarely used to the full the resources that are available to them.

In much of the discussion of central–local relations it is implicitly assumed that purposive, homogeneous organizations face one another each with policy instruments clearly geared to their own purposes, and with the resources to sustain those purposes. It could be argued that such assumptions underlie the debate about whether local authorities are agents or partners of central government,[1] and also certain resource dependency models.[2] If central government and local authorities were such organizations, restraint would be inexplicable. The reality is very different. Central government both wants local choice and seeks to limit it. Local authorities may at times seek central direction and resist it at other times.

Multiple and conflicting aims can be contained within the same organization. A political institution may seek to avoid responsibility as much as to claim it; ambiguities in the relationship can serve the purpose of both central government and local authorities. The dilemma has been maintained both as the positive of local choice and the negative of the denial of responsibility.

To understand the relationship a model can be developed that assumes

(1)   central government is not a homogeneous decision-maker, but is composed of different interests and is subject to a wide variety of pressures;

(2) central government cannot be regarded as having a clear and consistent set of policy aims;

(3) the departments of central government can equally not be regarded as having clear and consistent aims for a large range of their activities, but are content to deal with issues 'on their merits', balancing interests and the extent of pressures at the time;

(4) at different times the balance of power and influence of the varying interests between and within departments of central government may and in fact does vary;

(5) the policy instruments available to central government for influencing or controlling local authorities have often not been designed for the purposes for which they are used;

(6) the information available to guide central government in the use of the policy instruments is imperfect and fragmented.

Similar assumption can be made about local authorities. These models can be elaborated in the experience of central–local relations.

A Divide in Understanding

The worlds of local and central government are separate each with its own patterns of understanding. The processes of central–local relations link these two worlds but do not necessarily bridge the gap in understanding.

It is often argued that within organizations it is difficult for those at the centre to communicate with or learn from those at the periphery, separated as they are by many levels in the hierarchies. Where the divides are not merely levels in an administrative hierarchy but rather divides between organizations, the gap in understanding is likely to be even greater. Each organization has its own culture and its own set of perceptions which cannot easily be grasped by another organization.

The organizational world of central government is very different from that of local government. It is formed by different forces and structured on different principles:

(1) The concern of a local authority is local. It focuses on a local area and is subject to immediate pressures from the locality. Central government has a national focus and is subject to wider, and indeed at times international, pressures.

(2) Local authorities and central government have a different scale of operation. One department of central government can employ more staff than most local authorities.

These differences are obvious, but perhaps more important are the differences in the organizing principles both of the political and of the administrative structures:

(1)   The structure of the civil service depends upon the administrator, not the professional. The structure of the local government service is based on the professional, not the administrator. In central government the most senior positions are held by generalist administrators. The chief officer in local government is likely to have moved from authority to authority, working in the same department and reinforcing his professionalism. The senior civil servant will have moved within and between departments reinforcing his administrative perspective.

(2)   Central government is based on the ministerial principle, with a minister personally in charge of a department and answerable to Parliament. In local government the chairman of a committee may aspire to a ministerial role but his formal position derives from being chairman of the committee which is important in the working of the local authority, bringing councillors of all parties much closer to the working of the administrative machine than ever an MP can be, unless he is also a minister.

(3)   The local authority takes action to deliver services and to provide functions directly to the public. It is structured to the requirements of that action. It operates directly through its own staff upon its environment. There is an immediacy in the decisions of the local authority, which sharply distinguishes them from those departments of central government concerned with local authorities – the very departments with which local authorities deal. For those departments are not structured for direct action; they do not act directly on the environment. They act through local authorities.

These forces and principles of organization create different worlds each with their own pressures and their own climate. Unless the gap of understanding can be bridged, the attempts by central government departments to influence local authorities are likely to fail.

If central government seeks, for example, to influence the budgetary process of local authorities, it should understand the nature of that process – both its timing and its internal pressures.[3] If central government seeks to influence the decisions of education committees, it should understand the working of education committees and the balance of influences and pressures upon them. The gap in understanding has to be bridged if there is to be effective influence on action.

Understanding can best be built on shared experience. It can be achieved by the movement of staff from local government to central government or vice versa, so that normal career patterns cover both central government and local government. It can be achieved by secondment of staff for limited periods. It can be achieved by a development of joint training. Yet the personnel policies of central government and of local government are grounded in separation. Except in a few limited professional fields, career movement is rare. There is no pattern of shared experience to bridge the divide in understanding.[4]

A Lack of Learning

Across a divide of understanding learning is not easily achieved, yet learning processes can be built.

In the policy processes that govern central–local relations there seems, however, to have been little attempt to build adequate mechanisms for learning. The circular – although now reduced in significance[5] – symbolized a lack of learning at the centre since it was communication from the world of central government to the unknown world of local government. Statistical returns demanded by the centre collect information on the problems that are known. Central government departments' learning does not extend to the problems and perspectives that are unknown to the centre, but that is where learning is most required.

Different departments have developed their own distinctive learning processes. The Department of Education and Science stresses the role of the Inspectorate; the Department of the Environment stresses regional offices. What is less certain is whether they are learning processes. They may themselves be too remote organizationally from the local authorities from whom they must learn, or from the central government departments to whom they have to convey that learning. The policy planning systems that are described later in this book can be regarded as, in part, an attempt to improve learning mechanisms.

Central government has built up machinery of consultation which can be argued to provide mechanisms for joint learning. This machinery has its culmination in the Consultative Council for Local Government Finance, where leading representatives of the local authority associations meet representatives of central government under the chairmanship of the Secretary of State for the Environment.

National machinery of consultation is no substitute for adequate mechanisms to learn about local government. Local government promotes diversity. In national consultation the diversity of local government has to be reduced to simple uniformities, and in that reduction understanding of local circumstances is lost.

Yet unless central government has adequate learning mechanisms about the world of local authorities and about the effect of its actions, it is difficult to see that it has the basis for anything beyond random intervention.[6]

The Fragmented Approach

Central government cannot properly be regarded as a unitary organization when dealing with local government. For the complexities of central–local relations, it is best regarded as a diverse collection of interests. These interests are marked by the divisions within and between departments.

There is no reason why the interests of the Department of Education and Science should coincide with the interests of other departments or of the Treasury. There will be times when the ally of that department will not be another department of central government, but education departments of local authorities sharing similar interests and concerns. The unitary image is inappropriate to central government but also to a local authority. Yet unless the unitary image can be regarded as appropriate, it is necessary to regard central government – as opposed to particular interests at particular moments of time – as having a fragmented relationship with local authorities. The interventions of one department may well frustrate the purposes behind the interventions of other departments.[7]

A Random Set of Instruments

Central government has a set of policy instruments which it uses to intervene in the affairs of local authorities. The instruments available to central government were mainly formed during the period of growth in local government expenditure.

The instruments worked – to a degree – because of the existence of an increment of growth, which makes possible change without political and managerial costs. Interests in central government found ready listeners among related interests in local authorities, who based their claim for a share in that increment of growth on national policy.[8]

Other policy instruments of central government were also

related to growth in expenditure. Controls over borrowing were of great importance because of the size of capital expenditure programmes. When revenue expenditure was growing largely through increased grant in the postwar period up to 1975, the grant gave central government a general influence over the increase in revenue expenditure.

The annual increment of growth provided the basis on which central–local relations worked. It enabled many interests within both central and local government to be met without fundamental problems. Those instruments were always best regarded as a random set of instruments which were not mutually consistent. They worked because the increment of growth absorbed the pressures in the relationship.

CENTRAL INTERVENTION OR CENTRAL GOVERNMENT CONTROL

Central intervention can take place without necessarily leading to central control. 'Central control' implies purpose and actions that secure that purpose. Central control implies that the central government intervenes in the activities of local authorities and secures their adherence to achieve central government policies or goals. 'Central intervention' implies merely intervention. Those interventions do not necessarily have to secure adherence to central government policies or goals, or even that there are policies or goals related to the interventions. Control entails interventions but many interventions may not imply control.

Much writing on central–local relations has implicitly assumed that central government is a purposive unitary organization with knowledge and capacity related to those purposes. The assumption made is that central intervention necessarily implies interventions that are purposive in intent and achieve that purpose. Central government control and central government intervention are treated as synonymous.

Thus Boaden in *Urban Policy-Making* (1971) examines the degree of central control by testing the hypothesis that 'Local authorities within any particular class of authority will display broadly similar levels of activity within any service area because of the operation of central controls and pressures.'[9]

The assumption is that the aim of central control is to secure uniformity, and in the form being tested, that is, range of spending per 1,000 population for selected services. It is by no means certain that central government is aiming for that uniformity, or conversely, if achieved, that it has come about by these means. What is being tested is a particular assumption as to the effect of increased central control.

Boaden deals with the issue fairly, for although he argues that 'This seems a reasonable assumption', he recognizes that 'It is possible, of course, to argue that variation is compatible with central control. The centre may welcome diversity' (ibid., p. 20). Boaden clearly recognized that he was not applying a definitive test of the effect of central control, but testing a particular set of assumptions about that effect – a set of assumptions which, as we have seen, have not necessarily been accepted by all those normally considered to subscribe to the 'conventional wisdom'.[10]

The issue is not whether Boaden was correct in assuming that central government aimed for uniformity or whether central government had other aims. The point is that central government interventions are seen as necessarily implying central government control. It is assumed that central government has clear purposes and its interventions will achieve those purposes. Local autonomy from central government can then be tested by examining the extent to which local authority activities conform to the purposes of central government. Leaving aside the issue of whether conformity to those purposes might not have been achieved by free choice,[11] this mode of analysis assumes that central government intervention corresponds to central government control.

The same assumption underlies other writing on central–local relations. It is assumed that central government interventions reflect the actions of a consistent decision-maker with clear aims and policy instruments that can be and are used effectively to achieve those aims. It is assumed that central government interventions achieve central control because it is assumed that central government interventions are undertaken as part of a rational purposive decision-making process. We have suggested a model of central government that implies very different decision-making processes.

AN APPARENT PARADOX

To those who work within central government local authorities can appear to possess a remarkable degree of autonomy. Local authorities have the apparent capacity to pursue many policies often without interference by central government. They determine their own level of revenue expenditure. The departments of central government and their ministers are conscious not of control over local authorities, but of lack of control.

Those who work in local government are not conscious of autonomy. They see rather control and constraint, their activities dependent on statutes which are seen as the instruments of central government. Their finances are greatly influenced by central government grants. They are conscious of the many and changing interventions of central government in the work of local authorities, and the constraints they create. To actors within local authorities limitations imposed by central government appear as an ever-present reality.

To central government local authorities can appear as 'out of control', while local authorities perceive their activities as constrained and controlled by central government. The apparent paradox reflects the different points from which the relationship is viewed.

At one level the explanation is simple. Power and the autonomy to exercise that power are elusive. Power never appears present at the point of action. There is inevitably greater awareness of the restraints upon action than upon the ability to act.

Where there is freedom, action is taken without thought upon the fact of freedom. Constraint, control and intervention attract attention. Thus actors in central and in local government are both more aware of constraints upon their actions than of their freedom to act.

It is often argued that education is 'a national system locally administered'.[12] It could as well be argued that education is a school-based system occasionally influenced by the local education authority or by the Department of Education and Science. The analysis depends upon the viewpoint. Power is elusive. It lies not at one point in the system, but is divided and fragmented between many actors. Each actor is more aware of the power he does not have and of the constraints on him. He need not be aware of the power he actually has; he merely uses it.

However, over and above that general tendency, if in practice central government intervention does not necessarily imply control, then it is consistent for actors in central government to perceive the lack of central government control, while actors in local government feel constrained by central government intervention. The apparent paradox can be dissolved in this way. It is only a paradox if intervention and control are treated as identical.

CONCLUSIONS IN AN ERA OF RESTRAINT

There is a dilemma in central–local relations, it is the dilemma of local authorities which make decisions with which central government does not necessarily agree. It is, however, a chosen dilemma. The dilemma follows from the creation of elected local authorities with a capacity for local choice in fields of activity which remain the concern of central government departments.

There are many policy instruments that structure central–local relations. These policy instruments are not designed or used by unitary organizations systematically deploying their resources in pursuit of clear goals. Models of central government and of local authorities that assume fragmented organization, with differing interests operating with imperfect instruments and uncertain knowledge, may better explain many of the characteristics of central–local relations such as the divide in understanding and the lack of learning mechanisms.

Central–local relations may as a result appear to local authorities to involve high intervention, while not appearing to central government to involve high control. The chosen dilemma is heightened, and this can create pressures for the conditions of the choice to be redetermined. Within an era of growth those pressures could be contained. An increment of growth provided the inter-organizational slack that limits friction. Pressures resulting from the dilemma are likely to be greater in an era of constraint and cutback than in an era of growth. The heightened dilemma raises the conditions of local choice. Much of this book is concerned with changes as the pressure grows for the conditions of local choice are to be redefined.

The lesson of this chapter remains that central–local relations are a chosen dilemma. The dilemma is heightened by the conditions of both central and local government and by the conditions of constraint. The author remains convinced, however, that the dilemma chosen is a necessary dilemma.

NOTES: CHAPTER 1

1 See Hartley, 1971, pp. 439–56.
2 See Rhodes, 1981, pp. 98–9.
3 The Layfield Report, 1976, annex 11, shows the different bases of resource planning by central and local government.
4 cf. Central Policy Review Staff, 1977, p. 57, para. 14.12.
5 cf. speech by the secretary of state, 18 July 1979, which recorded a marked reduction in formal letters.
6 The lack of learning mechanisms is also discussed in the Central Policy Review Staff Report, 1977, pp. 33–5; referred to in Boaden, 1971, p. 20.
7 Layfield Report, 1976, p. 83, para. 55.
8 The impact of the increment of growth is discussed at greater length in Wright, 1980, ch. 2.

9   Boaden, 1971, p. 12.
10 The 'conventional wisdom' and 'conventional critique' are described in Rhodes, 1981, pp. 14–17.
11 See Foster *et al.*, 1980, p. 255: 'If we reveal considerable uniformity in behaviour we cannot prove it was not freely chosen.'
12 This phrase is often used in the world of education; cf. Dudley Fiske, Presidential Address to the Society of Education Officers, 1978.

REFERENCES: CHAPTER 1

Boaden, N. T. (1971), *Urban Policy Making* (Cambridge: Cambridge University Press).

Central Policy Review Staff (1977), *Relations between Central Government and Local Authorities* (London: HMSO).

Fiske, D. (1978), Presidential Address, Society of Education Officers, London, 26 January.

Foster, C. D., Jackman, R., and Perlman, M. (1980), *Local Government Finance in a Unitary State* (London: Allen & Unwin).

Hartley, A. (1971), 'The relationship between central and local authorities', *Public Administration*, vol. 49 (Winter), pp. 439–56.

Layfield Report (1976), *Local Government Finance: Report of the Committee of Inquiry*, Cmnd 6453 (London: HMSO).

Rhodes, R. A. W. (1981), *Control and Power in Central–Local Relations* (Farnborough: Gower).

Wright, M. (ed.) (1980), *Public Spending Decisions: Growth and Restraint in the 1970s* (London: Allen & Unwin).

2

Policy Planning Solution

BOB HININGS

Central–local relations can be viewed as a series of continuing dilemmas which require solution. These dilemmas concern matters such as the appropriate distribution of functions between levels of government, the locus of control of policy formulation and resource allocation, the respective involvement of different agencies of government and the necessity of establishing national standards. That is, issues of central–local relations are enduring as a matter of both functional and political necessity because of the existence of tiers of government, multiple agencies and varying political interests.

Central–local relations also comprise a network of inter-organizational relations (Jones, 1980: Rhodes, 1981). That is, the agencies which are responsible for providing services, establishing and implementing policies and controlling resource allocation are linked together in a variety of ways. The network of relationships at any one time is the result of attempts to solve the dilemmas through particular organizational and procedural means. The nature of the inter-organizational relations between agencies is subject to continuous change, acting as responses to the permanence of the dilemmas.

Once functions have been distributed between tiers of government, there have to be organized arrangements of handling business between the agencies concerned. Such arrangements are limited by a series of constraints, including the resources available, the known and accepted ways of organizing government business, the tasks to be dealt with, and so on. The aim of this chapter is to examine one type of inter-organizational form which was meant to help solve these dilemmas, namely the policy planning system (PPS).

WHAT ARE THE DILEMMAS OF CENTRAL–LOCAL RELATIONS?

With a formally tiered system of government and its attendant distribution of functions, powers and responsibilities, there is a need to organize the relationship between the tiers. A continuing, unsolvable (in an absolute sense) dilemma is _how to distribute functions within a system of government_. The work of Griffiths (1966) and, more recently, that of Raine (1981) illustrates continuing functional issues which required organizational and procedural solutions.

Governments 'struggle' with the issue of what constitutes an appropriate distribution of tasks and activities between the various legally defined entities. Any particular distribution is subject to change either on a piecemeal basis or as part of a major reorganization of government, such as happened in 1974. An inter-organizational field develops because the activities, powers and responsibilities of government require co-operation between the separate organizations.

The distribution of powers and the relationships involved between different tiers and agencies of government are usually underpinned either by legislation and/or administrative regulation. The character of this underpinning is partly an indication of views about how the structure of powers should work, and partly a reflection of the relative priorities given to particular issues. The functional distribution of powers can, of course, take different forms. A power may be exclusive to one agency; powers may be shared between agencies, in either a sequential or reciprocal sense; or powers may be the same in different agencies. The actual formal, legal distribution of functions will influence the ways in which the relationships between governmental agencies will be organized (see Hinings, Leach, Vielba and Flynn, 1983).

Of course, the distribution of functions between the various agencies of government is not just a matter of what seems to be best on a rational basis. There is a second dilemma of _the locus of control in the system_. Both in distributing powers and in the nature of inter-organizational relations there will be a reflection of a push towards national control, local control, or attempts at equality of control. The idea of locus of control involves the point at which decisions are made, the nature of the decision-making process (in particular, who is to be involved in and in what way) and the time-span of decision-making. Answers to these questions are embodied in the co-ordination processes represented by organizational structures and processes (cf. Thompson, 1967).

The point at which decisions are made within an inter-organizational system has to do with relative centralization. The allocation of tasks provides a base of authority but the particular agency responsible may have to refer many classes of decision upwards. Also as the Layfield Report (1976) argued, the ability to control the distribution of resources necessary for the performance of functions may confer decision-making capacity. With a variety of agencies involved in government, the points at which particular decisions are made have to be identified. The actual location of these points is an expression of control.

A further aspect of the nature of control concerns the pattern of involvement in decision-making. With a range of agencies both public and private potentially interested in the outcome of decisions, and with expertise to contribute to the decision-making process, there is a dilemma of participation. In many ways it will express itself through the relative emphasis on the position of experts *vis-à-vis* the role of the public in some form. If there are a number of public agencies involved in a policy arena, the question of who represents the public interest and in what way is raised. The potential boundaries to any policy area are usually wide and some way has to be found to establish and manage boundaries. This requires managing the participation of organizations.

The third dilemma of central–local relations dealt with here concerns substantive rather than procedural matters. Any system of inter-governmental relations has to deal with *differences of policies and priorities between the agencies involved.* In a system of government which has formally independent institutions, such as central government and local authorities, it is likely that there will be times when the political directions are different. Even in a formally unified system where local units are part of the centre (as with regional offices), there will be differences of view to be resolved.

The dilemma to be solved for the centre is that of how far it insists on its role as 'guardian' of national standards and directions. A tiered, constitutionally established governmental system suggests that local agencies have a right to deviate from nationally laid down policies to some degree. Such potential deviations may become relatively strong realities when there is political opposition between central government and localities. It raises in sharp form how far the centre can and will go in trying to control the substantive direction of policy. In any inter-organizational network there are bound to be differences of substantive interest and consequent tension between those involved (cf. Benson, 1978).

Because, of necessity, central–local relations represent an inter-organizational network, they carry with them the dilemmas of controlling and managing such a network. Three dilemmas seem to stand out: how to distribute functions; where to locate control;

and how to resolve substantive differences. At any particular time there are inter-organizational relations and procedural statements, together with stated policies, which represent the current 'solution' to these issues. Policy planning systems represent a particular attempt to deal with these dilemmas.

HOW ARE POLICY PLANNING SYSTEMS MEANT TO SOLVE THE DILEMMAS?

In order to suggest how a policy planning system might be used to deal with the dilemmas of central–local relationships it is first of all necessary to define one. A policy planning system (PPS) 'is an instrument for making explicit, formalizing and regulating the relations between objectives, policies and finance in a particular policy sector' (Hinings, Leach, Ranson and Skelcher, forthcoming). Underlying it is the idea of rational policy-making with – at least a medium-term planning horizon. Policy planning systems attempt to be future-oriented and work to rolling programmes with mechanisms of review. There is an attempt to plan policy, emphasized by the future orientation. There is an attempt to be systematic, procedural and cyclical, emphasized by the programmatic nature of a PPS (Hinings, 1980).

A policy planning system, then, tries to develop explicitness, clarity, rationality, formalization and a programmatic approach to policy-making. It does this by specifying the nature of involvement, who is to be involved, in what way and at what point in the process. A PPS specifies the form and duration of the programme-process and where the points of control lie. A policy planning system is introduced into an existing policy area, usually as an attempt to specify more clearly what that system is and should be.

Such systems are very much a product of the planning mood of the 1960s and early 1970s (cf. Gunn, 1973; Greenwood and Stewart, 1975). Difficulties in central–local relationships were to be dealt with by a more co-ordinated and planned approach to policy-making. While there were many different kinds of policy planning initiative, the common element was to formalize and plan the network of relationships between governmental agencies at the centre and those at the locality. In detail, however, at the formal level different policy planning systems often emphasize rather different things. A detailed account of two policy planning systems – transportation policies and programmes (TPPs) and inner city partnerships and programmes (ICPPs) – is provided in Chapters 8 and 9.

WHAT ARE THE DIFFICULTIES INVOLVED IN THE SOLUTIONS?

Policy planning systems try to solve some of the basic dilemmas of central–local relations by means of co-ordinating functions, specifying the focus of control and nature of involvements in policy-making and settling differences in priorities through a formal process of resolution based on rational criteria. As with all formally rational approaches, they represent idealized solutions that will only be partially implemented. The purpose of this section of the chapter is to examine the extent to which two policy planning systems – TPPs and ICPPs – actually managed to solve the dilemmas in the expected way.

Managing an inter-organizational field is difficult, and it is largely because of this that a less than perfect implementation of policy planning systems has taken place. The dilemmas of central–local relationships are complicated precisely because they involve a variety of agencies both governmental and non-governmental. Indeed, as more is expected from organizations in general and government in particular (Bennis and Slater, 1968), and as the diagnosis of problems becomes more complex, so the paradox of the need for inter-agency planning and the difficulty of such planning becomes more sharp. Within a single organization, although control is not entirely straightforward, there are single chains of command, lines of authority and, as a result, the possibility of authoritative direction. With multiple organizations involved in a policy system, a key element becomes the possibility of conflicts of interest enshrined in units that have their own cohesion, direction and 'logics of action' (Karpik, 1978). It is because of this that Rhodes (1981) has developed the concepts of interests, strategies and games as part of his framework for the use of inter-organizational analysis in central–local relations.

We have seen that policy planning systems may contain a high level of symbolism; that rationality itself is used in a symbolic manner. Such symbolism has the function of glossing over variations in interest between organizations and demonstrating that unified solutions to dilemmas and issues are possible. As soon as a division of labour occurs either within or between organizations differences of interest, outlook and strategy will occur (Selznick, 1949; Lawrence and Lorsch, 1967; Benson, 1978). It is in the *inevitability* of such conflicts that the dilemmas arise. The implementation difficulties of policy planning systems come from their relative failure to solve them either through an appropriate division of labour, a clear locus of control, or the resolution of policy differences.

In terms of the *division of labour* TPPs and ICPPs had rather different purposes. As primarily a 'tidying up' operation, TPPs were concerned with the specification and formalization of who was to do what. But aspects of the machinery decayed because some of those expected to take part found more effective ways of presenting their interests. Many of these ways represented the continuation of already established ways of acting. As such, they underlined the general point that the introduction of a policy planning system requires *changes* in behaviour and attitude, even when, as with TPPs, the emphasis is on tidying up. Similarly, there has to be a structure of incentives to enhance task involvement. The incentive of 'better' and 'more rational' policies and resource allocation is not one that has a great deal of potency for those on the edges of the process. As a result, elements of the TPP machinery decayed through the absence of incentives.

This is partly the case with ICPPs but we also see here the problems of difficulty of use. ICPPs wanted to clarify and specify task responsibility and involvement. As part of this there was an attempt to bring a wider range of agencies into the stage of policy discussion and formulation. Some of the working party and committee machinery has not worked as expected, that is, generated enthusiasm for the process and produced integrated plans, because it does not seem to be in the interests of those agencies to devote a great deal of time and energy to the process in relation to the likely return. The symbol of 'rationality' only retains its potency as long as the process produces tangible returns for those carrying out portions of the task.

Managing the task involvement of such a diverse set of agencies, not surprisingly, proved to be beyond the combined capacities of the agencies involved. The potent symbolism produced an over-ambitious inter-organizational system. As a result, decay occurred in two ways. The first was the non-attendance or low-profile involvement of many agencies and actors such as ministers, departments of state other than the DoE, health and water authorities. Their involvement was difficult to organize both in terms of tasks to carry out and interests to pursue. Secondly, decay occurred as the difficulties in managing complexity were handled by substituting 'simplicity'. That is, the major emphasis shifted from the consideration of strategies to the programming of packages of projects. A mutual awareness of the 'limits of the possible' soon became established and was manifested in a number of informal rules about 'priorities', 'balance', 'emphasis on scope of problems', and so on. While this was not quite so marked with regard to TPPs, the three potential criteria for judging submissions, namely, policy content, planning process and progress in implementation, relatively quickly became reduced to a mechanical rule of progress.

In terms of the *locus of control* both systems involved the widening of involvement on a formalized, specified basis through the structuring of a policy planning system. But with regard to other aspects of this dilemma, there are differences between TPPs and ICPPs. The former involve an essentially hierarchical process which in principle culminates in central government agreement (or not) over policy, and deciding subsequent resource allocation.

The development in TPPs of a formalized, specified planning system leads to an emphasis on hierarchical control. By developing a system which is multiple, substantive and programmatic, central government departments become involved in a level of information which was not previously open to them. The TPP system established a regular flow of information which is of greater use to the centre than the locality. It also provides a set of processes which sequence and specify decision-making steps that enable the centre to make decisive interventions. Ultimately the centre has the ability to change the rules and procedures to maintain its strategic advantage. Policy planning systems in general, and TPPs in particular, because of their degree of specification and initial hierarchical nature, work to the strategic advantage of the centre. Involvements become narrowed as a result of which the complexity reduces and central management of the system is enhanced. The process relies more and more heavily on simple rules of progress in implementation rather than policy analysis and the logic of the relationship between policy objectives and programmes. This makes it easier for the centre to evaluate and intervene. The collection of information about all transportation authorities over time gives the Department of Transport and its regional officers knowledge about where interventions are necessary from the point of view of the centre. All of this is backed up by the existence of a financial allocation as part of the policy planning system.

While the same processes are at work for ICPPs because of their rather different attempted solution to the locus of control dilemma, matters have turned out rather differently. The ICPP policy planning system had a strong symbolic base emphasizing non-hierarchical, joint decision-making with the aim of both producing specific policy objectives with the system and getting the various agencies to review their main policies and programmes.

With a complex inter-organizational system not only are *clear* integration devices necessary, but responsibility for ensuring that the integrative systems work has to be defined (cf. Lawrence and Lorsch, 1967). The machinery of ICPPs, particularly the partnerships, often failed to define that responsibility, producing something closer to an 'organized anarchy' rather than joint decision-making. With such situations, a movement away from joint decision-making towards a more bureaucratized mode of operation was attempted in order to provide the specification of control that tended to be missing in the original systems.

While the idea of joint decision-making is intuitively appealing its operation requires particular organizational styles and structures (Walton and Dutton, 1969), especially organic systems and styles emphasizing openness and trust. All of the agencies involved in ICCPs were internally bureaucratic in structure and climate. To expect major changes in a relatively small and unimportant part of their activity was to expect too much. A more specified and formalized process was seen as being more effective in operation. However, the potential implication that this should also involve a more hierarchical system of operation (as with TPPs) was resisted by the local agencies. For local authorities in particular, the idea of 'partnership' could be used to resist any movements towards centralization. The result was a continuous push–pull situation between the centre and the locality over control.

The centre has also been less able to use the financial allocations as a source of control. A number of local authorities have shown themselves either willing to forgo such resources or put up considerable resistance rather than accept more centralized control of allocations. As a result, there has been rather more negotiation and bargaining over the operation of the system than has been the case with TPPs.

Of course, the organizational solutions (and changes in those solutions) to the dilemmas of functional distribution and locus of control cannot be divorced from the ways in which the *dilemma of policy differences* between agencies is tackled. The existence of a variety of agencies presupposes differences of interest which have policy foci. A policy planning system is a technique for attempting to minimize eventual differences through rational planning. The appeal of PPSs was that through their process they would deal with, and perhaps even end, difficulties over differences in priority.

Transportation policy was seen as a technical area with an underlying consensus. TPPs were initially run by local government officers and central government civil servants with few substantial priority conflicts occurring. But this was not to be the case in perpetuity, and the system had to cope with overt political differences both between the centre and local authorities and between localities.

This happened initially with policies over the balance of activities between the revenue support (for bus fares), and spending on roads. When central government politicians wished to change policy direction away from revenue support, this was not a matter which could be handled on a technical/administrative basis. The system was unable to handle the subsequent political conflict. Face-to-face meetings between ministers and local politicians had to be set up and, in effect, the TPP system suspended until a political agreement (even if in at least one case it was an agreement to differ) had been reached. The idea of a technically rational process was exposed. Disagreements also arose over levels of spending. In other words, both because of its assumptions about technical rationality and its belief in the ability to find absolutely rational solutions, the TPP process is unable to deal with strong priority differences. So from time to time a parallel system is used, bringing politicians together in some forum after which the appropriate messages can be transferred into the TPP process.

This is quite dissimilar from ICPPs, which from the start recognized the existence of the policy dilemma and attempted to deal with it by a process of political involvement at the initial stages. This way it was thought that the necessary compromises could be reached through technical analysis.

The centre switched priorities towards economic regeneration and environmental rehabilitation and away from social welfare and recreation. Financially there was a decided move from revenue to capital spending. This involved changing some of the rules of the system and playing down the joint decision-making aspects. Individual local authorities complained there was little that they could do. It meant that in real terms the role of the centre as final evaluator and arbiter was stressed. Discussion was to take place within guidelines laid down by the centre. Of course, an offshoot of such changes and the distinctions that they masked was for local authorities to become skilled at packaging projects under particular headings. Because of the relative lack of detailed scrutiny, this could succeed. With a system that stressed political participation and the resolution of difference through discussion and joint decision-making, irresolvable conflicts could only be handled through a centralized approach. This, of course, struck at the heart and the symbolism of the system.

In short, both TPPs and ICPPs showed themselves unable to handle major policy differences within the system. In both cases they were essentially removed from the policy planning process. A policy planning system not only makes policy variations clear by formalizing information, it also presses for their resolution often within a one-year programme time cycle. Its rational, administrative, technical underpinning refuses to recognize the iterative; 'soft' processes of compromise and resolution that can be built into a non-specified system. A system which is more diffuse and fragmented can allow subterranean processes to occur without raising issues about legitimate involvement. The difficulty of such a system arises when policy changes are not just sharp, but when their implementation is required over a short period of time.

CONCLUSION

Policy planning systems are temporary solutions to enduring dilemmas of central–local relations. They are temporary in the sense that any particular organization and set of processes are temporary. It does not mean that they are not long-lasting, merely that they are subject to change as problem definition changes, as the original rationale for the particular organizational solution changes and as new practices become established.

Nor does it mean necessarily that policy planning systems make no difference to the process of policy formulation and resource allocation. To quote Hinings *et al.*,

> Policy planning systems have made a difference in an organizational and instrumental sense. They have specified sets of inter-organizational relationships and processes which represent genuinely new and different networks ... A prime purpose of policy planning systems has been to change and improve the process of policymaking. This is a difficult undertaking ... The fact that there will be difficulties does not nullify the attempts. (Hinings, Leach, Ranson and Skelcher, forthcoming)

What, then, does the analysis performed here say about the problems of instituting policy planning systems as one means of solving enduring dilemmas of central–local relations?

The attempt to solve the dilemma of the division of functions between tiers illustrates two problems. The first is that PPSs have to be introduced into existing networks of relationships. An aim of a PPS is the tidying up or redefinition of the network. To do this sufficient incentives have to be offered to the various agencies and the old network has to be rendered inoperative. Neither in the case of TPPs nor of ICPPs did this happen to the extent that was envisaged. Too much emphasis was placed on the inherent good of planning as an incentive. As a result, decay can occur in the system — through lack of perceived relevance.

The second problem is a related one. Setting up a new network is always an innovation. What is important is the extent of the innovation that is envisaged. In the case of TPPs the degree of innovation was limited, whereas for inner cities, it was quite major (especially for the partnerships). Underlying the structural arrangements were a series of assumptions about new ways of working. Without some agency taking responsibility for the efficient operation of the new system, decay occurs because of the difficulties of operation. While ICPPs were heralded as a new approach to problems of urban deprivation, no account was taken of the probable problems of developing satisfactory working relationships. This issue is taken up in relation to the introduction of new management systems in local government by Hinings (1981).

When turning to the dilemma of the locus of control, the issues centre around known ways of operating as against the attempt to change processes. Policy planning systems represent a mixture of bureaucratization, through procedural specification and the formalization of relationships and processes, and more organic forms through participation and non-hierarchical operation. Bureaucratic modes of organizing are more familiar to the participants in policy systems and so are likely to become the preferred style of operation. Also bureaucratizing the inter-organizational process and emphasizing its hierarchical nature clarifies the locus of control and tips it in favour of the centre. Implicitly at least a policy planning system requires a degree of ambiguity and flexibility for its successful operation. This is particularly true for ICPPs with their broad and almost indefinable policy area and the symbolism of partnership.

With the previous two dilemmas, while changes occurred in the operation, organization and management of policy planning systems, at the very least they showed themselves able to cope. Even if the process was not what was envisaged in pure form, the systems continued to operate within expected bounds. This is much less true with regard to the third dilemma, that of differences in policies and priorities between the agencies involved. The very rationality and specification of a PPS produce problems.

Setting up a policy planning system involves either the assumption that there will not be major differences or that the process can always handle them. The present analysis suggests that neither of these is true. In particular, there will be changes in the circumstances which such systems are meant to deal with which may come close to negating their purpose. For both TPPs and ICPPs, there have been major political differences and also basic changes in policy direction with which the systems *per se* have been unable to cope. In a sense this has been most apparent for ICPPs because they were designed to handle policy conflict. The fact that TPPs did not handle such issues is because, *qua* system, they were not designed to in any explicit sense.

However, with regard to managing policy differences, policy planning systems have demonstrated their usefulness to the centre when operated in a centralized, hierarchical form. Given their systematic, programmatic nature, they are available for crucial information to be passed up and directive messages to be passed down. Changes in policy direction can be signalled and the process of submission of programmes used to monitor the implementation of policy changes. This does not necessarily involve the resolution of policy variations in the manner envisaged by the PPS, but it does allow authoritative decisions to be made. Changing circumstances require adaptive organizational and procedural responses. Policy planning systems were a response to the situations of the 1960s and 1970s, as they impinged on the dilemmas of central–local relations. The dilemmas continue; the circumstances in which they are located and the appropriate responses change.

REFERENCES: CHAPTER 2

Bennis, W. G., and Slater, P. E. (1968), *The Temporary Society* (New York and London: Harper & Row).

Benson, J. K. (1978), 'The interorganizational network as a political economy', *Administrative Science Quarterly*, vol. 20, no. 2 (June), pp. 229–49.

Edwards, J., and Batley, R. (1978), *The Politics of Positive Discrimination* (London: Tavistock).

Greenwood, R. G., and Stewart, J. D. (eds) (1975), *Corporate Planning in English Local Government* (London: Knight).

Griffiths, J. G. (1966), *Central Departments and Local Authorities* (London: Allen & Unwin).

Gunn, L. A. (1973), 'Technology and planning in Britain', in D. O. Edge and J. N. Wolfe (eds), *Meaning and Control* (London: Tavistock), pp. 83–110.

Hinings, C. R. (1980), 'Policy planning systems and central–local relations', in G. Jones (ed.), *New Approaches to the Study of Central–Local Government Relations* (London: SSRC/Gower), pp. 59–68.

Hinings, C. R. (1981), 'Organizational change and organizing for change', *Local Government Studies*, vol. 7, no. 6 (November–December), pp. 45–57.

Hinings, C. R., Leach, S., Ranson, S., and Skelcher, C. K. (1983), *Policy-Planning Systems and Central–Local Relations*, Report to the SSRC (London: SSRC).

Hinings, C. R., Leach, S., Ranson, S., and Skelcher, C. K. (forthcoming), 'Implementing policy planning systems in central–local government', in *Long Range Planning*.

Hinings, C. R., Leach, S., Vielba, C., and Flynn, N. (1983), *A Framework for the Study of Inter-Authority Relations* (Birmingham: INLOGOV, University of Birmingham).

Jones, G. (ed.) (1980), *New Approaches to the Study of Central–Local Government Relationships* (London: SSRC/Gower).

Karpik, L. (1978), 'Organizations, institutions and history', in L. Karpik (ed.), *Organization and Environment* (London: Sage), pp. 15–68.

Lawrence, P., and Lorsch, J. (1967), *Organization and Environment* (Cambridge, Mass.: Harvard University Press).

Layfield Report (1976), *Local Government Finance: Report of the Committee of Inquiry*, Cmnd 6453 (London: HMSO).

Raine, J. (ed.) (1981), *In Defence of Local Government* (Birmingham: INLOGOV, University of Birmingham).

Rhodes, R. A. W. (1981), *Control and Power in Central–Local Government Relationships* (London: Gower).

Selznick, P. (1949), *TVA and the Grass Roots* (Berkeley, Calif.: University of California Press).

Thompson, J. D. (1967), *Organizations in Action* (New York: McGraw-Hill).

Walton, R., and Dutton, J. (1969), 'The management of interdepartmental conflict; a model and review, *Administrative Science Quarterly*, vol. 14, no. 1 (March), pp. 73–84.

PART TWO

Controlling Resources

3

Expenditure

JOHN RAINE

After some five years of almost relentless pressure from central government on local authority expenditure, it is hard to recall the state of central–local financial relations which existed before the election of the Conservative government in 1979. Certainly the period beforehand is now viewed as a relatively halcyon one, and any tensions and conflict which might have existed are all too easily forgotten. But the control of local government expenditure is not, of course, new: successive governments have taken the opportunity of the annual rate support grant announcement to regulate spending to levels considered appropriate to macro-economic policy. Traditionally this regulation has been achieved through changes in the proportion of 'relevant expenditure' which central government decides to support with grant. In times of economic expansion local expenditure has been allowed to move upwards in response to more money being provided by a larger proportion. Conversely, in periods of restraint a cut in the proportion, and therefore a smaller grant, has been used to put pressure on local expenditure. A further means of regulation employed by the centre has been in the decision about the level of 'relevant expenditure' itself. While this involves an element of consultation with the local authority associations, the final total is a government decision, and may be deliberately 'squeezed' again to put pressure on local government spending. In this context central government has often made insufficient provision for pay and price increases expected over the forthcoming year, which when inflation has been higher than forecast has meant cuts in the quality of services, below the levels assumed at the outset.

The measure of the success of such traditional means of regulation has been the extent of accord between the level of local government expenditure in a particular year and the level which was provided for by central government in the annual White Paper on Public Expenditure published in advance of the financial year in question. During the 1960s and early 1970s local government expenditure was almost invariably within a few percentage points of levels that government considered desirable, in some years exceeding the plans in others falling short. However, these were years of relative economic prosperity when the government's plans made provision for annual 'growth'. What would happen in the new era of national economic stagnation and decline, which became all too apparent in the mid-1970s, and how would local government expenditure react to the newly elected Conservative government's commitment to make immediate and substantial reductions in public spending in 1979?

In fact the government hardly waited to see; it took a succession of steps to toughen the impact of the existing means of control and to introduce new and more far-reaching ones. The first of these was the introduction of changes in the rate support grant system, particularly the introduction of a 'block grant' to replace the previously existing 'needs' and 'resources' elements. Like its predecessors, the amount of block grant paid to each authority would seek to take account of the differences in local taxable capacity between different authorities because of variations in rateable values, and differences in expenditure needs because of differing economic, social and geographical circumstances, together with differing populations to be served and other local factors.

But the approach especially to this latter aspect was markedly different. And at the heart of the new block grant lay the calculation for each authority of a 'grant-related expenditure assessment' (GREA), which would represent the government's estimation of the level of expenditure required by each authority to provide, to a common level, the services for which it was responsible. Having taken account of the financial contribution to be expected from each authority's local ratepayers, it was on these assessments that shares of block grant would be allocated. The assessments themselves were to be made on the basis of a service-by-service analysis of the need for expenditure. The principle here was to define the client group for which each service would be provided, for example, the number of children to be educated, the number of dwellings from which refuse had to be collected, and so on. The number of such clients was then multiplied by the unit cost of each service, or in other words the cost per pupil of education, the cost per dustbin of refuse collection, and so on, to arrive at the expenditure required in each authority on each service. By summing those separate costs for each authority, the GREAs would be attained.

All this, however, was merely the principle underlying the approach. In practice it proved far more complicated. In the first place, since 'need' is a subjective notion, the level of provision in each service for which the government would make provision was inevitably open to challenge. And certainly a government seeking economy in public spending generally was bound to distribute a predetermined total of grant through the GREA method which would imply a diminished level of provision. Secondly, it was difficult to identify the client group for most services. While it might seem fairly straightforward in the examples given above, it was, in practice, not so easy, and in many others such as the environmental and leisure and recreation services no specific client groups are served. As a result, reliance was placed in many cases on a number of 'indicators', which were considered likely to affect the need for expenditure but which were essentially proxies for need and, therefore, hardly consistent with the 'client group' principle. The most commonly used indicator was simply population size. While this is obviously related to some extent to the need for expenditure on different services, it failed on its own to take account of the standard of facilities available (for example, how well is the library stocked?), and of particular local circumstances which affect usage (for example, is the average library readership for the area high or low?) and, of course, of local preferences for the level of provision (for example, does the community want a larger record collection in the library?).

Nor did the derivation of unit cost figures for each service prove any more straightforward, if only because the client groups themselves were ill-defined. Again while some such information might have been available for certain statutory services like education, it was less easily attainable for others. As a result, the government had to rely to a great extent on national average costs, which would clearly be less accurate and, of course, would take no account of variations in the costs of providing the services resulting from local circumstances. And to circumvent this problem use has been made of a number of other indicators such as population density and sparsity, and measures of economic and social stress. In fact after several years of refinement, the present formulas employ more than fifty different indicators and, therefore, demand an immense amount of time and effort in compilation. And even then the figures are consistently challenged by local authorities as being unrealistic and, therefore, an inappropriate basis on which to calculate the shares of block grant.

To be fair, central government, acknowledging the potential for error in the assessments, does not merely pay grant in support of expenditure up to the GREA level, but allows for continued grant support above this, albeit at a tapered rate to those authorities which are heavily dependent on it. But this hardly ameliorates the criticisms, given the consequences at stake and the fact that the choice of indicators and their weightings are crucial to the pattern of allocation. For evidently choice of certain indicators or the attachment of high weightings to them could be beneficial to certain types of local authority, for example, 'density' and 'social stress' indicators to urban authorities, while others could favour those in different areas such as a 'population sparsity' indicator in rural authorities. That this difficulty is omnipresent is illustrated by the fact that prior to the introduction of block grant and GREAs when a more statistically oriented approach was used for calculating shares of the predecessor grant, the very same controversies were experienced. While the Secretary of State for the Environment argued that the new method would be more objective and rational than the old needs element, this was clearly debatable. And the important point is that no amount of technical sophistication could ever subsume the essentially political, and therefore subjective, nature of the grant distribution problem.

But in any case the block grant was not, of course, introduced with only technical improvements in mind. From the very start it was apparent that expenditure restraint was a principal motive. This was evident in the new notion of reductions in the rate of grant support for authorities fixing their expenditure significantly above the published GREAs. The concepts of 'overspending', and 'penalties' for the same, had been formally adopted! At the same time, the announcement of tough inflation allowances to be used in calculating the expenditure on which the government would pay grant, and the imposition of tight 'cash limits' on the actual amount paid out, demonstrated the strength of government commitment to local expenditure cuts.

And when it became clear that these measures would not be sufficient to ensure that all authorities reduced their expenditure at least to their GREA, a further set of measures were adopted and superimposed on the grant system. These took the form of a set of expenditure 'targets' for each authority, and more stringent grant loss penalties for expenditure above them. Those authorities spending above their target would thus have to finance both the grant loss and the extra expenditure from local rates, implying large increases in rate levies, which the government hoped would be a sufficient disincentive. The introduction of 'targets' in addition to the GREAs was said to be only temporary, and necessary because many councils who were spending in excess of the GREAs could not achieve the desired reductions fast enough without a drastic impact on services. The idea was that the targets would pressure those 'overspending' authorities to reduce their budgets towards their GREA levels by a 'realistic' margin each year until the 'overspend' had been eliminated. Unfortunately the actual method employed for calculating the targets and the penalty rules were ill-conceived and meant that, in practice, many Conservative-controlled and traditionally low-spending councils found themselves facing grant losses without apparent justification. Civil servants, it seemed, were unable to find a method which would penalize only those authorities which the government wished to. It was a case of a generally applied system being wholly inappropriate to the situation which, as the government acknowledged, amounted only to a handful of recalcitrant authorities. But Parliament had never sanctioned a grant system for England and Wales that entitled central government selectively to penalize authorities, unlike the situation in Scotland where the secretary of state gained powers to withdraw grant from any authority whose expenditure was deemed 'excessive and unreasonable' (Miscellaneous Provisions (Scotland) Act 1982).

Harsh though such measures might seem, the critical question was again whether they would produce the expenditure reductions which the government sought. And here the evidence was mixed. The fact that about two-thirds of the local authorities were spending within 2 per cent of the targets after two years of the new system might have indicated that considerable influence was being exerted. On the other hand, many of these councils were traditionally 'low spenders' and meeting targets involved little hardship, indeed in some cases even allowed for an increase in provision. At the same time, research into the impact of targets on budget decisions in Scotland suggested that the approach 'had only limited impact ... and remains relatively insignificant for influencing local spending decisions' (Midwinter, et al., 1984, pp. 21–31). In comparison, the issues of the level of rates, service levels and the maintenance of employment appear to have been more influential on local politicians of all parties.

Nevertheless, grant penalties were not the only action taken to effect reductions in local authority budgets. In parallel a tight control was imposed on capital expenditure, on such items as housing, school and road building programmes, by limiting the amount that each authority could spend each year. Moreover, in 1982 the power of local authorities to levy supplementary rates once the rate levy had been announced at the beginning of the financial year was abolished to prevent any opportunity for increases in budgets. This was followed by the announcement of the intention to abolish the six metropolitan counties and the Greater London Council, all of whom featured prominently among the shrinking list of authorities continuing significantly to 'overspend' their targets. And following the re-election of the government in 1983 on an enhanced majority, a still more controversial step was taken in preparing legislation for a scheme to limit the level of rates which individual councils could levy (Rates Bill, 1983).

Ironically the need for the Bill was owed in large part to the grant controls themselves. For a consequence of large grant loss penalties to overspending councils was that a number received no grant at all and were left dependent for almost all their revenue on the rates. In such circumstances they would be able to ignore central dictates and to assert their new-found independence through radical localism, under the banner of local accountability.

At present it remains to be seen how Parliament will decide, but in the conception of the proposals for rate limitation lay the view that control of the grant alone would not be enough to achieve the government's public expenditure policies. Central control of the finance of local government, it was felt by the government, would now have to be sought in that traditional and most cherished symbol of local financial autonomy – the rates.

So what, then, can one conclude on the experience of a traumatic five years of central–local financial relations? Without doubt one of the most striking features has been the unsuccessful nature of most of the actions taken, necessitating a continuing succession of attempts to tackle the single problem of control. A second, related feature has been the hastiness with which the actions were conceived and implemented, many of the practical consequences being unconsidered and unintended. Whatever was in fact expected of the various grant controls instigated in the early 1980s, it is the ill-effects which stand out so clearly. There is the element of *grantmanship* in the way individual interests have been pursued in working the formulas to advantage, whether on the part of central government in 'fixing' the distribution to suit political demands or on the part of local authorities in pressing for particular factors to be included or excluded. There is the establishment of *creative accounting* as a science in its own right within local authority finance departments, with its aim simply 'to beat the system' and avoid grant penalties. There is the temptation which the grant system has provided for *serious irresponsibility*, with some councils already heavily penalized opting to increase spending still further and simply blame the government for high rate bills. There is the *increase in local rates* itself which has resulted directly from government grant reductions and has had an unequal and for some burdensome impact on ratepayers. And enveloping it all, there is the cynicism which has become rooted among local authorities about the whole business and has undermined so much of what limited goodwill ever existed in central– local relations.

Whatever one thinks about the need for restraint in public expenditure and the contribution which local authorities should make in this direction, and whatever one thinks about the justification for central control over local authority expenditure, it is hard to conclude other than critically on the experience of recent years. The system of local accountability which is a necessary precondition of local government has always been fragile, but it is now seriously weakened. And the institutional and financial uncertainty which has at various times upset local government's capacity to fulfil its functions to best effect is now an unhappy fact of life for the foreseeable future at least.

REFERENCE: CHAPTER 3

Midwinter, A. F., Keating, M., and Taylor, P. (1984), 'Current expenditure guidelines in Scotland – a failure of indicative planning', *Local Government Studies*, vol. 10, no. 2, pp. 21–31.

4

Why Block Grant Failed

JOHN GIBSON

THE CRISIS IN CENTRAL–LOCAL RELATIONS

The crisis in central–local relations of the early 1980s occurred because (1) the Conservative government set local authorities an expenditure reduction objective which it was almost inevitable that they would fail to achieve if the previous expenditure response by local authorities to grant incentives was maintained, and then (2) proceeded to blame local authorities for this failure, claiming that central government had been confronted by a new phenomenon of local authorities who would not conform to central government's expenditure plans. Failure was inevitable primarily because of the Conservative government's inept handling of the new grant system; it did not reduce the level of grant by anything like the extent required to deliver the level of expenditure reductions requested.[1] The result has been that the government has now requested a major increase in the instruments of central control by seeking powers to limit or 'cap' the rate and expenditure levels of individual local authorities.[2] The government also plans to abolish that group of authorities who are regarded as being the highest overspending local authorities – the metropolitan counties and the Greater London Council.[3]

In this chapter we provide an analysis of the failure of the new block grant system, and the system of expenditure targets and grant penalties which were added in 1981. As stated above, the inept management of the grant system by the government is regarded here as the major reason for this failure. After this analysis, we will also explain the importance of a second factor – the changes in local political control in the early 1980s, particularly in the county elections of May 1981 which resulted in the emergence of several local authorities with politicians far less keen than their predecessors to cut levels of expenditure. A final section will analyse whether there previously existed a constitutional convention of conformity by individual local authorities to the central government's public expenditure plans, as was increasingly asserted by government ministers during this period of crisis in central–local relations. Before doing so, however, we will spend some time examining the background of the crisis in the centre–local relationship and the ultimate lurch in the direction of greater central control via the rate-capping proposals.

The major issue in central–local relations became the repeated failure of English local government to spend at levels in accordance with the government's public expenditure plans. This failure was regarded by the government as a breach of an alleged constitutional convention that local government had previously accepted the government's right both to set levels for local government spending and to have them conformed to by local authorities.

The Treasury regarded local government overspending as the main issue in central–local relations and local authorities' use of their discretion over rate levels as a major obstacle to government management of the economy. In hindsight the speech by the then Chief Secretary to the Treasury, Leon Brittan, to the Society of Local Authority Chief Executives in July 1982 can be seen as a final warning to local authorities to conform to their expenditure targets or face the legislative consequences:[4]

Central government *does* have responsibilities which do not allow it to concede total autonomy to local authorities. Yet there is clear, mounting evidence that the tensions that were always latent in the relationship of central and local government have worsened sharply. What has gone wrong?

The truth seems to be that the old implicit consensus about that relationship has broken down and that it has done so above all on the issue of public spending – the issue which, as I have explained, should rightly preoccupy us above all others. It used to be accepted that central government should take a view of and set out in published plans total public spending, including local authority spending . . . they [local authorities] accepted the right of central government to fix a total for local authority spending and the informal obligations to adhere to that total . . . local authorities have shown themselves less and less willing to accept that central government rightly and legitimately has the power to set effective targets for expenditure . . . it is not just the increasing levels of local government spending but the degree of local government *overspending* which is so worrying. Persistent spending above targets jeopardizes the whole balance which the government and only the government must determine between spending, borrowing and taxation ... [overspending] shows either that local authorities are unable to manage their budgets; or more probably, that they have no wish to do so in line with the overall guidance given by central government. (Brittan, 1982, p. 9)

After this analysis, which incidentally contains the major fallacy of past conformity and later to be demonstrated as such in this chapter, the Chief Secretary then proceeded to issue a threat relating to the performance of local government with respect to the targets published in July 1982 for the 1983–4 financial year:

Local government spending plays such an important part in our economy that a failure to overcome the problem of overspending is bound to lead ultimately to developments which the friends of local government will find extremely unwelcome. It is bound to cause central government to intervene ever more obtrusively and seek ever greater powers over local authority finances ... if overspending continues, whichever government is in power ... will ... take further steps in the direction of central control. The only way in which this process can be avoided is for the old and valuable consensus to be restored, and for local authority spending to be contained within limits set by what the nation can afford. (ibid., pp. 9–10)

The fact that the 'further steps' taken were to assert powers to control local rate levels does, of course, have a political as well as an economic explanation. It helped the present Prime Minister to escape from the dilemma of a perceived inability to act on the abolition of domestic rates. The abolition of domestic rates had been a manifesto commitment of the Conservative Party in the October 1974 general election when Mrs Thatcher was shadow Environment Secretary and it had remained as a high priority in the 1979 manifesto. Rate reform re-emerged as a top political issue when rate increases in London accelerated during 1981. However, in the period after the publication of the Green Paper on Alternatives to Domestic Rates of December 1981 (DoE, 1981c) the idea of rate abolition hit the predictable historical, administrative and political obstacles – especially the widespread aversion at the centre to giving local government a local income tax. The *Guardian*'s local government correspondent admirably summarized the potential situation in December 1982:

We all know that the Conservative commitment to abolish domestic rates cannot be made to work without a local income tax (a tool Mrs Thatcher is not prepared to put in the hands of 'Red' Ken Livingstone and friends) or nationalising education. Ministers failed to admit it, and we are rather scared that they may do something silly next year to mark the abandonment of the rate abolition promise. (Carvel, 1982)

We can now see that the Prime Minister had a potential power alliance with the Treasury and a ready excuse for rate-capping (other than vulgar considerations of vote-grabbing) in the failure of some English local authorities to achieve their 1983–4 expenditure targets.

THE IGNORED THEORY OF EXPENDITURE CONTROL

The most simple explanation of the failure of the block grant and the expenditure targets is that the new instruments were operated too leniently.

There had been in existence a theory of the use of grant to control local authority expenditure which could be readily derived from the literature on the expenditure effects of intergovernmental grants.[5] The practical implications of the theory have recently been restated both by a major politician and a top Treasury civil servant. Joel Barnett, who served as Chief Secretary to the Treasury in the Labour government of 1974–9, recalls in his recent memoirs the problem of controlling/reducing local government spending during that period:

> My main concern was with total local authority expenditure . . . we were always discussing how best to exercise control . . . The main source of control was the size of the Rate Support Grant. As Chief Secretary, I would be arguing for as low a grant as possible, on the grounds that it would squeeze local authorities, who, not wanting to increase rates excessively, would be compelled to cut expenditure. (Barnett, 1982, pp. 75–6)

The Treasury civil servant, Leo Pliatsky, in his memoirs writes:

> the only instrument which the central government had for influencing the scale of revenue expenditure by local authorities was the size of the rate support grant . . . the only inhibition on their . . . expenditure . . . is . . . the need to raise more rate revenue from the local electorate. (Pliatsky, 1982, pp. 117–18)

The theory tells us that if the desired objective is to cut local authority expenditure, then the grant system presented in the annual rate support grant (RSG) settlement must place local authorities under sufficient fiscal pressure. Local authorities must be forced to ask for rate increases which involve real sacrifices in terms of ratepayers' disposable incomes. In line with this stance let us use as a measure of toughness the percentage rate increase imposed on local authorities if they spend to meet the government's expenditure target or plan compared to other important indicators such as the rate of increase in the retail price index, earnings, or local authority costs. In fact it is obvious that the larger the year-on-year cuts requested, the larger must be the rate increase forced on local authorities to meet these expenditure plans compared to the current and anticipated rate of inflation.

Table 4.1   *Computation of the Necessary Increase in Use of Rates and Balances If Government's Expenditure Plans Had Been Met by English Local Authorities, 1981–2*

	1980–1 budgets (£m. cash)	1981–2 settlements (£m. estimated out-turn prices)	Percentage change (in local expenditure to be met by rates and balances)
(1) Total relevant expenditure *plus*	17,851	18,423	—
(2) Net non-relevant expenditure plus mandatory student awards *equals*	656	818	—
(3) Total rate and grant-borne expenditure *minus*	18,508	19,241	—
(4) Mandatory student awards grant *minus*	501	625	—
(5) Estimated specific and supplementary grants *minus*	1,596	1,868	—
(6) Block grants (needs and resources element in 1980–1) *equals*	8,100	8,364	—
(7) Local expenditure to be met by rates and balances	8,311	8,384	0·87

Sources: CIPFA (annual), 1980; Local Authority Associations (annual), 1981.

How do the government's RSG settlements measure up on the criteria? Let us examine the situation at the time of the settlement for 1981–2. The cuts requested were very large – 8·3 per cent in current expenditure compared to original 1980–1 budgets, and anticipated average inflation between 1980–1 and 1981–2 was in excess of 10 per cent. But as row 7 in Table 4.1 shows, local authorities were on average only pushed into a 1 per cent nominal increase in the use of rates and balances – equivalent to a real reduction in the burden of rates of at least 10 per cent! Local authorities could have given their ratepayers a 'holiday', and it is not surprising that the expenditure plans for 1981–2 were not met. Anyone who has absorbed the message of the theory of control expounded by Barnett and Pliatsky can see that this was a ridiculous RSG settlement.

Let us jump the 1982–3 settlement (which was also a conspicuous failure) and concentrate on the 1983–4 settlement. This has the appearance of a more realistic regime – a 3·3 per cent reduction in the proportion of planned relevant expenditure to be met from grant, from 56·1 in 1982–3 to 52·8 per cent in 1983–4, combined with a much more modest 1·8 per cent requested year-on-year reduction in current expenditure. However, as Table 4.2 shows, the settlement was still inappropriately lenient – on average local authorities could have reduced their rates by nearly 2 per cent at a time when the expected rate of price inflation was in excess of 5 per cent. Once again a rate holiday was made available. On this occasion there was an additional reason for local authorities not meeting their targets. This was the appearance within the methodology of constructing targets of a possible feedback from higher budgeted expenditure into higher targets. We discuss this point in the next section.

Table 4.2 *Computation of the Necessary Increase in Use of Rates and Balances If Government's Expenditure Plans Had Been Met by English Local Authorities, 1983–4*

	1982–3 budgets (£m. cash)	1983–4 settlements (£m. estimated out-turn prices)	Percentage change
Local expenditure to be met from rates and balances	11,599	11,404	−1·7

Sources: CIPFA (annual), 1982; Local Authority Associations (annual), 1983.

THE FAILURE OF THE TARGETS

A possible response to the above analysis is to claim that application of the simple Barnett–Pliatsky theory of control is invalid because the analysis so far ignores the fact that the grant system has changed since 1981 and has provided the government with new instruments of control which, according to the basic theory, should have acted as additional expenditure disincentives to spending. The new instruments were (1) the taper on the marginal rate of grant given to expenditure by any local authority above its threshold level of expenditure, and (2) the grant penalties (known as holdback) on expenditure by any local authority above its target level of expenditure. Both instruments involved a reduction in the marginal rate of grant support, which depended under the block grant formula on the size of the 'rate poundage price' of extra spending, and the effective rateable value per head of a local authority.

It has been shown elsewhere that the potentially greater equalization powers inherent in the structure of the block grant – powers achieved by placing all local authorities within a common class on the same rate poundage price function for expenditure in relation to GRE – were modified by the use of multipliers.[6] Thus many London authorities received multipliers of protection which reduced the severity of the negative marginal rates of grant which would otherwise have applied because of their large rateable values per head. It has been shown that marginal rates of grant under the basic block grant structure were thus not dramatically altered in most local authorities and this left the system with the domestic ratepayer sector still paying a small proportion of the marginal costs of extra expenditure.[7] However, the target-related grant penalties for overspending targets were much more severe, and the task remains here of explaining why these grant penalties did not succeed in reducing the expenditure of local authorities to their target levels.

The task of explanation is an arduous one because the imposition of targets made the grant system a great deal more complicated. The method of construction of targets and the rules and severity of application of grant penalties for expenditure above target differed from year to year. The 1981–2 targets were wholly unrelated to the new measures of the spending needs of each local authority, the GREs, being 5·6 per cent below 1978–9 out-turn current expenditure. However, penalties were paid only if expenditure was above target *and* above GRE. This allowed many local authorities, especially a large proportion of the non-metropolitan counties, to spend above target without incurring grant penalties because their GREs tended to be larger than their targets. (The opposite was the case for many London and metropolitan authorities whose targets tended to be well in excess of their GREs. However, their expenditure tended to be much further above their GREs.) There was also a limit/ceiling on the grant penalties in both 1981–2 and 1982–3. This limit was removed for 1983–4 as was the GRE exemption from grant penalties, and also grant penalties were made much more severe. The 1983–4 targets also showed that a major principle of targets seemed to be establishing itself: easier targets for authorities who were classified as low-spenders, more severe targets for high-spending authorities.

As the failure of a number of local authorities to conform to their 1983–4 targets (called 'expenditure guidance' by the secretary of state) resulted in the final crisis in central–local relations, we will devote some space to describing the 1983–4 targets.

One innovation with respect to the 1983–4 targets was that they were issued in a statement by the secretary of state to the Consultative Council on 27 July 1982 (see DoE, 1982), well in advance of the RSG settlement when targets had previously been released. The idea behind the earlier release of targets was to 'give . . . detail of the Government's intentions . . . sufficiently ahead of the next year to leave no excuse for those authorities that fail to take the necessary action to avert significant rate increases' (ibid., p. 2). The basic principles underlying the targets were simple:

> all authorities must restrain their expenditure. But the high spending authorities that have so far failed to respond to the Government's request for economy will be asked for more restraint than those which have already made efforts to spend in line with the Government's plans. (loc. cit.)

The actual method of constructing targets and the basis for categorizing an authority as a past high-spender or low-spender is shown in Table 4.3. The constraints applied in fact meant that many high-spenders were given targets which were 1 per cent below their 1982–3 budgets. (The second constraint applied only to the Greater London Council (GLC) which had increased its net expenditure dramatically since Labour took control in May 1981 – it was given a target 19·9 per cent below its 1982–3 budget.) In fact the differentiation between high-spenders, who were given the 1 per cent cash reduction target (or slightly higher in some cases), and the other authorities, who were given a 4 per cent cash increase target, tended to coincide with the differentiation by Labour and Conservative political control.

Table 4.3   *Method of Constructing 1983–4 Expenditure Targets*

Category of authority	Those budgeting to spend up to 1% above the higher of GRE or target in 1982–3	Those budgeting to spend more than 1% above the higher of GRE or target in 1982–3
1983–4 target =	1982–3 budgeted total expenditure *plus* 4%	The higher of 1982–3 target and GRE *plus* 5%
Constraints	None	1 No target to represent more than a 1% cash reduction from 1982–3 budgeted total expenditure, subject to 2 No target to allow more than a 25% cash increase from an authority's 1981–2 minimum volume budget

Source: DoE, 1982, p. 6.

The penalties which were applied for 1983–4 overspending in relation to target were much more severe than in previous years. Penalties at ratepayer level were an addition to the rate poundage (GRP) at the rate of 1p per 1 per cent overspend up to 2 per cent above target and 5p per 1 per cent overspend above this level. At the average target per head figure of £435 in 1983–4 and at a fairly average rateable value of £150 per head the 5p penalty gives negative marginal rates of grant per £1 per head of expenditure of minus £1·85 (that is, a need to charge ratepayers £2·85 for each £1 of expenditure). This dwarfs the effect of the basic block grant taper.

It has been shown elsewhere that the 1981–2 target-related grant penalties did exert quite significant expenditure reduction effects – although not sufficient to meet the government's objectives.[8] However, the 1983–4 penalties, even though much more severe, seemed on analysis of 1983–4 local authority budgets to have been largely ineffective.[9] The failure of the 1983–4 targets can be measured in two ways. First, English local authorities actually increased their volume of current expenditure provision by 1·7 per cent in their 1983–4 budgets[10] when the government was asking for a 1·8 volume reduction.[11] Secondly, the actual excess of total expenditure over targets was £771 million or 3·8 per cent, as shown in Table 4.4.

Table 4.4 *1983–4 Budgets: Comparison with Expenditure Targets and Provisional 'Holdback' Penalties, English Local Authorities*

| | Excess over target | | Authorities penalized | |
	(£m.)	(%)	(number)	(amount, £m.)
GLC	301	53·2	0	0
ILEA	97	12·8	0	0
Metropolitan Police	0	0·0	1	0
Inner London boroughs	57	6·4	7	31
Outer London boroughs	37	2·1	11	27
Metropolitan counties	72	6·5	6	65
Metropolitan districts	61	1·5	23	41
Non-metropolitan counties	147	1·6	25	99
Non-metropolitan districts	–1	–0·1	75	11
Total	771	3·8	148	275

Source: CIPFA (annual), 1983, table F, p. 5.

Why were the 1983–4 targets with their more severe grant penalties so ineffective? First, two authorities were responsible for over one-half of the excess – the Greater London Council and ILEA – and these authorities were immune to the grant penalties because, ironically, they lost all their entitlement to block grant at levels of expenditure below their targets. Secondly, many authorities could spend above their 1983–4 targets without imposing large rate increases. This was mainly due to the fact implied by our earlier analysis that the RSG settlement was too lenient. However, in addition many Labour authorities, besides having tougher targets in 1983–4, were already suffering from holdback penalties in 1982–3 and this, as shown by Pauley (1983), reduced the impact on rate increases in 1983–4 even when the new holdback penalties applied. Finally, the eventual holdback penalties are based on out-turns, and given that a principle of basing targets on previous budgets appeared to be established, there was an incentive to local authorities to 'budget up' to target or the 2 per cent overspend level. This effect appears to be particularly important among the non-metropolitan counties where less than £40 million of the £147 million excess is due to budgeting in the above 2 per cent overspend/heavy penalty region. Such budgeting up will probably exaggerate the usual fall in expenditure levels recorded between budgets and out-turns, and thus the provisional estimate of holdback penalties shown in Table 4.4 will prove to be a large overestimate.

It is perhaps ironical that an overspend which may out-turn at less than £400 million or 2 per cent in relation to targets has proved to be sufficient excuse for the Conservatives to make their 1983 election pledges to take action to abolish the Greater London Council and the metropolitan county councils and also to cap local authority rate and expenditure levels. In fact given that the budgeted overspend was predictable due to the general leniency of the 1983–4 RSG settlement, and even financially prudent given the emerging methodology of target construction, it is perhaps not outlandish to view the 1983–4 grant/expenditure plans as a machiavellian plot to assist Mrs Thatcher with respect to her political weakness on domestic rates and give the Treasury long-desired direct control over local authority expenditure.

THE IMPORTANCE OF CHANGES IN
LOCAL POLITICAL CONTROL

The national–local political cycle has also been of much importance. Jones and Stewart write:

> The task facing a Conservative government in calling for restraint and cutback is inherently more difficult than for a Labour government. Because of the extent of swings against the central government, as local elections take place, central government as time goes on increasingly faces authorities of a different political complexion. This trend may for a Labour government work in favour of constraint, since its appeals for constraint will usually strike a sympathetic chord in Conservative local authorities. However, the trend may work against a Conservative government which finds itself confronted by Labour local authorities totally out of sympathy with its calls for expenditure reductions. (Jones and Stewart, 1982, p. 52)

Certainly the experience of the early 1980s has proved the truth of these sentiments and many of these who know local government would agree with Jones and Stewart. However, their assertiveness of the importance of local political control contrasts with the quite considerable degree of scepticism which existed among political scientists on this issue,[12] especially with respect to the largest population and spending authorities – the non-metropolitan counties.

The experience of 1981 provides a particularly interesting demonstration of the importance of local political control. Local authority budgets for 1981–2 indicated a planned overspend of 5·3 per cent, despite the unexpected introduction in January 1981 of expenditure targets published for each individual local authority. This innovation in central–local financial relations was backed up by the threat of grant penalties for those local authorities who overspent their targets.

Against this background Mr Heseltine took the unusual step in June 1981 of asking local authorities to submit revised budgets for 1981–2:

> I must also give a warning of the further steps that I may have to contemplate if the response is not satisfactory. If the revised budgets were to show no aggregate reduction my proposal would be to ask Parliament to approve in the autumn a supplementary report which would reduce the total of grant for 1981/82 by about £450 m. (DoE, 1981a, p. 2)

The warning was followed by a letter which specified the structure of holdback penalties, and the penalties which would be paid by each local authority if original budget levels of expenditure were unchanged.

This unprecedented degree of intervention by the secretary of state had, however, been preceded by the county elections of May 1981. The 1981 results conformed to the expected national–local political cycle. The main features were:

(1) All four metropolitan counties not under Labour control during 1977–81 – Greater Manchester, Merseyside, West Midlands and West Yorkshire – returned to Labour control. The GLC also changed from Conservative to Labour control.

(2) Nine non-metropolitan counties moved from effective Conservative control to Labour control – Avon, Cleveland, Cumbria, Derbyshire, Humberside, Lancashire, Northumberland, Nottinghamshire and Staffordshire; only one – Durham – of the thirty-nine English non-metropolitan counties had been under Labour control prior to the elections.

(3) Six non-metropolitan counties moved from effective Conservative control to either no party having overall control

or Liberal control – namely, Bedfordshire, Berkshire, Cheshire, Isle of Wight, Leicestershire and Northamptonshire.

The extent of these political changes was ominous for the government's objectives for the revised budgets exercise. The counties experiencing change in control had current expenditure plans of £4,255 million for 1981–2 (at November 1980 prices); this was over 26 per cent of the current expenditure plans (£16,284 million) of English local government.

In fact it was the rapid and dramatic readjustment of spending policies by the Greater London Council, Merseyside and West Midlands which effectively throttled the revised budgets exercise. The policy change which led to immediate increases in budgeted current expenditure was the same in each case – the lowering of urban passenger transport fares. These had been manifesto commitments and were implemented despite the fact that it could be seen from the June letter that the resulting holdback penalties would be quite severe for all three authorities.

The Department of the Environment's press notice of 3 September 1981 summarized the failure of the revised budgets exercise as follows:

> Most local authorities (257 out of 413) have . . . reduced their expenditure . . . from . . . original budgets by £196 m in line with the Government's request . . . a small number of authorities have ignored the Government's request for economy . . . The total increase by these local authorities is £211 m of which £167 m is attributable to just 3 authorities. (DoE, 1981b, p. 1)

The experience of the revised budgets exercise led, of course, to the government's proposals for referendums contained in the Local Government Finance Bill. It also led ministers into more ambitious assertions with respect to the existence of a constitutional convention that local authorities had previously conformed to the wishes of central government with respect to aggregate expenditure plans. It was felt that for the first time, as Environment Minister Tom King said in the House of Commons on 12 November 1981, '[This] voluntary understanding [is now] under threat from people who are no longer prepared to accept the basic tradition on which local government has stood – the acceptance of the Government's responsibility to set overall public expenditure targets'. We return in the final section to an analysis of this alleged constitutional convention. In this section, however, the main priority is to demonstrate the actual importance of local politics and we will show that the effects of changes in political control were not confined to the three urban authorities who most seriously damaged the revised budgets exercise.

The GLC and metropolitan counties were able to increase expenditure so rapidly simply by forgoing revenue from transport fares by lowering charges. For the non-metropolitan counties, there was no equivalent large revenue source to forgo and obviously their main budgetary item – expenditure on schools – could not be increased rapidly. However, if we examine the evidence provided by the revised budgets exercise summarized in Table 4.5, we can see that the impact of changes in political control was also significant for the non-metropolitan counties. In Table 4.5 we split the non-metropolitan counties (excluding Durham) into three groups, classified according to the result of the May 1981 elections: (1) Conservative to Labour; (2) Conservative to no overall control; and (3) Conservative before and after. There was a difference of over 3 per cent in the change in current expenditure between the Conservative group and the other two groups. However, the Conservative group were slightly more overspent with respect to targets at original budgets – the revised budgets reversed this position. If all three groups had achieved the Conservatives' 2·55 per cent overspend with respect to targets, then the budgeted current expenditure of the non-metropolitan counties would have been £84 million lower at £7,259 million.

A CONSTITUTIONAL CONVENTION?

We have previously given two quotations from the many made by government ministers during this period which alleged that there had existed a constitutional convention towards conformity by individual local authorities with the 'informal obligation to adhere' to the total for local authority spending. Certainly the statistics in Table 4.6 show a conformity at the aggregate level during the latter half of the 1970s, with the government's expenditure plans embodied in the RSG relevant expenditure total and with the first signs of increasing divergence after the Conservatives came to office. However, critics of the government have argued that it is a major error to assert that the aggregate statistics show either: (*a*) the existence of a constitutional convention towards conformity at the individual authority level, or (*b*) the emergence of a unique new breed of local authority bent

Table 4.5 Current Expenditure, 1981–2: Budgets and Current Expenditure Targets, English Non-Metropolitan Counties (November 1980 prices)

'Group' of authorities	Current expenditure 1981–2		Percentage change in current expenditure between budgets	Current expenditure target (£m.)	Percentage overspend in relation to expenditure targets	
	Original budget (£m.)	Revised budget (£m.)			Original	Revised
Labour	2,096·964	2,113·823	0·80	2,002·966	4·69	5·53
No overall control	987·903	999·371	1·16	950·802	3·90	5·11
Conservative	4,335·148	4,229·805	−2·43	4,124·802	5·10	2·55
Total non-metropolitan counties*	7,420·015	7,342·999	−1·04	7,078·570	4·82	3·74

* Excluding Durham.
Source: DoE, 1981 a, memorandum, and 1981 b, exemplifications.

on flouting this convention. This is because it is argued that local government has always been composed of high-spending and low-spending authorities. Also it was argued by critics that the divergence of the early 1980s was due to the fact that the government was calling for much larger cuts than those requested by the previous Labour administration.

Table 4.6 *Relevant Expenditure: Comparison between RSG and Out-turn (England and Wales)*

	RSG £m.	Out-turn £m.	Percentage overspend
1975–6	9,986·8	10,055·5	0·7
1976–7	11,445·6	11,243·0	−1·8
1977–8	12,358·8	12,173·4	−1·5
1978–9	13,655·3	13,542·0	−1·8
1979–80	16,363·5	15,866·0	−3·0
1980–1	19,155	19,181†	0·1
1981–2*	18,673	19,881†	6·5

* England only.
† Provisional out-turn.
Source: Local Authority Associations (annual).

Ministerial response to such criticisms, as witnessed by their repeated reassertion of the existence of the conformity convention, has been zero. In fact ministers had a most useful source of support in former Labour Treasury Minister Joel Barnett, who provided the following observations on the behaviour of local authorities in the latter part of the 1970s:

> Labour local authorities which we had in greater preponderance at the outset (almost all were eliminated by 1978 after four years of Labour government), were not surprisingly eager to maintain regular increases in expenditure to sustain and improve public services. Conservative local authorities were more amenable to cutting expenditure, although they were as sensitive of their democratic rights as any Labour authority. All in all, we began the Consultative Council with some trepidation. In fact, we were remarkably successful, with both Labour and Conservative Councils, even though the Associations' chiefs had no control over their individual council members. (Barnett, 1982, pp. 75–6)

In fact we will show below that this interpretation by Barnett is wishful thinking. A later statement from the same section of *Inside the Treasury* contains a Freudian slip which gets us closer to the truth. In discussing the theory of control the quote given earlier p. 61) continues:

> Tony Crosland (as Secretary of State for the Environment) for his part, while reluctantly recognizing the need to cut expenditure, feared that the squeeze of a lower grant would simply lead to very large rate increases. I shared his concern, because of the possible effect on the Retail Price Index (RPI), but I had to balance that worry against the fact that this was virtually the only means we had of influencing the difficult local authorities. (ibid., p. 76)

Reference to 'the difficult local authorities' arouses suspicion with respect to Barnett's earlier assertion that Labour as well as Conservative authorities assisted the Labour government in meeting their expenditure plans. It also arouses suspicion with respect to the present assertion by Conservative ministers of a previous conformity convention.

However, it only arouses suspicion. What is unsatisfactory in this whole debate is that no evidence has been produced about individual local authority expenditure during previous periods when the alleged conformity convention operated. It is obviously of major interest to consider the period discussed by Barnett. Thus we will analyse the expenditure data for English local authorities at almost the exact opposite point in the national–local political cycle to 1981. Once again we will consider year-on-year changes in expenditure. The years chosen are 1978–9 compared to 1977–8. 1978–9 is chosen because it is the first budget available to show changes in the expenditure policies of those county authorities who had changes in political control in the 1977 county elections. In that year the Labour government was still concerned to see expenditure increases kept as low as possible and we may judge the extent of conformity by comparing the expenditure increases of the following groups of authorities.

(1) Non-metropolitan counties. Compare the six counties (Cleveland, Derbyshire, Humberside, Northamptonshire, Nottinghamshire and Staffordshire) which moved directly from Labour to Conservative control in 1977 with the twenty-nine counties which remained under Conservative control throughout. Here the expectation is that if conformity is a myth, we will observe expenditure readjustment policies among the six 'Labour-to-Conservative' counties such that their increases in expenditure

are significantly lower. This is confirmed in Table 4.7 where the Labour-to-Conservative group increased rate- and grant-borne expenditure by 2·95 percentage points less than the Conservative group, despite receiving larger increases in the main element (needs element) of rate support grant which is usually regarded as stimulating expenditure increases.

(2) Metropolitan counties. Compare the four authorities (Greater Manchester, Merseyside, West Midlands and West Yorkshire) which moved directly from Labour to Conservative control with the two counties which remained under Labour control throughout. Here again the expectation is that if conformity is a myth, the former group will exhibit lower expenditure increases. This again is confirmed by the data, where there is a difference of over 5 percentage points between the increase in rate- and grant-borne expenditure for the 'Labour throughout' group (16·48 per cent) and the 'Labour-to-Conservative' group (11·36 per cent).

We could observe similar differences among authorities not subject to election in 1977. Labour metropolitan districts increased their budgeted rate- and grant-borne expenditure between 1977–8 and 1978–9 by 11·66 per cent compared to the 8·36 per cent increase by Conservative metropolitan districts.

The refutation of the conformity myth will not be surprising to those with some knowledge of English local government. If it had not been refuted, we should find it hard to explain why the Conservative members of the Association of County Councils repeatedly complained that they were bearing the brunt of the cuts in the late 1970s and that there were authorities who were failing to cut expenditure. That this was the case is implicitly admitted by the Labour government in the Joint Departmental Circular of 29 December 1976, when in answer to the mounting pressure for discriminatory action against high-spending local authorities they stated that:

> The Government are aware of the view of some authorities that across-the-board reductions in grant are unfair to those authorities who have kept within the Government's expenditure guidelines. But there would be serious practical difficulties in seeking to identify those authorities who are overspending, and any attempt to do so would involve the Government more closely in the day-to-day affairs of individual authorities than has previously been contemplated. (DoE, 1976, para. 19)

Also the Conservative government did not act as if they believed in a conformity myth when they took office in 1979. As part of the

Table 4.7 Rate- and Grant-Borne Expenditure and Needs Element, English Non-metropolitan Counties, 1977–8 and 1978–9

Group of Authorities	Rate- and grant-borne expenditure			Needs element		
	1977–8 (£m.)	1978–9 (£m.)	Percentage increase	1977–8 (£m.)	1978–9 (£m.)	Percentage increase
Labour to Conservative control in 1977 elections	1,025·059	1,102·353	7·54	311·351	401·386	8·09
Conservative before and after 1977 elections	4,184·976	4,623·611	10·48	1,384·190	1,457·376	5·28

Sources: CIPFA (annual), 1978, 1979; Society of County Treasurers, 1980, p. 35.

justification for introducing a new grant system they emphasized that there were overspending local authorities. If they had felt that conformity ruled, then it was unnecessary to change the grant system and provide new disincentives to spending.

CONCLUSIONS: IS RATE-CAPPING NECESSARY?

The public posture adopted that conformity was the previous pattern, backed up by important previous Labour ministers such as Joel Barnett, provided a rationale (albeit an unsatisfactory one) for expecting cuts in expenditure without removing large amounts of grant. The hope was to achieve cuts without large rate increases.

We have shown here that despite the introduction of targets and grant penalties, the policy was doomed to failure. The inevitable consequence, given Mrs Thatcher's embarrassment with respect to her commitment on domestic rates and the Treasury's pre-occupation with local authority expenditure, has been the proposals for rate-capping and abolition of some of the major overspending authorities.

However, given the present intentions of the government, we finally review some of the major arguments offered in support of the rate-capping proposals. The major argument is the need for the government to be in greater control of the level of aggregate demand in the economy. Here we may recall the emphasis in Brittan's SOLACE speech on the level of overspending in relation to expenditure plans. However, such overspending is rate-financed and has no effect on the PSBR, and Jackman (1982) has shown that rate-financed additional expenditure by local government has far less effect on aggregate demand than has been asserted by the Treasury. It has, of course, been argued that extra rate finance by reducing the level of private savings will increase the level of interest rates. However, given the likely small size of reduction in savings, say, a small fraction of the £770 million present revenue overspend, it is hard to take this point seriously: as a determinant of the level of interest rates this seems to be an obvious minnow compared to the dominating influence of American and world interest rates. Further, the claimed unpredictability and level of local government overspending is very small compared to that surrounding the PSBR.[13] We agree with Jones *et al.* (1983) when they state that 'To manage the economy the Government needs to control its own expenditure, which includes its grant to local government, and to control borrowing by local authorities. There is no economic justification for controlling local government current expenditure if it is financed by local taxation'.

The other major argument put forward in the Rates White Paper is the heavy burden of local rates on commerce and industry. However, we must note that rates represent only 2·7 per cent of the costs of wages and salary of industry.

This leads us to the alternative strategy to rate-capping – reform of the system of local government finance with the objective of increasing local accountability and responsibility. Here one ingredient would be to reduce the level of central grants and replace the reduction in grant income by a local income tax which would result in local voters bearing a larger direct share of local expenditure. Also there are good reasons for equalizing actual non-domestic rate poundages, and this could be achieved by treating this as a national tax. The list of desirable potential reforms is large, including the major need to update domestic rateable values and transfer from the anachronistic practice of basing them on notional rental values rather than capital values.

Rate-capping is, we argue, an inappropriate response to a minor problem of centrally defined local 'overspending'. The major problem is how to increase the effectiveness of local democracy, and rate-capping unfortunately will lead to a dramatic reduction in the need for local responsibility and substitute a lobbying process for greater use of general fund (Exchequer) finance in support of local services.

NOTES: CHAPTER 4

1   Among previous papers which suggested this are Harrison and Lee, 1981, and Jones and Stewart, 1982. The extent of the inadequacy has been shown in Gibson, 1983a, 1983b.
2   See Department of the Environment, 1983a.
3   See DoE, 1983b.
4   See Brittan, 1982, p. 9.
5   For a useful statement of the basic theory see Wilde, 1968, or Gramlich, 1977.
6   See Gibson, 1982.
7   See Foster and Jackman, 1982.
8   See Gibson, 1982.
9   See Smith and Stewart, 1983.
10 See CIPFA, 1983, table C, p. 5.
11 See AMA, 1983.
12 See, for example, Newton and Sharpe, 1977.
13 Jones and Stewart, 1983, p. 10, note the evidence of a permanent under-secretary of the Treasury to a Select Committee that £1 billion of extra spending would have negligible effects on the economy.

REFERENCES: CHAPTER 4

Association of Metropolitan Authorities (AMA) (1983), *The RSG Settlement 1983/84* (London: AMA).

Barnett, J. (1982), *Inside the Treasury* (London: Deutsch).

Brittan, L. (1982), speech to the Society of Local Authority Chief Executives (SOLACE), Viking Hotel, York, 16 July.

Carvel, J. (1982), 'Local government', *Guardian*, 29 December.

Chartered Institute of Public Finance and Accountancy (CIPFA) (annual), *Finance, General and Rating Statistics* (London: CIPFA).

Department of the Environment (DoE) (1976), *Rate Support Grant Settlement 1977/78*, Circular 120/76 (London: DoE).

DoE (1981a), 'Local government expenditure 1981–82', statement by the Secretary of State for the Environment to the Consultative Council on Local Government Finance, 2 June.

DoE (1981b), 'Local government expenditure', statement by the Secretary of State for the Environment to the Consultative Council on Local Government Finance, 3 September.

DoE (1981c), *Alternatives to Domestic Rates*, Cmnd 8449 (London: HMSO).

DoE (1982), 'Local government expenditure and exchequer grant, settlement by the Secretary of State for the Environment to the Consultative Council on Local Government Finance', Department of the Environment, 27 July.

DoE (1983a), *Rates: Proposals for Rate Limitation and Reform of the Rating System*, Cmnd 9008 (London: HMSO).

DoE (1983b), *Streamlining the Cities: Government Proposals for Re-organising Local Government in Greater London and the Metropolitan Counties*, Cmnd 9063 (London: HMSO).

Foster, C. D., and Jackman, R. A. (1982), 'Accountability and control of local spending', *Public Money*, vol. 2, no. 2, pp. 11–14.

Gibson, J. G. (1982), 'The block (and target) grant system and local authority expenditure – theory and evidence', *Local Government Studies*, vol. 8, no. 3, pp. 15–31.

Gibson, J. G. (1983a), 'Block grant and holdback penalties – the manipulated grant system', *Local Government Studies*, vol. 9, no. 4, pp. 12–16.

Gibson, J. G. (1983b), 'Local "overspending": why the government have only themselves to blame', *Public Money*, vol. 3, no. 3, pp. 19–21.

Gramlich, E. M. (1977), 'Intergovernmental grants: a review of the empirical literature', in W. E. Oates (ed.), *The Political Economy of Fiscal Federalism* (Lexington, Mass.: Lexington Books), ch. 12.

Harrison, A., with Lee, G. (1981), 'Local authority budgets 1981', *Public Money*, vol. 1, no. 2, pp. 35–53.

Jackman, R. (1982), 'Does central government need to control the total of local government spending?' *Local Government Studies*, vol. 8, no. 3, pp. 75–90.

Jones, G. W., and Stewart, J. D. (1982), 'The Layfield analysis applied to central-local relations under the Conservative government', *Local Government Studies*, vol. 8, no. 3, pp. 47–59.

Jones, G. W., and Stewart, J. D. (1983), 'The Treasury and local government', *Political Quarterly*, vol. 54, no. 1, pp. 5–15.

Jones, G. W., Stewart, J. D., and Travers, T. (1983), *Rate Control: The Threat to Local Government* (London: Local Government Chronicle).

Local Authority Associations (annual), *Rate Support Grant* (London: Association of County Councils).

Newton, K., and Sharpe, L. J. (1977), 'Local outputs research: some reflections and proposals', *Policy and Politics*, vol. 5, no. 3, pp. 61–82.
Pauley, R. (1983), 'Most rate bills will rise more than inflation', *Financial Times*, 17 January.
Pliatsky, L. (1982), *Getting and Spending* (Oxford: Blackwell).
Smith, P., and Stewart, J. (1983), 'Local authority spending 1983/84', *Public Finance and Accountancy*, vol. 10, no. 5, pp. 35–9.
Society of County Treasurers (1980), *Needs Element Statistics 1980–81* (Reading: Society of County Treasurers).
Wilde, J. A. (1968), 'The expenditure effects of grant-in-aid programs', *National Tax Journal*, vol. 21, no. 3, pp. 340–8.

5

Law

OWEN LOMAS

The purpose of this chapter is to examine, by reference to a selection of recent court cases, the nature of the constitutional and legal resource and its effects on the centre–local exchange process (cf. Rhodes, 1979, 1981). The idea of law as a resource has already received some attention from public lawyers, notably Elliott (1981). While not seeking to challenge the efficacy of characterizing law as a resource in the centre–local relationship, Elliott draws attention to a number of difficulties that this creates from the standpoint of public law. First, he points out that central government's prerogative and dominium[1] powers, and its virtual legislative monopoly, mean that this resource is not distributed equally between the parties.[2] Rather bargaining 'is on terms dictated by the centre'. Secondly, he notes that traditionally the role of public law has been seen as 'a method of providing redress for the grievances held by a fundamentally disadvantaged individual against the State' rather than 'as a method of regulating a bargain struck between two institutional bodies', as envisaged by its characterization as a resource in the centre–local relationship. He suggests that, as a result, the courts are unsuited to performing such a regulatory role. Thirdly, Elliott argues that central and local government rarely use litigation as a resource in the exchange process, and that the *ad hoc* nature of court actions which arises from other sources makes them of little use to either party. He therefore, sees the court's role in determining the legality of central and local government action as having little bearing on the centre–local relationship. Finally, Elliot makes an observation of paramount importance to the understanding of the role of the law as a resource. He points out that although the constitutional and legal resource must be derived from public law, the very concept of public law in Britain today is a problematic one. The argument here is that although the powers, duties and functions of local government and to a large extent central government are laid down by statute, the process of determining their extent and how the powers may be used is based upon highly uncertain and problematic 'rules and principles' of administrative law, which owe their existence to the common law developed by the courts.

Although some of Elliott's comments on the idea of law as a resource are open to criticism,[3] they provide a very useful point of departure for further analysis of its nature and effects. His last point, in particular, demonstrates that since it must be derived from public law, the constitutional and legal resource itself is not a fixed and unproblematic commodity and cannot simply be listed alongside other resources as something which each party either has or does not have in a given situation. Nor is it quantifiable. One cannot talk about units of this resource in the same way that one talks, for example, about finance. Rather the constitutional and legal resource is highly complex, and like the centre–local relationship itself, it has a dynamic life of its own. It is, therefore, susceptible to the manifold influences which are brought to bear on the public law upon which it is based. Of particular importance here are a variety of complex and often conflicting ideologies which underlie the subject-matter of public law. Thus, for example, there is an ideologically grounded conflict concerning the purposes of administrative law which has traditionally centred on whether its primary role is to protect private rights, or to facilitate government action in the public interest, although more recently a third role as a means of promoting public participation in decision-making has been asserted.[4]

From where, then, do these ideological inputs materialize? From the judiciary certainly. The dual role of judges as adjudicators and developers of the law renders them of paramount importance. But the judiciary is passive and cannot act alone. It can only be activated by a litigant, seeking support or redress from the courts. Here, then, is another potential ideological input. If, for example, litigants are disproportionately individuals seeking to protect private rights, all other things being equal, this is likely to reinforce the ideological presumption that this is the primary purpose of administrative law. Academic lawyers by what they write, and practising lawyers by the advice they give and the arguments advanced, may also provide an ideological input.

What is being asserted here, then, is that the legal and constitutional resource is a problematic, dynamic multi-faceted commodity and that this must be recognized and analysed if its role in the exchange process between central and local government is to be understood. This is particularly so since the whole bargaining process between central and local government, in so far as it involves the constitutional and legal resource, is dependent upon and conditioned by the parties' understanding of law and its application to the subject-matter of bargaining. And it is precisely in the areas of greatest uncertainty, namely, those relating to the extent of local and central government powers and the ways in which they may be properly exercised, that bargaining is likely to be at its most intense. It is also in these areas that the influence of the courts and the judiciary, through previous case law, is likely to be greatest because, as we have already noted, they have been and continue to be almost exclusively responsible for the law's development here. In other words, the uncertainties and conflicting ideologies inherent in the legal and constitutional resource which arise, in part, from the role of the courts and the judiciary penetrate right into the heart of the exchange process between central and local government. In this respect Elliott's contention that the role of the courts in determining the legality of central and local government action has little bearing on the centre–local relationship seems inaccurate.

THE CASES

When the courts are called upon to determine the legality of central or local government's exercise of their statutory powers, and therefore the nature and extent of those powers, they are essentially concerned with two questions. Has there been an excess of power, and/or has there been an abuse of power? We shall, therefore, examine the cases under these two headings. Our concern will be to see what 'rules and principles' of administrative law were employed to determine whether power had been exceeded or abused, and to consider what ideological premises may have been involved and the implications this may have for the legal resource in the centre–local relationship. It will be seen that under each heading great scope is provided for judicial discretion.

An Excess of Power
In order to determine whether a power has been exceeded the courts must interpret the relevant statutory provisions.

Local authorities' powers of subsidy. In *Bromley* v. *The GLC*[5] the House of Lords declared unlawful a supplementary precept raised by the Greater London Council in order to implement its 'fares fair' policy of reducing London Transport's bus and tube fares on the basis, *inter alia*, that the Council had exceeded its

discretionary powers. The statute in question was the Transport
(London) Act 1969. Under section 3 of this Act the GLC was
empowered to give subsidies to the London Transport Executive
(the transport providers) 'for any purpose'. It might be thought,
therefore, that at least as far as the GLC's statutory powers were
concerned, no exception could be taken to any subsidy on the
ground that it was for an unlawful purpose. The House of Lords,
however, decided otherwise for two reasons. First, because the
Council's power to give subsidies (and the LTEs' to receive them),
had to be interpreted in the context of their other powers and
duties and the statute overall. Of relevance here[6] was the financial
duty imposed on the LTE to 'break even' as far as practicable (a
duty to which the GLC was to 'have regard'), and their general
duties and powers to provide public transport services 'with due
regard to efficiency, *economy* and safety of operation' (the LTE)
and 'to promote the provision of integrated, efficient and *economic*
transport facilities and services' (the GLC). These provisions,
taken together, led the House of Lords to conclude that the statute
overall required the LTE 'as far as practicable to carry out its
functions on ordinary business lines by meeting operating
expenditure out of their income',[7] and thus circumscribed the
GLC's power to make subsidies accordingly. The words 'for any
purpose' used in section 3 did not, therefore, mean for *any*
purpose.

This conclusion was not inevitable. The provisions of the 1969
Act were capable of a variety of interpretations, as was
demonstrated by Lord Diplock, who interpreted them differently.
He saw nothing in the provisions 'that should lead to the
conclusion that the revenue account of the LTE ... is limited to
income [from fares] ... so as to exclude grants made by the GLC
... under the power contained in section 3 to make grant to the
LTE "for any purpose" which on the face of it is unfettered'.[8] The
effect of the majority's decision, however, was to alter radically the
commonly understood meaning of the expression 'for any
purpose' and, by implication, phrases like it used in other statutes,
and thus throw into doubt the nature and extent of statutory
powers of this kind.

The second reason for the House of Lords decision was their
finding that there was a general principle in law that transport
undertakings were to operate on 'ordinary business principles',
unless the terms of any statute provided otherwise. This finding
was not inevitable either. It arose from the court's interpretation of
the case of *Prescott* v. *Birmingham*[9] in 1955, in which a scheme to
allow free travel to elderly people had been declared unlawful on

the basis that the statute governing the transport undertaking required that fares be fixed 'in accordance with business principles'. If one examines this case, however, it is clear that the court was not laying down a general principle. It was only concerned with the interpretation of the statute relevant in that case (cf. Loughlin, 1983, p. 42). Yet the effects of the House of Lords finding was to elevate this decision to a general principle of law, the applicability of which was to be presumed unless the relevant statute provided otherwise. The importance of this finding cannot be overestimated. Once made, the outcome of the case was inevitable and the highly controversial issue of whether public transport should be run on semi-business lines or as a social service was effectively closed.

It is apparent from the judgments that the primary consideration which led the House of Lords to their decision was that any departure from 'ordinary business principles' would involve additional subsidies, the cost of which would have to be borne by the ratepayers. By interpreting the statutory provision in the way that they did, and by making the 'ordinary business principles' presumption, this could however be avoided and the interests of the ratepayers protected. The ideological basis of their decision can, therefore, be seen to be the desire to minimize the amount of private financial resources which could be legitimately appropriated to contribute to the cost of providing public transport and thus the redistributive dimension of the statutory provisions. Ultimately, then, the decision was based upon the ideology of private property.

The House of Lords decision, and its implications, came as a great shock to transport authorities, who had seen their functions as including a social service dimension. However, potentially their decision had far wider implications, particularly bearing in mind the ideological considerations upon which it was based. If the functions of local authorities in relation to public transport could be interpreted in this way, could their other statutory functions be given similar treatment? The answer to this question was no longer certain. Nor could it be said, with any confidence, what provisions or words were required in statute, in order firmly to establish that what was intended was essentially a social service rather than a quasi-business operation.

Clearly the 'discovery' of the 'ordinary business principles' presumption also had direct political ramifications in the context of the centre–local relationship. It was consistent with central government's monetarist policy of cutting public expenditure and reducing the role of the welfare state. As such, it provided the government with a useful legal resource to be used in the exchange process with local government, in the context of financial controls and the lack of legitimate financial needs for public transport provision, and potentially in the provision of other services as well.

Following the *Bromley* v. *The GLC* case, the fare subsidies of a number of local authorities were thrown into doubt, and one authority, faced with a challenge to the legality of its fares reductions, capitulated and increased them again.[10] In *R. v. Merseyside C.C. ex. parte Great Universal Stores Ltd*,[11] however, the council successfully resisted a challenge to the legality of a supplementary precept it had raised to finance a cut in fares. The relevant statute here was the Transport Act 1968, the provisions of which the Divisional Court described as having a 'very marked similarity' to the 1969 Act but with 'an important distinction as to emphasis',[12] namely, that the general powers and duties of the council and the PTE were wider than those of the GLC and the LTE. As a result, the court was able to determine both that the duty to avoid deficits was not of the same paramount importance as it was under the 1969 Act and that this displaced the 'ordinary business principles' presumption sufficiently to allow the reduction in fares decided on by the council.

The provisions of the 1969 Act itself were further examined by the Divisional Court in *R. v. LTE ex. parte GLC*.[13] This case was brought by the GLC as a result of its inability to reach a mutual agreement with the LTE about the nature and limits of their respective powers and duties under the 1969 Act. The GLC proposed to cut fares by 25 per cent, thus returning to the fare levels that had existed prior to their abortive 'fares fair' policy, and had been advised by their counsel that this would be lawful. However, the LTE were advised by their counsel that if they were to receive such a subsidy, they would be in breach of their duties under the 1969 Act. The Divisional Court found unanimously in favour of the GLC. This decision was remarkable, in view of the findings of the House of Lords in *Bromley* v. *The GLC*, which was binding on the Divisional Court. The way the court arrived at this decision was ingenious, to say the least. Essentially what the court did was to accept that the LTE had 'as far as practicable' to operate on 'ordinary business principles' but then went on to find that the statute afforded both the GLC and the LTE considerable discretion in determining *how far* this was practicable. This enabled the court to overcome the 'ordinary business principles' presumption and conclude that the GLC *did*, in the circumstances, have statutory power to impose a cut in fares of 25 per cent and to make up the deficit by grants to the LTE.

In some respects the decisions in the Mersyside and *GLC* v. *LTE* cases were seen as reassuring for local authorities. They appeared to represent a retreat from the position taken by the House of Lords in *Bromley* v. *The GLC*. It should, however, be appreciated that these were Divisional Court decisions and that the House of Lords judgment remains the law. Their chief significance, therefore, is that they demonstrate how uncertain and unpredictable the court's interpretation of critical statutory provisions can be. The ability of transport authorities to depart from 'ordinary business principles' and subsidize as an object of social policy, for example, could, it seems, depend upon small variations in the wording of a statute.

Central government's powers of intervention. Two cases involving the courts' interpretation of statutory provisions relating to the powers and duties of central and local government are compared and contrasted here. In *Secretary of State for Education & Science* v. *Metropolitan Borough of Tameside* (1976)[14] the minister sought unsuccessfully to have a direction issued against the council under section 68 of the Education Act 1944 enforced by the courts. The case arose from the decision of the newly elected Conservative council to reverse the plans of the previous Labour administration to 'go comprehensive' in September 1976. The minister believed that it was too late to reverse this decision and, therefore, used his powers under section 68 to direct the authority to implement the plans for comprehensive education, and applied to the courts to have this order enforced. Section 68 allows the minister to act where he 'is satisfied ... that any LEA ... have acted or are proposing to act *unreasonably*'. The House of Lords decided that the word 'unreasonably' meant 'conduct which no sensible authority acting with due appreciation of its responsibilities would have decided to adopt'.[15] The Lords found, on the evidence, that Tameside's actions did not amount to such conduct, with the result that the minister's direction could not be enforced. The concept of 'unreasonableness', defined in this way, is familiar to public lawyers. It provides one of the grounds upon which the courts will find that discretionary power has been abused and that a decision taken in reliance upon it is, therefore, unlawful. What the House of Lords did was to take the definition used in this context and apply it to the wholly different context of section 68 of the Education Act 1944. The effect of this was greatly to narrow the scope of the minister's powers. Essentially it turned his power to issue directions where he was satisfied that the authority was acting or proposing to act unreasonably (in the ordinary meaning of the word) into the power only to review the *legality* of the authority's actions, the latter of which he in all probability did not doubt anyway. It also shifted the whole emphasis of the case away from a review of the minister's directions and on to a review of the legality of the authority's actions. That this was not the relevant issue in relation to the minister's powers under section 68, and that the definition given to 'unreasonableness' was not the appropriate one, is made clear if one looks at section 99 of the Act. Under this section the minister is empowered to make a default order, enforceable by the courts, if he is satisfied that any LEA has 'failed to discharge any duty imposed upon them'. It will be appreciated that this section would apply whenever an LEA acted unlawfully by breaching its statutory duty, including where it engaged in 'conduct which no sensible authority acting with due appreciation of its responsibilities would have decided to adopt'. Thus if the same narrow interpretation is given to unreasonableness in section 68, the section becomes superfluous. It is only possible, therefore, to make sense of section 68 if 'unreasonableness' is given its ordinary, everyday meaning, and the minister has the power to issue directions where he is satisfied that an LEA is acting 'unreasonably' even though it is *not* acting unlawfully.

The failure of the House of Lords to interpret section 68 in this way appeared to deprive central government of an extremely important legal resource in its relationship with local government. As such, the decision had potentially far-reaching implications and generated considerable alarm and uncertainty. One effect of the decision which could not, however, have been envisaged at the time is the way in which central government has been able to turn the Lords' narrow interpretation of the section 68 powers to its own advantage. This occurred when cuts in local government expenditure, encouraged by central government, led to concern being expressed about declining educational standards. Faced with demands to use the section 68 powers to intervene, central government was able to claim, following the Tameside case, that they could do so only where an LEA was acting *unlawfully*. The consequences of this were described by the House of Commons Select Committee on Education[16] as 'profoundly disturbing'. It meant that the only safeguards on maintenance of standards in education were the minimum legal duties and responsibilities, expressed in very general and vague terms, in the Education Act 1944. This was, however, very convenient for central government in its single-minded pursuit of reduced local government expenditure. Ironically it was able to use the decision in Tameside as a legal resource which legitimated its refusal to intervene. As a result, it was able to avoid placing itself in the embarrassing situation of having to intervene to maintain educational standards, while demanding the cuts in expenditure which threatened those standards. What had started life as a decision which appeared to favour local government, at the expense of central government, therefore turned out to be exactly the opposite, thus providing a clear illustration of how unpredictable such legal resources can be.

The other case to be considered here is *Norwich C.C.* v. *Secretary of State for the Environment* (1982),[17] in which the Court of Appeal dismissed an application by Norwich City Council to have quashed an order made against them by the minister under section 23 of the Housing Act 1980. This Act gives council tenants a statutory 'right to buy'. Under section 23, where it appears to the minister that 'tenants have or may have difficulty in exercising their right to buy effectively and expeditiously', he is given exceptionally wide powers to 'do all such things as appear to him to be necessary and expedient' to enable tenants to exercise this right. These powers were described by the court as 'coercive'[18] and 'draconian'.[19] It was, therefore, of critical importance to determine in what circumstances the minister could lawfully make an order under section 23. Here the court decided that as the ability of a minister to use his powers rested on a belief that tenants were having or may have difficulty in exercising their right to buy effectively and expeditiously, the conduct and circumstances of the local authority had no bearing on the legality of any order made against them. This decision was in stark contrast to the one in Tameside where, as we have seen, the reference in section 68 of the Education Act to the 'unreasonableness' of the local authority's actions made their conduct and circumstances the central issue in the case. It is easy to account for these contrasting decisions by simply drawing attention to the different drafting of the respective statutory provisions – the one placing emphasis on the local authority's conduct, and the other on the tenants' difficulties. There is little doubt that central government's object in drafting the latter provision in this way was to avoid the need for any consideration of the local authorities' conduct. However, to let the matter rest here would be to miss a further contrast in the treatment given to the two statutory provisions which is of considerable importance and cannot easily be explained by reference to the different ways in which they are drafted. In Tameside the courts subjected the provision and the word 'unreasonably' to minute examination, and not content to give the latter its ordinary, everyday meaning, they proceeded to define it very narrowly. In Norwich, however, no consideration was given to what was meant by 'difficulty' for tenants in exercising their right to buy 'effectively and expeditiously'. Rather, then, it is apparent from the case that the court was content to give these words their ordinary, everyday meaning. Had they instead followed the approach adopted in Tameside, it would have been open to them to take the view that the meaning of these words had to be judged in the context of what it was reasonably possible for the local authority to do, having regard to their statutory duties overall and their limited resources. If this was not the case, it might have been argued, then taking matters to their logical conclusion it would have been possible for the minister to intervene whenever a tenant could not complete his purchase on the same day as he requested it, and such a result clearly could not have been intended by Parliament.

Had the court taken this course, it is not suggested that it would necessarily have affected the outcome of the case. What is being suggested, however, is that it is significant that the courts avoided taking it, despite the precedent in the Tameside case. In trying to account for this one is driven to the conclusion that ideological considerations relating to the institution of private property were, once again, at work. Evidence of this comes from the words of one judge, in particular, who stated that 'The concern of the court, as always is to protect the individual from the misuse or abuse of the power by those in authority. The individual here is the tenant'.[20] The tenant's right to acquire private property was, therefore, seen as paramount. Although there can be little doubt that it was the intention of the legislation that this should be so, what is interesting is that the courts were so clearly responsive to Parliament's intentions in a way which they had not been, for example, in the Tameside case. This can only be explained, it is suggested, by the high value placed upon private property interests and the low value afforded other interests which it was the council's responsibility to protect. Once it is appreciated that the court saw the case in these terms, it becomes possible to explain why the judges had no difficulty in overcoming any doubts they might have been expected to have about sanctioning the use of such wide powers by central government without reference to the conduct of the local authority concerned. This was because the case was not seen as being concerned primarily with the relationship between central and local government. The overriding importance attached to the private property interests of the tenants meant that the issue was seen instead as being one between tenants and 'those in authority' (that is, the council), with the minister coming into the picture only as an agent of the tenants in order to protect their interests.

While the court, then, did not see the case as being primarily concerned with the centre–local relationship, there is no doubt that their decision had major implications for it. It resulted in a reallocation of legal resources in favour of the centre, the importance of which lies not only in the increased powers it gave to the latter in relation to housing policy; the decision approved also a legislative formula which could be used in the future greatly to increase the power of central government in the control of other functions of local government. Following the judgment, it became apparent that if central government's powers of intervention were based upon the inability of service recipients to obtain their rights rather than on the failure of local authorities to provide them, then this would be likely to maximize the power and discretion of the minister. In particular, the effect of this would be to avoid the need to consider the council's duty to provide a service and the minister's powers to enforce this duty in the context of the council's overall duties and responsibilities and its available resources. The implications of this for local government were serious. It meant that, as is now the case in relation to the duty to sell council houses, local authorities would lose the power they currently have to determine priorities and allocate resources as between competing statutory duties and functions, provided they comply with their minimum legal obligations. The consequences of this for services not protected by ministerial powers of intervention, expressed in these terms, could be very damaging. As an increasing proportion of local authorities' resources were taken up in providing 'maximum' services over which they had no discretion, such unprotected services could be expected to receive less and less. Again evidence of this is already available in the area of housing, where the concentration of resources (in particular, manpower) on selling council houses is accompanied by minimal allocations of resources to processing rent and rate rebates or to the administration of other housing services such as repairs or transfers, despite the demand for these services. It should be noted, however, that since the court's approval of this legislative formula in the Norwich case rested on its commitment to private property interests, it is, therefore, open to question as to whether a similar approach would be adopted where such interests were not at stake.

AN ABUSE OF POWER

One of the grounds on which the courts may decide that there has been an abuse of discretionary power is where a decision is based on irrelevant considerations or is made without regard to relevant considerations. Statutes rarely specify what these considerations are. The courts are left to decide, and this confers wide powers upon them. Here we examine the courts' treatment of two such considerations.

Local Authorities Fiduciary Duty to Ratepayers

In the *Bromley* v. *The GLC* case the House of Lords decided that the council had failed to take into consideration, or had breached, a fiduciary duty it owed to its ratepayers 'not to expend [their] . . . money thriftlessly but to deploy the full financial resources available to the best advantage'.[21] The concept of a fiduciary duty to the ratepayer is not statutory; it was created by the courts. It has a long history, but prior to the GLC case, it had not been used for over twenty-five years and its continued relevance was open to doubt. In the GLC case, however, it assumed a critical importance to the legality of local authority decisions. The case well illustrates how the courts can select relevant considerations after the event, and on finding that a body has failed to have regard to them declare their decisions unlawful.

The GLC was deemed to have breached its fiduciary duty to the ratepayers because its decision to reduce fares not only involved an increase in rates to make up for the reduced fares income, but necessitated nearly doubling that increase because of the grant penalty implications of the additional expenditure. Ironically although central government was not a party to the case, it was the operation of its own block grant penalties which had played a major part in rendering the GLC's policy unlawful. The decision was, therefore, very helpful to the centre. It supported the government's policy of reducing local government expenditure and suggested that while grant penalties did not control local authorities' total expenditure, they could operate to make additional expenditure unlawful.

In order to support its decision the court sought to draw a distinction between ratepayers and transport users and to suggest that there was a conflict of interests between them. It was pointed out,[22] for example, that only 40 per cent of residents in Greater London (that is, the potential transport users) were ratepayers and that they contributed only 38 per cent of the total rates burden (the balance being contributed by commercial ratepayers). The validity of this distinction has been rightly criticized as unduly narrow and formalistic.[23] But the fact that it was drawn brought into question the very role of local authorities as redistributors of resources except where statutes, as interpreted by the courts, expressly authorized it. It raised the possibility, then, that when service recipients might be seen as a different category of people to ratepayers, any provision for them over and above that required to fulfil statutory duties and obligations might be a breach of the local authority's fiduciary duty to its ratepayers. It was, therefore, profoundly disturbing to local government and generated maximum uncertainty. This uncertainty was further magnified by the wide terms in which several judges appeared to define the scope of the fiduciary duty consideration. Rather than suggesting that it was a consideration which local authorities must have regard to in exercising their discretionary powers, they appeared to interpret fiduciary duty as an *overriding* consideration. In other words, they created the impression that it was not enough merely for a local authority to take into consideration the interests of ratepayers; in order to avoid breaching the fiduciary duty owed to them it had to ensure that the ratepayers' interests came first.

The fiduciary duty consideration overlapped in the GLC case, with the 'ordinary business principles' presumption which the House of Lords decided should also apply to the case. In considering the ideological basis for this decision it was suggested that the judges were influenced by their desire to protect private property, the interests of which were implicitly at stake. The court's concentration on the GLC's fiduciary duty to the ratepayers provided further and more direct evidence. The concept of such a duty to the ratepayers is itself synonymous with a duty to protect private property interests, and the definition and scope which the House of Lords gave to it well demonstrates their strong commitment to such interests.

The fiduciary duty aspect of *Bromley* v. *The GLC* was not at issue in the later case of *GLC* v. *LTE*, and was not therefore considered. It was, however, an issue in the Merseyside case. But here the Divisional Court, influenced by the fact that there were no additional grant penalty implications in the authority's fares policy, decided that the duty had not been breached.

The House of Lords' rediscovery of the fiduciary duty concept has had major effects on the centre–local relationship, as the following three examples illustrate. The first concerns the government's implicit use of the concept in the Transport Act 1983 as a means of controlling transport subsidies without formally appearing to do so. This Act enables the minister to lay down guidelines for subsidies. Provided transport authorities keep within these guidelines, they are immune from legal challenge. They are, however, free to exceed the guidelines if they so wish.

But if they do so, they lay themselves open to challenge on the basis, *inter alia*, that they are in breach of their fiduciary duty to the ratepayer. This operates as a powerful restraint on subsidy levels and encourages transport authorities to comply with the guidelines. Yet central government is able to maintain that it has not taken legal powers to control subsidies.

The second illustration concerns the effects that the 'rediscovery' of the fiduciary duty concept has had in other areas of local authority activity. Wherever discretionary decisions involve expenditure over and above that which is necessary to comply with minimum statutory obligations, the question now arises as to whether such decisions might constitute a breach of this duty. Obvious examples are the permissible levels of subsidy for council housing and school meals. Discretionary decisions of this kind have now become the subject of counsel's opinion, with local authorities seeking advice as to the legality of alternative courses of action.[24] These examples demonstrate how far uncertainty over the scope of their legal resources has penetrated local authorities' decision-making, and can serve even to dominate it, thus undermining their ability to exercise their discretionary powers on the merits of the issue before them. Such uncertainties in local government's legal resources have themselves become a legal resource for the centre within the centre–local relationship.

The final illustration concerns local government's powers under section 137 of the Local Government Act 1972. This section permits local authorities to spend up to the product of a 2p rate on activities which because there is no specific statutory authority for them would otherwise be unlawful. This power has been much valued by local authorities because it is free from central government restriction and control, and proposals to give specific powers in areas where they are currently reliant on section 137 have, therefore, traditionally met with a cool response. The effect of the House of Lords' 'rediscovery' of the fiduciary duty concept, however, has been to cast doubt on whether all activities pursued by local authorities under this section can be justified as consistent with this duty. As a result, a remarkable change in attitude has occurred, with a number of authorities now favouring specific powers – albeit subject to central government restriction and control, and to the legal uncertainties of section 137. One of local government's most valuable legal resources has therefore been undermined, thus buttressing central government's policy of controlling its activities and expenditure, and the prospect now exists for a further reallocation of legal resources in favour of the centre.

Local Authorities' Electoral Mandates

Although the concept of an electoral mandate is unknown in law, it is possible that it may be a relevant consideration to be taken into account when central or local government are exercising their discretionary powers. Evidence of this comes from the Tameside case. Here the House of Lords stated that the status of the council as an elected body was 'vital' to the interpretation of the minister's powers to intervene on the basis that it was acting unreasonably. The court went on to say that in a 'strongly fought' election the new administration's policy had been 'approved by the electorate and massively supported by parents' and that the minister had 'failed to take into account that it [the authority] was entitled – indeed in a sense bound – to carry out the policy on which it was elected'.[25]

This view, however, is to be contrasted with the treatment given to the GLC's mandate for its 'fares fair' policy in *Bromley* v. *The GLC* when the case was before the Court of Appeal. There the court talked in very disparaging terms about the importance of election manifestos and suggested that if an electoral mandate was a relevant consideration at all (and even this seemed to be in doubt), it need not be given undue weight or importance.[26]

Although it is possible in legal terms to reconcile these two views of the electoral mandate,[27] the fact remains that remarkably different attitudes to its importance and relevance are displayed. Further support is, therefore, lent to the suggestion that the courts in these cases were heavily influenced by their attitudes and ideology concerning the substantive issues involved, tailoring their arguments accordingly on the relevance of the electoral mandate and on the other questions before them. This demonstrates once again how the courts' ability to determine the relevant considerations can radically affect the legality of the exercise of discretionary power and, in turn, legal resources.

CONCLUSION

The analysis of the above cases demonstrates how susceptible is the legal resource to the vagaries of the judicially created and applied 'rules and principles' of administrative law. Thus it is seen how the judicial freedom they afford to the courts in interpreting statutory provisions, and determining the relevant and irrelevant considerations, enables decisions to be made which may have major repercussions far beyond the instant case, sometimes resulting in sudden reallocations of the resource between central and local government.

The analysis also illustrates two other characteristics of the resource attributed by Elliott (1981). Firstly, it highlights the unequal distribution occasioned by central government's superior ability to legislate – as evidenced by the Housing Act 1980 and the Transport Act 1983. Secondly, it demonstrates the courts' lack of awareness and insensitivity to the nature and functions of local authorities and the needs of public administration, and a consequent inability to regulate effectively the centre–local relationship. Examples here include the attitude evinced towards social policy considerations inherent in *Bromley* v. *The GLC* and the narrow and formalistic distinctions drawn between ratepayers and transport users; and the failure to comprehend the realities of the respective roles of central and local government in education policy in the Tameside case. Moreover, there is an obvious inability of the judiciary to appreciate the major implications which their decisions, in all the cases considered, may have for central–local relations.

The final point to emerge from the case analysis concerns the nature of judicial attitudes and ideologies and the influence they can have on court decisions and therefore on the legal resource. An ideological pattern is seen clearly to emerge from the decisions of the higher courts,[28] which is based upon the desire to protect and further the interests of private property[29] and, in wider terms, private rights. Thus in *Bromley* v. *The GLC* we saw how the court's interpretation of the statutory provisions and the 'ordinary business principles' presumption, together with the concept of fiduciary duty and the attitude taken to the Council's electoral mandate, were all brought to the aid of the ratepayers; and how in the Norwich case the court was pleased to embrace the tenants' 'right to buy' by interpreting widely the minister's powers of intervention on their behalf. Similarly, in the Tameside case we saw how the court's narrow interpretation of the minister's powers of intervention and the importance attached to the council's electoral mandate was used to promote parental rights to selective education for their children. These examples illustrate that the role of public law is seen, primarily, as a method of providing redress for disadvantaged individuals against the state (both nationally and locally). As one judge said in the Norwich case, 'the concern of the court, as always, is to protect the individual from misuse or abuse of power by those in authority'.[30]

However, a corollary to this desire to protect private rights is an antipathy to public service provision and to local state intervention, which is intensified by the perceived distinction between such rights and the rights of service recipients – as evidenced by the ratepayer–transport user distinction in *Bromley* v. *The GLC*. The antipathy is illustrated by the use of the 'ordinary business principles' presumption and the fiduciary duty concept, which militate against any provision above the statutory minimum; and again in the Tameside and Norwich cases, acting against comprehensive education and public sector housing respectively.

What are the effects of these ideologies on the centre–local relationship? Whether one looks at the diminished powers of local authorities and the legal uncertainties afflicting them or at the reduced service provision occasioned by the enhancement of private rights, and also the impairment of their ability to determine priorities in the allocation of resources, the result is the same. A shift of legal and other resources to the centre, given its existing policy. What is of critical importance to appreciate, however, is that this does not represent a *deliberate* reallocation to the centre of legal powers and resources. Rather it is incidental. Indeed, the overwhelming concern of the courts and the judiciary to protect private rights means that they have a tendency to be as wary of central government power, and the dangers of increasing it, as they are about the powers of local government. As a result, if the courts were to be faced with litigation concerning central–local relations, unrelated to other ideological considerations, their attitude would likely be ambivalent. There would be no basis on which to favour one side or the other. This is particularly so since the courts have no concept of local democracy equivalent to their conception of private rights. Instead they see their role in relation to local government, like that in relation to central government, as being one of control. However, if private rights are involved, the position is entirely different. Indeed, it is likely to determine the issue. Thus, in the Norwich case the outcome was favourable to the tenants, and therefore to the centre, whereas in the Tameside case the positions were reversed and a favourable outcome for the parents (as the court saw it) was also favourable to the locality. The role of private rights can, therefore, be seen to be of critical importance, and it is this rather than any predisposition to the centre on the part of the courts which accounts for the reallocation of resources to the centre that has occurred.

It should be noted, however, that this reallocation of resources to the centre will only occur when the policies of central government coincide with the ideologies of the courts, as represented by their commitment to private rights. Thus we can see that the outcome of the Tameside case was, at the time, unfavourable to the centre, given its commitment to comprehensive education. Today the position is reversed. Central government policy is now in conformity with court ideology, and the outcome of a case is therefore favourable to these policies.

Today, then, there is effectively an identity of ideological objectives between the higher courts and central government. This is evidenced by the willingness of the courts to approve such wide powers for central government in the Norwich case. It is also demonstrated by the way in which government policy and developments in the courts, though separate, are running in parallel and feeding off each other. Central government's block grant penalties, for example, provided the court in the GLC case with the grounds it needed to determine that there had been a breach of the Council's fiduciary duty to its ratepayers. Equally the courts' 'rediscovery' of the fiduciary duty concept assisted central government in its policy of reducing local authority expenditure and public services – as illustrated by its implicit use in the Transport Act 1983.

It is seen, then, that central government and the higher courts are currently partners on a course which the latter have steered for many years. Arguably the courts have pursued this course with less confidence and assertiveness than they do today. But it should not come as a surprise to find that judges can be sensitive to the political climate, or that potential litigants should be influenced by this same climate in deciding whether to proceed with their litigation upon which the courts depend before they can assert themselves. There can be little doubt that the courts will continue to follow the same road in the future. Consequently, the partnership with central government will last only for as long as the latter steers the same course. For as long as it does, however, the two together are a powerful combination, eroding local autonomy and discretion.

NOTES:CHAPTER 5

1 Elliott borrows this term from the work of Daintith: 'dominium' power is derived from the ownership and ability to use and dispose of resources. It is to be distinguished from 'imperium' power, which is the power to rule.
2 Rhodes concedes this: see Rhodes *et al.*, 1983.
3 See below, p. 96; and on 'dominium' powers, Loughlin, 1983, pp. 98–9.
4 See McAuslan, 1980.
5 *Bromley London Borough Council* v. *The Greater London Council.* [1982] 1 All E.R., p. 129.
6 See sections 7(3), 7(6), 5 and 1 of the 1969 Act.
7 L. J. Oliver in the Court of Appeal (see n. 5, above, p. 140) approved by the House of Lords.

8 See n. 5, above, p. 163.
9 Prescott v. Birmingham Corporation [1955], ch. 210.
10 *R. v. West Midlands C.C., ex. parte Solihull B.C.*, 1982 (unreported).
11 (1982) LGR 639.
12 ibid., p. 650.
13 *R. v. London Transport Executive, ex. parte Greater London Council; The Times*, 28 January 1984.
14 [1976] 3 WLR, p. 641.
15 ibid., p. 681.
16 *Second Report on Education*, Science and Arts Committee, 1981, para. 9.17.
17 [1982] 1 All E.R., p. 737.
18 ibid., p. 744.
19 ibid., p. 748.
20 ibid., p. 747.
21 See n. 5, above, p. 165.
22 See ibid.
23 See Lomas, 1983, p. 23; Loughlin, 1983, p. 44.
24 The GLC took advice on the legality of six options for council house rents. The ILEA took advice on the legality of different prices for school meals.
25 See n. 14, above, p. 668.
26 See n. 5, above, p. 135.
27 On the basis that it is relevant to the *reasonableness* of a local authority's actions (as in Tameside) but is *not* relevant to, and cannot be relied upon, in any question as to the *legality* of such actions (as the GLC had tried to do).
28 The decisions of the Divisional Court show some variation from this pattern, but since both the House of Lords and Court of Appeal are hierarchically superior, their decisions are unaffected by subsequent cases in the Divisional Court. Future litigants, dissatisfied with decisions of the Divisional Court, can also be expected to take their cases, on appeal, to these higher courts.
29 See Griffith, 1977, especially chs 5, 8 and 9.
30 [1982] 1 All E.R., p. 747.

REFERENCES: CHAPTER 5

Education, Science and Art Committee (1981), *Second Report: Session 1981–2* (London: HMSO).
Elliott, M. (1981), *The Role of Law in Central–Local Relations* (London: SSRC).
Griffith, J. A. G. (1977), *The Politics of the Judiciary* (London: Collins/Fontana).
Lomas, O. (1983), 'Local government, the courts and the law – a growing acquaintance', *Local Government Studies*, vol. 9, no. 4, pp. 23–38.
Loughlin, M. (1983), *Local Government, the Law and the Constitution* (London: Local Government Legal Society Trust).
McAuslan, P. (1980), *The Ideologies of Planning Law* (Oxford: Pergamon).
Rhodes, R. (1979), *Research into Central–Local Relations in Britain: A Framework for Analysis* (London: SSRC).
Rhodes, R. (1981), *Control and Power in Central–Local Relations* (Farnborough: Gower).
Rhodes, R., Hardy, B., and Pudney, K. (1983), 'Power dependence theories of central–local relations: a critical assessment', Discussion Paper No. 7, Department of Government, University of Essex, July.

6
Workforce
KIERON WALSH

Local authorities are predominantly engaged in the delivery of services which are labour-intensive and in which the possibilities of technological development and advances in productivity are limited. These characteristics had two effects on the postwar development of local government. The rapid expansion of services entailed a rapid rise in the number of people employed by local authorities. Between 1952 and 1975 local authority employment doubled from 1·45 million to 2·9 million, and the proportion of the working population employed by local government rose from 6·2 per cent to 11·3 per cent.[1]

The second effect was that identified by Baumol (1967), who argued that technological advance is difficult within the public services. Wages and salaries tend to rise at the same rate as in the technologically progressive sector because of unionization and the use of comparability in pay settlements. Unit costs in the public sector will, therefore, tend to rise compared with those in the more technologically progressive private sector – the 'relative price effect'. The thesis is difficult to evaluate empirically, given the lack of output measures for public services, but there are indications that it has some validity. The price index for the public services has risen faster than that for consumers' expenditure.[2] The rise of local government expenditure was greater than that of employment; while employment doubled between 1958 and 1975, expenditure in real terms rose by 260 per cent. The significance of employment is greater in local government than elsewhere in the public sector because it is relatively *more* labour-intensive, as is shown in Table 6.1. It is significant, though, that wages and salaries as a proportion of total expenditure fell in the 1970s. Financial constraint does not necessarily lead to a greater proportion of expenditure on labour.

Bacon and Eltis (1976) have argued that the failure of the British economy has resulted from productivity advances being used to expand public services rather than 'productive' activity. They maintain that if productivity and economic growth are to be increased, labour must be moved from the non-productive to the productive sector. The empirical evidence for this thesis is weak[3] and it seems much less plausible in a time of high unemployment,[4] but it is only in the light of such arguments that one can understand why central government has shown as much concern to reduce local government employment as to reduce expenditure. Central government not only wants to reduce expenditure, but to shift real resources from less to more productive uses.

Table 6.1 *Proportion of Wages and Salaries in Government Expenditure, 1980*

Service	Percentage
Total	62·0
Central government	51·9
Local government	78·2
National Health Service	56·8

Source: Gretton and Harrison, 1982, p. 27.

There are two further aspects of the government's argument. Local authorities may choose to reduce expenditure by cutting areas of expenditure that are indirectly productive. Capital expenditure, which will generate activity in the private sector, is seen by the government as being cut in order to maintain less economically important spending on staff. The response to local government arguments that capital spending has labour implications has been that there are areas where this is not so (for example, roadbuilding).

There is a further government argument for employment cuts. It assumes that lack of market incentives necessarily means that resources are not used effectively in the public sector. Pressure to reduce staff will, therefore, produce greater internal efficiency. The transfer of services to the private sector will be the most effective solution. Even where services must be provided within the public sector, the market should be brought in as far as possible through charging or vouchers. Efficiency will also be enhanced, in the government's view, by importing private sector methods into local government, and the Audit Commission has been created to further this trend, acting more like an authoritarian management consultant than an auditor of accounts.

These arguments, however theoretically tendentious and empirically unverified, may explain the government's concern for employment levels. There may be more pragmatic reasons. Mrs Thatcher has attached great significance to reducing the number of civil servants. Michael Heseltine cut manning levels enthusiastically at the Department of the Environment. Cutting the numbers employed gives a tangible sign of effectiveness, especially if levels of public expenditure are not cut as fast as the government wishes. The reduction in the number of local authority employees or civil servants can be cited as a sign of progress irrespective of what they were doing.

EMPLOYMENT DECLINE

Central government has little formal control over local authority employment, and it is somewhat surprising that there has been far more reduction in employment than in expenditure. Government statistics illustrate that between 1979 and 1983 manpower numbers fell by about 4 per cent, while expenditure in volume terms rose by about 3·5 per cent.[5]

Table 6.2   *Employment in Local Government in England and Wales: Full-time and Full-time Equivalent, 1979 and 1983 (Thousands)*

	1979	1983	Percentage change, 1979–83
Education – teachers and lecturers	574,570	549,131	–4·4
Education – others	431,235	387,475	–10·1
Construction	135,638	117,220	–13·6
Transport	22,220	19,846	–10·7
Social services	205,944	215,432	+4·6
Public libraries and museums	33,281	32,707	–1·7
Recreation, parks and baths	73,623	74,056	+0·6
Environmental health	21,773	20,425	–3·9
Refuse collection and disposal	49,571	43,376	–12·4
Housing	49,305	54,031	+9·6
Town and country planning	22,380	21,103	–5·7
Fire service – regular	34,642	35,641	+2·9
other	5,372	5,169	–3·8
Miscellaneous	267,772	253,081	–5·5
Total	1,927,326	1,829,193	–5·1
Police – all ranks	110,529	120,946	+9·4
Total	2,093,901	2,013,882	–3·8

Source: Manpower watch returns, *Local Government Manpower.*

In part the difference in the behaviour of expenditure and manpower can be understood by examining the pattern of fall in manpower numbers. Table 6.2 illustrates the distribution of local authority employment in 1979 and 1983.

The major areas of cutback in employment have been construction, transport, non-teaching education staff and refuse collection and disposal. Manual workers have suffered much more than non-manual. They are more likely to be part-time and, therefore, to be less protected by employment legislation and easier to dismiss. The areas in which manual workers predominate are those more susceptible to privatization. In the construction area there have been large numbers of redundancies as a result of the legislation on direct labour organizations. Making manual workers redundant is also, of course, cheaper than is the case for non-manuals, who tend to have greater continuity of employment, to be higher paid and consequently more costly to dismiss in terms of redundancy payments. The government's attempts to impose expenditure cuts on local authorities have led to disproportionate cuts in the most vulnerable sections of the workforce, manuals rather than non-manuals, part-timers rather than full-timers, female workers rather than male workers and the newly employed rather than the established employee.

These unintended consequences, whether or not they are thought desirable by the government, arise because central government, although it may influence expenditure, has little influence over employment. Even in the case of teacher numbers, where it has a direct input through control of the teacher training system, Blackstone and Crispin (1982, p. 76) argue that 'At best there is only half-control, and this largely accounts for the mismatch between the numbers and specialism of those trained and the numbers subsequently employed'.

The remainder of this chapter analyses the nature and limitations of central control and influence over local government employment, and the changes that have followed from the cuts. It shows that the pattern of influence varies from service to service but that specific controls tend to increase rather than decrease employment. The government has, therefore, been more concerned to influence negotiations over pay than the employment required for service delivery, in order to exert a general downward influence on employment costs.

THE FRAMEWORK OF CONTROL

Local authorities *must* provide certain services and *may* provide others, so they must make provision for people to be employed to provide these services. In very few cases does statute provide that local authorities must deliver services by themselves employing workers. Large-scale privatization is possible with local authorities co-ordinating, rather than directly providing, services. Statutes require that local authorities shall provide efficient library, fire and education services; they do not necessarily require that authorities shall themselves employ librarians, fire officers and teachers. The level of service to be provided by authorities is rarely specified. Statutes tend to use vague phrases such as 'efficient' or 'adequate'. Minimum, maximum, or uniform standards on levels of staffing, training, or expertise are rarely specified. All teachers, for example, must hold qualified teacher status which is dependent on specified training, but little else is specifically required of authorities on staff qualification or training. Government takes an interest in but does not control the training of some local government professions such as social workers. And an intermittent interest is taken in raising the quality of staff; in the 1970s, for example, the DoE became interested in the professional development of housing officers. Such guidelines on staffing levels as do exist, for instance, in the social services are not normally met. In other cases manning standards exist by implication through the specification of service standards. For example, there are advisory standards on fire cover which have implications for the number of fire appliances, and advice is given on the manning of appliances. Teacher establishments are indirectly determined by requirements on class sizes which still pertain in Scotland, having been abandoned in England and Wales in 1969. Manning standards for the careers service were specified by the Department of Employment in 1975 but have been withdrawn by the present government. Professional bodies frequently make recommendations on levels of service which normally go beyond those actually pertaining. As Dunleavy and others have noted, the professional community in many services crosses the boundaries between central and local government. A common professional consensus may well emerge on staffing standards which is separate from statutory requirements or government exhortations. None the less, as Laffin's (1982) work shows, professional networks are of limited value in the face of a government requiring financial cuts and adopting a more managerialist stance.

Almost all legislation with an impact on local government has employment implications which are rarely explicitly considered when it is drawn up. Civil servants do not have the detailed knowledge necessary to assess the levels of employment required in implementing legislation, and any estimate made will normally be guesswork. The proportion of legislation relating *directly* to local government employment is small; Page (1982) has calculated that only 9 per cent of the legislation in the period 1970–9 was concerned with employment in the case of Scotland. Unlike many other countries Britain has no specific body of law governing public employment, but general employment legislation creates a framework of constraint within which local authorities must work. Specific legislation exists for some matters. Although super-annuation in local government is financed by the individual pensions funds of local authorities, the scheme is by statute uniform throughout local government. Separate statutory provision is made for the pensions of teachers, police and fire officers. Even with pensions, local authorities are free to operate their own early-retirement schemes for teachers, manual and APT&C staff, which vary considerably from authority to authority. Central government has arrogated to itself relatively few controls over local authority employment. As Poole states (1978, p. 28), 'Although the 1972 Act is the principal Act relating to the employment of local authority staff, the relevant provisions are few'. Only at a very minimal level, therefore, does central government have specific control over any aspect of local authority employment. The framework of constraint within which local authorities operate as employers is little different from that faced by any other employer. Government attempts to influence local authorities more through letters, circulars and other advisory mechanisms than statutory controls.

The only service areas in which central government has significant specific controls over local government employment are education, fire and police. In education, under the Remuneration of Teachers Act 1965, local education authorities are required to pay teachers in accordance with prescribed salary scales, and the overall cost of any salary settlement must be approved by the Secretary of State. Under the Police Act 1964 the Home Secretary must approve the appointment of chief constables, deputy chief constables and assistant chief constables. He must also approve the establishments of individual forces and may make regulations on the conditions of service of police officers. Under the Fire Services Acts 1947 and 1959 the Home Secretary may make regulations on the maintenance of discipline, on appeals against dismissal or disciplinary action, on the method of appointment of chief fire officers and on the qualifications for appointment and promotion of other ranks. Establishment schemes must be notified annually to the Home Secretary, who must approve any planned staff reductions. The greater concern for detailed employment controls in fire, police and education may reflect central government's perception that they are national services locally administered.

The powers of central government in education, fire and police have been used to varying degrees. The government has never refused to accept the pay recommendations of Burnham Committees, although it has used its veto during negotiations. Close control is exercised over the police and may involve detailed consideration of employment in individual posts.

Specific funding has been made available for the employment of careers officers. The Secretary of State for Education has taken the power to make specific finance available for the in-service training of teachers. Specific funding is made available by the Home Office under section 11 of the Local Government Act 1966 for the appointment of teachers of ethnic minorities.

In education the government has in the past also attempted to exercise control over the recruitment and distribution of teachers through the quota system and special payments for teaching in difficult areas. In 1956, worried by the apparently inequitable distribution of teachers, it introduced a quota system intended to help those authorities facing shortage of teachers. It suggested a limit on the number of teachers that could be appointed by those authorities with below-average pupil–teacher ratios. Whether for this or other reasons, there was a narrowing in the differences between pupil–teacher ratios across local authorities. Essentially the scheme was voluntary, introduced by the local authorities themselves and administered through the DES. The Social Priority Allowance began as the allowance to be paid to teachers in 'schools of exceptional difficulty' (SED) in 1968. Authorities submitted lists of schools to the DES which made the final choice of SED schools. In 1974 the scheme was changed from a flat-rate addition to teacher salaries to a sum that varied with years of experience.

There are explicit attempts to influence establishments both in the police and the fire service. For education, there is no such power, but specific measures on manpower have been taken, and the government is showing an increasing interest in teachers. For these three services, the government mentions 'planned' employment levels in its expenditure plans each year, indicating that it feels it has a right to some say in the numbers of teachers, police and fire officers.

Government controls over local authority employment are

inherited from the period of growth in local government expenditure. They operate in one of three ways. They encourage growth through setting targets; they encourage employment in particular categories; or they set upper or lower limits to employment. DHSS guidelines on employment levels are of the first type, employment under section 11 of the Local Government Act 1966 of the second, and controls on police and fire establishments are examples of the third. Such controls are essentially positive in encouraging rather than reducing employment. They do not, therefore, allow the government to enforce employment cuts upon local authorities. If powers were to be taken specifying where cuts were to be made, then the government would have to be specific about the areas of service it wished to see reduced rather than, as at present, specifying those it does not wish to see reduced.

PLANNING EMPLOYMENT LEVELS

The only local government service in which central government plays any planning role on levels of employment is education, and then only over schoolteachers. The Secretary of State's responsibility for the supply and education of teachers derives from the Education Act 1944. Central government has attempted to expand its concern for supply into control over demand. However, local government has failed to meet central government aggregate targets as expressed in White Papers on Public Expenditure, and authorities have chosen to spend more on employing teachers than is assumed in central government plans. Without taking more direct powers, the government has no instruments beyond financial controls to ensure that its plans are implemented. As Blackstone and Crispin (1982, p. 76) say: 'If the present planning system cannot cope readily with demographic and economic vicissitudes leading to changes in financial policies it is mainly because of the strict division of responsibility between those who plan but do not employ, and those who employ but have little say in planning.' On the other hand, local authorities' planning for the decline in numbers of teachers and other staff as school rolls fall has been thrown into disarray by the process of cash limits and cash planning. Salary awards higher than those assumed in the plans lead to severe, unplanned cuts in employment or to the preservation of employment levels by cutting other areas of expenditure or to large rate rises.

The PESC process is carried over into the RSG because the various expenditure subgroups of the Central Consultative

Council on Local Government Finance consider the implications of central government expenditure plans for local government employment. These subgroups include both central and local government officials. The whole exercise is shadowy and ultimately futile because local authorities choose to avoid the most extreme scenarios for redundancy. Plans are seen as unrealistic, impossible to fulfil because they would involve massive redundancies.

There are two choices if the relation between plans and reality is to be closer – either local government should be brought more into the central expenditure planning process or central government must impose its will by fiat. If central government will do neither, its assumptions on local government employment are likely to be meaningless. Until now the tendency, as one White Paper on Public Expenditure succeeds another, has been for the government to adjust its plans for numbers employed to the reality of local authorities' collective decisions by increasing planned future employment levels.

The PESC system has gradually changed from being a planning to a control system. As Wright argues:

> by the end of the 1970s PESC had become less a process for planning public expenditure in the medium term than a means of restraining the growth of the size of the public sector and controlling the cash flow of spending authorities; there has been a switch in emphasis from volume or resource planning to cost control, from the use of physical resources to the financing of those resources; and ... the approach of the Treasury has become more short term, more ad hoc and more incremental. (Wright, 1980, p. 88)

This trend has become more marked under Mrs Thatcher's government, especially since the introduction of cash planning in 1982. None the less, the control is financial, not a control over the way in which money is spent. There is less manpower planning since employment levels, given cash limits and cash planning, are a residual decided after the determination of financial limits and pay settlements.

PAY BARGAINING

The government's attempts to use the PESC process as a control rather than a planning mechanism is limited by the separation of financial planning from pay bargaining. Local authorities are independent employers who cede to a central negotiating system the right to make national agreements binding on individual local authorities. Authorities are represented by members of Provincial Councils, which are regional groupings of authorities, and the national Local Authority Associations, which come together to form National Joint Councils for negotiating purposes. Central government has a formal voice in only two areas – education and the police. In education the DES has two representatives on the Burnham Committee with a weighted vote of fifteen as against twenty-five local authority representatives. The role of the DES is mainly negative, using its veto to control the overall level of the settlement. For police services, the Home Secretary is represented on the Police Committee since he is the police authority for the Metropolitan Police and, therefore, the employer. Therefore, in theory local authorities bargain as independent employers with their employees; in practice there are a number of means of influence available to central government. They may overlap. Three seem significant:

(1)   incomes policies;
(2)   cash limits and cash planning;
(3)   political influences.

Incomes policies had their beginning in the 'pay pause' adopted by Selwyn Lloyd in 1961 when faced with a sterling crisis. It was aimed at controlling public sector pay. Since then there has been an almost continuous series of incomes policies of various forms under both Labour and Conservative governments. The present government claims not to have an incomes policy even in the public sector, but in practice it has a policy on public sector pay. Central government assumes a norm for the overall level of pay rises in local government, and that figure is a major determinant of the RSG. Negotiations take place in the shadow of the norm. The employers' side may choose to settle for a higher figure for one group of workers by recouping the expenditure through lower pay settlements for others, by spending less on non-manpower areas, or reducing levels of employment. Since the grant is cash-limited, local authorities' only other option is to raise more through the rates, but this option is limited by the increasingly severe grant penalties that have been imposed in recent years. It will be even more limited should the 'rate-capping' proposals become law. The norm gains especial significance from cash limits and cash planning, which ensure that the government is continuously involved. The contact between central and local government in negotiating was more marked under the Labour government of 1976–9, when there was a chance of the government raising cash limits to accommodate a pay rise. The result was much informal contact in the negotiating process. Contact has been less under the present government but does still take place.

Incomes policies establishing government norms for pay on a statutory, voluntary, or informal basis have a number of implications for local government. They have given central government a general and indirect influence over local government pay. There have been attempts at direct influence. Under the Labour government's incomes policy of 1976–9 the 'sponsor' departments – the departments with oversight of a given group of local government employees – became more active in attempting to control pay offers. During Stage Three of the policy central government tried to operate the rule that no offer was to be made until the sponsor departments had had two clear weeks to examine the costs involved. Local government fought against this rule which never operated, although government departments were informed of what was being done. During Stage Four of the policy the Department of the Environment set up a working group of officials, meeting informally, to monitor and exercise influence over local government pay bargaining. The breakdown of bargaining meant that this group's activities came to naught.

Central government may influence local government bargaining through party political linkages. Such pressure is limited but what government wants on pay is clear, and local government members of the party in control at the centre will take its wishes into account in making decisions. Political influences have become more likely since 1974 when the local government bargaining system became more party- and councillor-dominated. The employers' side of the bargaining process is likely to find itself split on party political lines as has happened in recent negotiations. This factor contributes to the antagonism between the central representative associations of local authorities, the ACC, the AMA and the ADC. The Conservative-controlled associations, the ACC and ADC, have tended to follow the central government line, while the AMA has resisted it. Kessler and Winchester (1982) cite a number of examples of party-based clashes between the AMA and the ACC in the negotiating process in the 1980–1 and 1981–2 wage rounds.

The development of greater central government influence on the local government bargaining system has the effect of requiring far more integration between bargainers. If local authorities want to be able to play off rises above the norm for one group of workers against rises below the norm for another, co-ordination between different negotiating bodies is required. There are attempts at integration within the Local Authority Associations, and the Local Authorities' Conditions of Service Advisory Board (LACSAB) plays something of a co-ordinating role. In 1979 the AMA proposed that LACSAB should be amalgamated into the AMA and ACC so as to improve the co-ordination of bargaining. The move was resisted by the other associations and was dropped. Equally there have been attempts at integration on the employee side, particularly through the work of the TUC Local Government Committee, formed in 1971. These developments have been limited. There is no effective co-ordination in bargaining.

It is difficult for a highly centralized bargaining system such as those which operate in local government not to be strongly influenced by central government, given the financial dominance of the centre. The development of a more independent system of local authority financing might allow movement to a system of more localized bargaining. Flexibility and innovation in pay systems are difficult to develop within the present centralized system. More independent local bargaining would be possible only if authorities had the financial independence to implement the results of such bargaining.

Another effect of central government playing a greater role in local government bargaining is the desire by the unions for a more direct relationship with the government. This desire was partly attained under the last Labour government. Leopold and Beaumont (1982, p. 53) state that during the social contract period of 1976–9 the Local Government Committee of the TUC 'was regularly meeting government ministers and taking the initiative in setting agendas and bringing forward business of direct concern to the Committee. This close relationship with government which some commentators have interpreted as signs of a developing corporatism, ended suddenly and abruptly with the election of a Conservative Government in May 1979.'

The election did not change the *desire* for a more direct relationship with central government. That desire is strongest among teachers, fire officers and police officers all of whom see themselves as part of a national service. During the acrimonious negotiations over police pay in 1976 and the firemen's strike in 1977 there were calls for the nationalization of the respective services. With the teachers, there have been more recent calls for teachers' salaries to be paid centrally, for example, by a number of NAS/UWT representatives during the 1982 discussion on a block grant for education. It is difficult to see how the union side could benefit from direct negotiation with a central government which might be expected to be more single-minded in the pursuit of low pay settlements and redundancies than the more diffuse local government employers. In the present circumstances it is difficult to see any but the Treasury view dominating. None the less, some think that centralizing pay would be advantageous.

The greater part played by central government in local government bargaining has made it more difficult to reach settlements. Claims are now more likely to be referred to arbitration or to lead to disputes, sometimes extended and bitter. In recent years there have been strikes among manual workers, social workers, fire officers and many others in the 'winter of discontent' of 1978–9. The police considered balloting on the possibility of a strike in 1976, even though it would be illegal for them to go on strike. Such disputes are more likely as the government tries to downgrade comparability as a means of determining pay and to introduce market criteria. The quiescence of police and fire officers has only been bought at the cost of indexing their pay to national average earnings. The bargaining process has, therefore, effectively been short-circuited, although decoupling of pay from average earnings is always possible at some point. With the firemen, according to Kessler and Winchester,

> While the employers' side of the NJC is less fragmented than in many other local government negotiating bodies, it still exhibits tension between central and local government control and political divisions between association members. The most notable illustration can be seen in the attempt by the ACC, under central government pressure, to rescind the pay formula for 1980–81. This was resisted by the threat of union strike action until, following local elections, the employer's side changed to Labour control; in the 1981–2 negotiations, a settlement of 10·1 per cent based on the indexation formula was implemented in November. (Kessler and Winchester, 1982, p. 29)

The police have found themselves paying a higher proportion of their pay in superannuation contributions.

PAY AND THE THIRD PARTY INQUIRY

The effects of incomes policies are particularly felt in the public sector but relative pay is not necessarily eroded in the long term.

While being held back at times of the operation of an incomes policy, there is afterwards a rapid catching-up period. Although it is argued that overall the 1970s was a period of relative gain,[6] local authority pay has fluctuated in relative terms between 1970 and 1983.

Table 6.3 *Local Authority Average Earnings as a Percentage of Average Earning in All Industries and Services, 1970–83*

	1970	1971	1972	1973	1974	1975	1976
Male manual	79·0	81·6	80·5	80·8	80·7	86·9	86·0
Male non-manual	101·0	100·3	102·9	102·9	102·0	105·8	108·2

	1977	1978	1979	1980	1981	1982	1983
Male manual	83·1	86·1	83·9	89·4	89·3	85·3	83·9
Male non-manual	104·3	99·4	100·2	100·7	102·8	101·5	96·5

Source: DES, *New Earnings Survey* (annual).

The experience of different groups in local authorities varies; as Table 6.3 shows, manual workers have done better than non-manual. More important, as Heald (1983) has argued, public and private sector pay have become desynchronized, that is, the linkages between private and public sector pay have been broken. The fluctuation of local government pay relative to that of the private sector has been greater than in the rest of the public sector, creating the conditions for continuing discontent and disagreement. What would appear to be happening is that local authority workers are hit by incomes policies more than the private sector, and there are fewer ways round the policy since most bargaining is carried out centrally.

Very often the catching up process at the end of an incomes policy has to be mediated and legitimated by a third party. References to arbitration have been increasing and there have been a number of committees of inquiry. In 1974 the Houghton Committee was established to report on teachers' pay. In 1976 the unrest in the police force resulted in the Edmund-Davies Commission and more recently there was the Clegg Comparability Commission which reported on a number of categories of local authority workers. The reference of disputes to third party inquiries reflects the inability of local government employers and employees to bargain effectively within the constraints laid down by central government. Reference to an independent third party can then save face both for central and local government.

A further result of the limitations of bargaining in local government is that there has been a growth of local bargaining and local settlements. In the 1979 manual workers dispute there was a small number of local settlements – and similarly in the dispute over white-collar workers' pay the following year. In the latter case a number of authorities felt that the employers' side was foolish in not settling since they had expected, and budgeted for, a higher pay settlement than the employers nationally seemed willing to offer. The right of local authorities to make settlements that go beyond national agreements has been tested and upheld in *Pickwell* v. *LB Camden*, but the effect of the limitation of pay bargaining both through incomes policy and cash limits is that there is little room for negotiation of pay at the local level. Partly in consequence bargaining over everything else becomes much more important for increasingly union-conscious employees. The result has been a rapid expansion in local trade union and negotiating activity in non-pay areas.

CONCLUSION

The powers of central government over local government employment are limited, haphazard and frequently contradictory. Even where powers are most extensive – police, fire and education – controls are so incomplete as to prevent effective national manpower planning. There are many controls but no effective control. As Stevenson says in the case of the fire service,

> The authority can make a scheme which sets out how many firemen it is going to employ. For that purpose it does not need to consult the Home Secretary at all, although it must advise him afterwards. However, if it wishes to amend the scheme by reducing the number of firemen, the Home Secretary has a power of veto. (Stevenson, 1982, p. 21)

The powers of central government sponsor departments are weak. The Secretaries of State for Education and Social Services, and the Home Secretary, have no specific control over the expenditure by local authorities in their service areas. The Inspectorates are advisory, providing information rather than acting as a mode of control, although the control element is increasing. Moreover, the secretaries of state are extremely unwilling to take action against authorities accused of providing an inadequate service, as a number of recent cases in the education service have established. The various influences of central government over local government employment may be categorized as falling along three dimensions.

General v. Specific

The majority of central government's influences on local government employment operate at the general level, and relate to the totality or the large majority of local authority employees. Examples of such influences would include incomes policies and superannuation regulations. These major influences operate simply because local authorities are large employing organizations. Specific influences on employment develop in areas where government is interested in particular developments which it sees as unlikely to proceed without direct funding. Such developments are more likely in a period of contraction than of growth, to protect rather than to promote. Recent examples of such specific funding would include money earmarked for in-service training of teachers and Department of Employment grants for careers officers.

Positive v. Negative

Central government's general interest is now negative, in that it is concerned to reduce local government employment. In particular areas it will have a positive interest in encouraging manpower and recruitment as, for instance, recently with the police. Particular controls inherited from the past are likely either to be oriented to growth or to prevent decline. The problem for local authorities is to accommodate the tension between general negative influences and positive encouragement to spend in certain areas.

Direct v. Indirect

Most of central government's influence over local government manpower is indirect, deriving from its general control over finance. Direct mechanisms are strongly resented by local authorities as intrusions upon their rights as independent employers. Again central government is likely to operate direct influences where it is encouraging preservation or growth of services.

Central government's influence over local government employment is mainly general, negative and indirect. The attainment of specific ends, whether negative or positive, entails a degree of direct control that even an interventionist government such as the present one is loath to take. The financial powers are not easy to translate into manpower outcomes. While it might be expected that there will be a growth of specific initiatives of a positive and direct sort using earmarked funds, it seems unlikely that central government will actually enforce staffing levels on local authorities. The sad saga of the GREs has shown the pitfalls of attempting to set levels of service centrally for local authorities, and the establishment of variable manning standards would be as difficult.

The powers of central government over local authority manpower illustrates the weakness of the central government's resources of present law and finance. Legal constraints on local authorities are so broad as to allow large variations on manning standards. The financial constraints are limited because local authorities choose to protect certain categories of staff at the expense of other aspects of expenditure. But if central government powers are sufficient for it to plan local government expenditure, the way that it exercises its influence prevents local authorities from engaging in coherent manpower planning. In financial decline manpower planning must follow from financial planning. But authorities faced with the vagaries of the block grant and cash planning by central government are not able to plan expenditure. As John Kay says of the 1982 White Paper on Public Expenditure,

> Buried somewhere between the quoted figure of £13410m for education spending in 1984–85 are implicit or explicit assumptions about what will happen to prices between now and 1984–85 – two or three years ahead. Unless the numbers are simply plucked from the air, there is no way in which it could be complied with without such assumptions. These assumptions will certainly be falsified; it would be a brave man who would confidently forecast within 10 per cent or so the general price level in 1985, far less the price of chalk in that year. When these assumptions are falsified, these plans will presumably be revised; none of us thinks that teachers should be sacked because the Treasury's forecast of the inflation rate was too low, or that educational administrators should be paid more because some civil servant's guess as to what would happen to the price of blackboards was pessimistic. (Kay, 1982, pp. 105–6)

In practice the gap is likely to be bridged by revising plans upwards. The gap between central government plans for local government employment and practice might be reduced in a number of ways. Central government could take statutory powers to ensure that its policies were carried out by setting establishment levels and centralizing pay bargaining and determination. In its plans for the abolition of the GLC and the metropolitan counties it has moved this way since the secretary of state will set manning levels for the joint boards which are proposed to replace them. Alternatively, local government might be brought into the policy planning process perhaps through the preparation of manpower plans for a number of years ahead. Both these approaches would involve a considerable tightening of the relation between central and local government directly or through incorporation. The alternative is to decouple local government finance from central government control, leaving local authorities free to plan their own expenditure and choose how to spend it on manpower and pay. Such an approach could be coupled with a considerable decentralization of local government pay bargaining. It is clear that the present system provides for neither planning or control.

NOTES: CHAPTER 6

1 These figures are taken from the Layfield Report, 1976, annex 10, table 22, p. 381.
2 See Elliott and Fallick, 1981, p. 16.
3 See Thompson, 1979.
4 Some of these arguments are advanced in Eltis, 1982.
5 DoE/Welsh Office, 1983, p. 7.
6 This argument is made by Thompson and Beaumont, 1978, among others.

REFERENCES: CHAPTER 6

Bacon, R., and Eltis, W. A. (1976), *Britain's Economic Problem: Too Few Producers* (London: Macmillan).

Baumol, W. J. (1967), 'Macroeconomics of unbalanced growth: the anatomy of urban crisis', *American Economic Review*, vol. 57, no. 2, pp. 415–26.

Blackstone, T., and Crispin, A. (1982), *How Many Teachers? Issues of Policy, Planning and Demography*, Bedford Way Paper No. 10 (London: London University Institute of Education).

Department of Education and Science (1983), *Teaching Quality* (London: HMSO).

Department of the Environment/Welsh Office (1983), *Rates: Proposals for Rate Limitation and Reform of the Rating System* (London: DoE/Welsh Office).

Elliott, R. F., and Fallick, J. L. (1981), *Pay in the Public Sector* (London: Macmillan).

Eltis, W. A. (1982), 'Do manpower cuts correct deficits when the economy is in deep recession?', *Political Quarterly*, vol. 53, no. 1 (January–March), pp. 5–15.

Gretton, J., and Harrison, A. (1982), *How Much Are Public Servants Worth?* (Oxford: Blackwell).

Heald, D. (1983), *Public Expenditure* (London: Martin Robertson).

Kay, J. (1982), 'The new framework for public expenditure planning', in J. Kay (ed.), *The 1982 Budget* (Oxford: Blackwell), pp. 101–8.

Kessler, I., and Winchester, D. (1982), 'Pay negotiations in local government – the 1981–82 wage round', *Local Government Studies*, vol. 8, no. 6 (November–December), pp. 19–31.

Laffin, M. (1982), *Professionalism in Central–Local Government Relations*, SSRC Report (London: Social Service Research Council).

Layfield Report (1976), *Report of the Committee of Inquiry into Local Government Finance*, Cmnd 6453 (London: HMSO).

Leopold, J. W., and Beaumont, P. B. (1982), 'The local government committees of the TUC – a decade of activity', *Local Government Studies*, vol. 8, no. 6 (November–December), pp. 49–68.

Page, E. (1982), *Laws and Orders in Central–Local Government Relations*, Studies in Social Policy No. 102 (Glasgow: Centre for the Study of Social Policy, University of Strathclyde).

Poole, K. P. (1978), *The Local Government Service in England and Wales* (London: Allen & Unwin).

Stevenson, B. (1982), 'De-controlling the fire service', *Public Money*, vol. 1, no. 4 (March), pp. 21–2.

Thompson, A. W. J., and Beaumont, P. B. (1978), *Public Sector Bargaining: A Study of Relative Gain* (London: Saxon House).

Thompson, G. (1979), *The Growth of the Government Sector* (Milton Keynes: The Open University).

Wright, M. (1980), 'From planning to control: PESC in the 1970s', in M. Wright (ed.), *Public Spending Decisions: Growth and Restraint in the 1970s* (London: Allen & Unwin), pp. 88–119.

7

Direct Labour Organization

NORMAN FLYNN

For Whitehall to establish control over hundreds of independent building and civil engineering contractors spread throughout the country would seem a formidable task. Such a strategy of control pursued in relation to the private sector through nationalization would undoubtedly produce criticisms based on the difficulties of lines of communication, rules of behaviour, performance targets and the inevitable remoteness of Whitehall from the sites where the work is done. In fact the Department of the Environment has taken control of hundreds of public sector contractors. They are the direct labour organizations (DLOs) of local authorities and other public bodies. This chapter examines the procedures which were established to exercise central control over an extremely diverse set of organizations involved in building and maintenance of buildings and structures. The organizations range from those which have thirty jobbing maintenance workers to those with over 3,000 workers, from those whose biggest task consists in reroofing a house to those constructing major highways and bridges.

In addition to the great variety of organizations to be controlled, there were further complexities. First, in the great majority of cases the organizations did not exist in the sense that the people performing the building and (especially) maintenance tasks were integrated within departments whose responsibility it was to specify the work to be done and to supervise its execution. Although the *work* to be controlled could be specified, the *people* and the organizational units could not. Secondly, there was already a very clear line of accountability for the work which was to be controlled from Whitehall. Accountability in local authorities was to the elected members of the authority and through them to the electorate. This accountability would not be superseded by a new accountability to Whitehall, but would have to continue alongside it.

Given such diversity and complexity, there had to be a strong motivation from the centre to establish a control mechanism. On the face of it the pre-existing decentralized structure with local accountability provided a control mechanism of sufficient variety and with sufficient channels to cope with the differences and peculiarities of local circumstances. What was the motivation for change?

WHY THE DRIVE FOR CONTROL?

One interpretation of the process of legislation and regulation is that it was not designed for control purposes, but was rather aimed at transferring work from the public to the private sector. The incoming Conservative administration of 1979 had a general commitment to reducing the size of the public sector. It has also made a specific commitment in its manifesto to saving money by transferring work from the allegedly inefficient DLOs to the private construction sector, which was said to be 30 per cent more efficient. One motivation, then, was the reduction of the amount of work performed directly by public sector labour. This motivation did not appear in official pronouncements until the announcement of a draft set of revised regulations in December 1983 when the Minister for Housing and Construction, John Stanley, said: 'Ministers . . . would wish to see a reduction in dependence on DLOs by highway authorities, so far as this is practicable.'[1] This motivation was fuelled by a campaign conducted by the construction industry against building industry nationalization and against specific direct labour organizations. This campaign and lobby were welcomed by the government. One member of the volume builders' lobby, Mr Tom Baron, was employed later by the secretary of state as an adviser. Some of the revisions to the regulations follow closely the published recommendations of organizations such as the Federation of Civil Engineering Contractors.

There were also ideological constraints on the government's actions. Privatization is presented as part of an ideology of competition, efficiency achieved through the pursuit of profit and individual skills of entrepreneurs. The underlying political objective may be to counter the 'crowding out' of the private sector by the public sector and the desire to open up more sectors of the economy to private accumulation, but the mechanisms to achieve that objective have to be constructed from competitive, market-oriented components.

Since there was likely to be resistance from many authorities to the privatization drive, local decision-making had to be curtailed. Rules of behaviour had to be established which would ensure that local decisions were in accord with central objectives. Competition was to become mandatory, DLOs were to operate like business with a centrally imposed criterion of success and penalty for failure. To ensure that competition took place authorities had to be made to adopt accounting practices which allowed cost comparisons to be made and internal tenders produced.

In this the government had an ally in the Chartered Institute of Public Finance and Accountancy (CIPFA). They had advocated accounting practices which moved away from the practice of recharging work done at cost towards a practice which allowed cost to be compared with some valuation. This was an essential step in the move towards a measurement of efficiency. If output is only measured by costs of production, no definition of efficiency is possible. Before legislation was introduced, the CIPFA had produced sets of voluntary guidance on accounting practices.[2] This guidance was produced to achieve measures of efficiency, not to encourage privatization, but it suited the government's purposes.

Privatization through competition and the imposition of penalties for failure to compete could only be achieved through mechanisms which allowed the centre to impose its will. How did the centre go about designing the control mechanisms?

THE CENTRE'S STRATEGY

The requirements for a system designed to achieve the government's objectives were varied. There was a constraint that control should be exercised without a large number of civil servants carrying out detailed checks on individual operations. There had to be developed, therefore, a simple set of performance measures which could be calculated universally and used objectively.

A second requirement was that the measures used had to relate to work performed and not to organizations since independent organizational units did not, in most cases, exist. The rules had to apply to the standard of performance in the production of a set of outputs, which had then to be related in some way to a set of standard costs. The requirement was for strictly defined output measures linked to a satisfactory way of arriving at comparable standard costs and of matching standard costs with actual costs. This comparison clearly could not be done by a system of central checking of individual outputs and costs because of the scale of work involved. For example, Glasgow District Council Building and Works Department performs over 600,000 individual operations each year.

The third requirement was speed. Ministers wanted legislation during 1980 and an operating control system which could be installed by 1 April 1981. Consultations with professional bodies and local authorities produced a plea for delay in implementation because of the large upheavals involved. Such pleas went unheeded, except in Scotland where implementation was delayed until April 1982.

The drafters of the legislation did not start with a blank sheet. Already in existence were the advisory accounting codes of practice produced by CIPFA (1975, 1978) and a report in 1978 from a DoE working party.[3] In these, accounting principles had already been established. The CIPFA was clearly an important ally in drawing up a set of rules. One reason for the financial orientation of the rules may have been the leading role played by CIPFA prior to the legislation and later in helping draft regulations and a new accounting code of practice. Certainly CIPFA was seen by local government as an important source of support for the government.

Without the detailed work of the CIPFA, legislation could not have been implemented. The shift of role of the CIPFA was a significant one: from offering guidelines to individual treasurers on how to keep accounts to the imposition of an accounting system which was different in principle from many existing systems. In return for enhanced status in relation to the government the CIPFA became part of the centre in opposition to the wishes of many local authorities. This was to have the effect in many authorities of the treasurer being seen as part of the central government initiative and as opposing the wishes of the authority.

The basic strategy, then, was to produce quickly a simple set of accounting principles and rules which would reduce a complex situation to a manageable one and ensure that consultation could be concluded speedily, so that opposition would have little chance to gather strength. The blunting of opposition was reinforced by the inclusion of the direct labour organizations legislation in a Bill which contained far-reaching constitutional and financial issues for local government. Opposition to the Bill as a whole concentrated on these constitutional and financial aspects.

THE PROCESS

A consultation paper was issued by the DoE in August 1979, setting out the main proposals. The paper proposed legislation 'with the double objectives of improving DLO efficiency and of reducing waste in local government, and of ensuring that DLOs are fully tested in fair and frequent competition with private sector contractors'. The principles to be adopted in the legislation were said to be:

(1) every local authority employing its own construction or maintenance labour force shall have to keep separate accounts of all work done by that labour force;

(2) direct labour accounts shall be maintained on a trading basis, giving a true financial picture of their operations;

(3) authorities will be obliged to publish prompt annual accounts and a report giving a full assessment of DLO performance and prospects;

(4) every council shall be required to ensure that its DLO covers the opportunity cost of its capital by earning a real rate of return equivalent to the average private sector rate;

(5) every council shall ensure that its DLO wins a substantial proportion of its work in fair competition with private contractors.

In addition to these principles, there was a shift in the ultimate decisions about the continued existence of DLOs from the council to the secretary of state:

there may be cases where some authorities, over a period of years, show themselves unable to comply with the requirements. The Bill will therefore enpower the Secretary of State to remove or curtail the powers of an authority to employ its own direct labour where it has shown itself to be consistently unsuccessful. (DoE press release, no. 352, 20 August 1979, p. 2)

These principles were adopted in the legislation and the subsequent regulations. They meet the requirements of simplicity and of a calculable performance target. The main question which arises is: how good a measure of performance is the rate of return on capital employed? The CIPFA in its response to the consultative paper pointed out that 'the magnitude of capital employed may be so small as to render the concept of a return on capital as irrelevant and misleading'. DLOs are not especially capital-intensive. The work, particularly maintenance, is such that the greatest cost is labour. Indeed, the ratio of capital to turnover is so low that very small variations in charges may produce very large fluctuations in the percentage rate of return on capital.

There was no great opposition to the consultation paper from the Local Authority Associations. The AMA, ACC and ADC all agreed with the proposal to account as trading organizations. Objections were mainly centred on the power of the secretary of state to close down DLOs, the definition of work to be put out to competitive tender and the use of a return on capital, set at 5 per cent, as a requirement.

The ADC was 'concerned at the proposal that the Secretary of State should be given the powers to remove or curtail an authority's right to employ its own direct labour'. The AMA, also expressing 'concern' said, 'It must surely be for the local council, democratically responsible to the ratepayers, to decide on any appropriate action'.

Objection was also made to the scope of work to be included in the legislation. The ACC proposed a definition of highways work which would eliminate winter maintenance and very small works, while the ADC urged 'that the Government's proposals should not apply to maintenance work'. There was also some argument about the proposed value limits above which work had to be put out to tender: the limits suggested, first mentioned in 1975, should be revised upwards and should be inflation index linked.

Little account was taken of these objections, although certain concessions were made, for example, excluding winter maintenance from competition requirements. In essence part III of the Local Government, Planning and Land Bill as published followed the principles in the consultation paper. The main provisions of the Bill concerned: the publication of revenue accounts for four categories of work (highways, major new construction jobs of over £50,000, minor new works of less than £50,000 and maintenance work); a requirement that works of particular types should go out to competitive tender; a requirement to achieve a rate of return on capital on each of the four specified types of work; a requirement to publish accounts, a balance sheet and reports; and the power for the secretary of state to direct that authorities shall cease to have powers to undertake work by direct labour.

What was unusual about the Bill was the degree of discretion left to the secretary of state in making regulations about the detailed implementation of the law. One explanation may be the difficulty experienced in drafting the Bill in the time available. Another interpretation is that the secretary of state wished to retain the option of changing the rules if the results were not those desired. The frequency of the subsequent rule changes make the latter explanation more likely. The Bill was passed with minor amendments. What was then required was a series of regulations about detailed implementation and the new CIPFA code of practice on how to keep the accounts. There was a very short time between the passage of the Bill on 13 November and the secretary of state's desired implementation date of 1 April 1981. A circular[4] was issued on 19 March 1981, advising local authorities on decisions which had been made on detailed matters to be implemented on 1 April.

The civil servants had had some difficulties. They arose in applying the general principles contained in the Bill to individual DLOs. The civil servants' background and experience were not entirely appropriate. Their toil was revealed in a series of drafts. One of the problems arose over the definition of a 'job'. In maintenance all 'jobs' over £10,000 in value have to go out to tender. If a series of 'jobs' (for instance, repainting houses) adds up to more than £10,000, should the series go out to tender? One attempt at a definition produced the following: 'A job . . . shall be treated together with one or more other jobs if . . . each job was undertaken within three months, each relates to work of the same type and each relates to work to be performed on a single site or surface or on adjacent sites or surfaces whether separated horizontally or vertically.' This nonsense disappeared from subsequent drafts. It illustrates the difficulty in applying a general principle in an unambiguous way to a large number of diverse cases. The loose definition of a 'job' would allow much work to be divided up in such a way that no competition was required. Unable to arrive at any really satisfactory definition, Circular 10/81 nevertheless warns against abuse:

> If in the light of experience it appears to [the secretaries of state] that work is being artificially sub-divided to circumvent tendering requirements, they will not hesitate to revise the Regulations in order to eliminate such abuse, even at the cost of introducing a greater degree of rigidity and inflexibility than they would wish.

This sentence hints at the attitude of the centre towards local authorities. Councils are considered devious, prepared to cover up inefficiency and are in any case clearly subordinate to civil servants and ministers.

In the event the Regulations and Circulars required a good deal of interpretation by local authorities. Implementation of the new rules also caused a great deal of upheaval in local government beyond the changes which would be expected from changes to accounting systems.

THE LOCAL GOVERNMENT RESPONSE

The new law came into force on 1 April 1981 in England and Wales and one year later in Scotland. INLOGOV conducted a survey of all authorities in England and Wales during the summer of 1981 to find out the extent of the changes made.[5]

The most striking feature of the response is the admission by almost one-half of the non-metropolitan districts and almost one-fifth of the counties that they were not able to comply with the accounting provisions by the implementation date. They were unable mainly to produce prior written estimates of the cost of carrying out work. It was predicted in Circular 10/81 that it would be difficult for some authorities to comply fully with this requirement in the first year. There were still some authorities at the end of the second year who were unable to produce prior written estimates for some categories of work.

Although the Act had nothing to say about the organization of DLOs, the impact on structures was considerable: 40 per cent of non-metropolitan districts, 60 per cent of metropolitan districts and one-half of the counties which responded to the INLOGOV survey had carried out to some degree a reorganization of the DLO. The imposition of a trading account and a profitability target implied an organization for building and maintenance contracting which was separate from the organization responsible for housing or highways. Specification of work, supervision and authorization of payment represent the 'client' side of the work. Executing the work, tendering for jobs, providing estimates and controlling output and income to ensure a profit constitute the 'contractor' function. Many authorities are now organized in such a way that local authority staff are separated into client and contractor roles. In many cases nobody was previously occupying a management position purely responsible for contracting and new posts have been created.

New information systems had to be established. Financial information systems which were adequate for monitoring expenditure against budgets were inadequate for monitoring income and expenditure for jobs.[6] The provision of prior written estimates and tenders implied changes to costing systems.

Along with these changes in structures and systems went changes in attitudes. The move to a trading account from a system where work was recharged to the 'client' at cost implies that the monitoring of cost against income becomes crucial. Failure to keep costs at or below estimated costs would result in deficits and ultimately closure by the secretary of state. Profitability as a criterion of success was alien to many people in DLOs and implied a fundamental change in attitude. In some cases managers with those attitudes were imported from the private sector. The change in attitude among management has in many cases brought a change in management and a supervisory style alien to that prevailing in local authorities.

Previously management had concentrated on achieving an acceptable volume of work within an overall budget. Supervision of individual workers had been mainly directed at ensuring that work for which bonus payments were claimed had actually been carried out. In the new situation income is only credited to the DLO account at the agreed price for work performed. If cost exceeds income, the account will go into deficit. The emphasis of management and supervision has switched to output and cost considerations. This has led to a more aggressive style of operation.

There was little organized resistance to the legislation. There was some sharing of experience in devising or finding 'loopholes' in the rules. Counsel's opinion was sought in such matters as what was included in the definition of maintenance and the opinions were publicized. There was some co-operation among authorities by tendering for each other's work (for example, between Sandwell and Walsall boroughs).

One obstacle to organized resistance was the attitude of the client departments within authorities. In many cases the exposure to competition was welcomed by those responsible for school and housing maintenance. It was seen as a way of breaking the monopoly of supply of services by the DLOs. At a time of severely limited maintenance budgets any chance of achieving more work for less money was welcomed. Alliances were developed between clients and treasurers against the DLOs. These alliances were replicated in many cases among elected members.

Not all these changes happened immediately. In some authorities the impact of the legislation was slow. In others, where trading accounts had been in operation previously and where there was already competition with the private sector, no fundamental change was necessary. However, the overall impact was considerable.

CHANGING THE RULES

Central government, however, was not content with the changes that were taking place. Before the first financial year was over and before the Department of the Environment had received any of the reports specified, it changed the rules. On 15 March 1982 new competition regulations were issued, lowering the threshold above which highways work had to go out to tender and making it mandatory for 30 per cent of small maintenance jobs to go to tender. This change in the regulations cannot have been prompted by the objective of increasing efficiency. No reports were yet available about rates of return or comparative costs. It was directed only towards increasing competition with the private sector. The Federation of Civil Engineering Contractors had called for a reduction of the threshold to £50,000 on highways work. This new limit was announced in March. Further changes in the competition regulations were made in March and May 1983, which put more work out to tender. These changes in the competition requirements have caused further disruption to local authorities. Just as systems are being established to cope with the production of tender documents and procedures, more work is pushed through those systems.

MEETING THE TARGET

The first annual reports were produced six months after the end of the 1981–2 financial year. The regulations about the content of the reports were not mandatory in the first year, so a full appraisal of performance was not possible. However, all authorities reported their success or otherwise in meeting the main target, the rate of return on capital. Table 7.1 shows the distribution of rates of return for the four categories of work for the different types of authority.

The requirement to a 5 per cent return was met by the majority of DLOs. There were several reasons for the failure of the few. In some cases failure was because of technical errors in the procedure for producing estimates. In others failure was attributed to excess costs incurred deliberately, for example, by employing a higher than normal number of apprentices to provide job chances for school-leavers. Only in the case of DLOs where there was a high proportion of work won in competition with the private sector could losses be attributed to 'inefficiency'. In cases where work was not won in competition, profit could be made as long as costs were kept to within the submitted estimate. 'Efficiency' in these cases is a measure either of the ability to estimate accurately (or over-estimate) or the ability to control costs to within the level indicated in the estimate.

Table 7.1   DLO Rates of Return on Capital Employed, 1981–2

%	Districts				Metropolitan districts				London boroughs				Counties				Totals			
	a	b	c	d	a	b	c	d	a	b	c	d	a	b	c	d	a	b	c	d
<5	21	2	2	19	4	6	5	2	4	3	2	6	1	0	2	3	30	11	11	30
5–19	35	4	10	91	11	3	4	12	12	1	0	12	32	1	2	7	90	9	16	122
20–99	21	6	7	57	6	3	5	13	3	2	1	3	12	1	3	6	42	12	16	79
>100	4	4	5	7	0	5	1	1	1	0	0	1	0	0	0	2	5	9	6	11
No capital assets	15	0	0	18	1	0	0	1	1	0	1	1	0	0	0	0	17	0	0	20
No work	63	175	167	0	4	12	14	0	2	17	21	0	0	42	37	27	69	246	239	27

a = general highways.
b = capital over £50,000.
c = capital under £50,000.
d = maintenance.
Source: DLO Annual Reports sent to INLOGOV.

More significant perhaps is the fairly large number of DLOs which made apparently high rates of return. The 100+ category in the table includes one rate of return of 1,494 per cent. If rate of return on capital is a true measure of efficiency, then that work was carried out 299 times more efficiently than in the case of a 5 per cent return.

In the first year the use of a rate of return on capital as a measure of efficiency failed. It was the only target set by which the DLOs were to be judged by the DoE. If the targets were taken seriously, then it would have to be allowed that those DLOs with 20+ per cent returns were tremendously successful, if those with less than 5 per cent were to be condemned or closed.

Crucial to an evaluation of performance is the amount of work won in competition. Many reports contained examples of contracts which had been won in competition, but those authorities which declared the proportion of work won in competition showed a very low figure. The competition regulations had not stimulated much competition. The tendering requirements had been met, but there was enough work left over to allow the DLO to survive. Although the DoE had no figures on the amount of work won in competition at the time, this tendency led to the two major revisions in the competition regulations.

CONCLUSION

The DoE and its allies in the CIPFA operating in effect as an adjunct to central government sought a simple target to achieve their objectives of testing efficiency and increasing privatization where efficiency was shown to be inadequate. That search produced a set of accounting rules and a target, the rate of return on capital, which drew on economists' notions of productive efficiency. It produced a method of reporting which the DoE was able to cope with administratively. It also produced rules about performance which led to decision-making at the centre which was technically objective. A very complex problem had been reduced to a set of rules, targets and reporting procedures which allowed a high degree of central government control over local decision-making.

It remains to be seen how this control will be exercised. The major decisions about closing all or part of a DLO will not be made until the end of the third year, 1983–4. To date control is exercised through auditors who have to judge whether estimating, accounting and tendering procedures comply with the regulations and code of practice and through letters from the DoE about individual annual reports. Although there have been substantial reductions in the numbers of people employed in public sector building and maintenance work, the reduction has been even greater in the private sector. The rules were introduced to achieve privatization through competition. A continuous tightening of the rules indicates that central government was not satisfied with the rate of success.

The process of producing those rules demonstrated a lack of detailed understanding of the work being carried out in local authorities. The example of the search for a simple definition of a 'job' shows the inability of civil service and accounting draughts-men to comprehend the reality of building, civil engineering and maintenance work. It was left to the people responsible for carrying out the work to interpret what the rules meant. Indeed, at one meeting between DLO managers and the civil servants concerned, the managers were told that it was not the civil servants' task to interpret the regulations which they had written.

In these circumstances it was inevitable that the civil servants and ministers should keep their options open. They knew the *effect* which they were trying to achieve. They did not know precisely which rules and procedures would achieve those effects. They chose, therefore, to devise legislation which allowed the rules to be changed as the results became apparent.

The impact of the uncertainty which this openness to change created for local authorities was considerable. As one set of regulations was interpreted and working practices were changed in order to comply with it, so a new set arrived. This volatility made the planning of work and the achievement of efficient practices difficult, especially since in a large number of cases management structures and practices had been changed in order to comply with the general framework of the legislation.

The new rules were a fundamental change to the accountability for a major sector of local government. The target of achieving a 5 per cent return on capital is imposed by the secretary of state. Failure to achieve the target will result in the secretary of state withdrawing the power of the local authority to carry out work in that category by directly employed labour. This decision will be based on a report submitted by the local authority to the secretary of state regardless of the wishes of the elected members of the authority. If they decide that a smaller surplus or a deficit are acceptable to them, they may be overruled by the government.

The reports which the secretary of state requires take no account of the aspects of DLO performance other than profitability and the degree of competition. Quality of work, speed of response, the provision of continuity of work to the workforce and the provision of training opportunities are not his concern. Accountability for these matters remains in the hands of the elected members of the authority.

This dual accountability, one based on financial performance and the other on work performed and conditions of service, places managers in a difficult position. There are contradictions, for example, between a desire to achieve a profit in competition with the private sector and a desire to be a good employer. This applies to the treatment of older workers, the interpretation of health and safety rules, the employment of apprentices and the allowance of time for trade union activities. Many authorities wish to be model employers while being forced to institute cost-saving measures prevalent among the companies with whom they are in competition.

What are the lessons to be learned from this episode about the relationship between central and local government? To understand the outcome it is necessary to consider the resources available to the two sides and the balance of advantage and disadvantage.

A large parliamentary majority and the successful creation of an anti-public sector ideology were the most effective weapons central government had. The ideology of competition and entrepreneurship has allowed the development of a coherent privatization strategy among many parts of the public sector. From this position of strength the tactics of privatization have been chosen appropriately for each sector – sales of assets, ending of state monopolies and the introduction of competition from private contractors. Having chosen competition in this case, what was needed was a suitable set of instruments. This was partially available already. A report by the previous government contained most of the requirements on accounting procedures including endorsement of the CIPFA code of practice. In other cases firms of private accountants were used to produce evidence and advice. For DLOs, the local authority accounting profession was a natural ally; CIPFA is keen to enhance its status both within local government and in relation to central government and was a willing partner, though members did not acquiesce in all the government's wishes. The chairman of the code of practice working party saw his role, at least in part, as a defender of local government's interests. However, the alliance of CIPFA and central government proved a strong one. Individual treasurers found it more difficult to argue with a code of practice drawn up by their own profession than would have been the case if civil servants had drafted it all; and CIPFA's involvement was not limited to the code of practice. Civil servants also received help in drafting the regulations.

The major disadvantage the government had was that civil servants lacked direct experience of the operations for which they were required to provide legislation. This lack of detailed knowledge probably resulted in more loopholes than necessary. Certainly successive regulations have attempted to stop loopholes which had become apparent. This may have caused delays in achieving the government's objectives.

On the local government side the resources available were its professional skills, its lobby through the Associations and its local political support. Its professional expertise was compromised by the defection of treasurers and by internal divisions. Engineers were not universally in favour of the use of direct labour. Many prefer the use of contractors – because of the reduction of contact with trade unions which this involves and because of the relative simplicity of a contractual relationship compared with detailed day-to-day organization and supervision of a workforce. The building managers (most of whom are members of the Institute of Municipal Building Management) are not organized as a lobby, have few full-time staff and a weak presence. Client departments in many cases welcomed the legislation.

The lobby through the Associations won some concessions such as the exclusion of snow-clearing and gritting from the competition regulations. This was achieved during the consultation process as the regulations were formulated. Parliamentary lobbying was less successful and only in the House of Lords were objections seriously raised to this part of the Bill, and then only on matters of detail. More important central local battles were being fought and energy was naturally devoted to them.

Some authorities attempted to build support among the local electorate. Sheffield rallied support through its 'Building for people not profit' campaign. It was a difficult task. Among tenants alienation from the local authorities could not easily be reversed in response to a threat to one part of the authority from central government. The other potential allies were the unions whose members were particularly threatened by the legislation. The building workers' union, UCATT, organized a propaganda campaign but its industrial strength was limited by the scale of unemployment in the building industry and by the fact that the membership was divided between the public and private sectors.

Local government's major resource which has been deployed not to defeat the legislation, but to play the game according to the new rules, is the expertise of its staff. Major changes have occurred in management working practices to increase competitiveness.

The government is continuing its privatization strategy. Further use was made of the privatization through competition tactic in the health service in 1983.[7] Here competition rules were devised without the rate of return criterion. Again the competition rules have been introduced concurrently with much more pressing matters, in this case a reduction in funding and staff; and the work that is to be privatized is carried out by a relatively weak union.

NOTES: CHAPTER 7

1 See DoE press notice, 14 December 1982.
2 See CIPFA, 1975, 1978.
3 See Department of the Environment, 1978.
4 See DoE/Welsh Office, 1981.
5 See Flynn and Walsh, 1982.
6 Even by 1982–3 many authorities experienced problems. An auditor's note on the City of Birmingham's DLO accounts remarked that the origins of the surplus achieved were 'obscure' because of the difficulty of relating prices quoted to costs.
7 See Health Circular HC(83), 18 September 1983.

REFERENCES: CHAPTER 7

Chartered Institute of Public Finance and Accountancy (CIPFA) (1975), *Direct Works Undertakings (Accounting)* (London: CIPFA).
CIPFA (1978), *Direct Works Undertakings (Maintenance)* (London: CIPFA).
Department of the Environment (DoE) (1978), *Working Party of Direct Labour Organisations* (London: DoE).
DoE/Welsh Office (1981), *Local Government Planning and Land Act 1980: Direct Labour Organisations*, Circular No. 10/81 (DoE); Circular No. 7/81 (Welsh Office) (London: DoE/Welsh Office).
Flynn, N., and Walsh, K. (1982), *Managing Direct Labour Organisations* (Birmingham: INLOGOV, University of Birmingham).

PART THREE

Restructuring Policy Sectors

I   Infrastructures

8

Inner Cities

STEVE LEACH

INTRODUCTION

Inner city partnerships (ICPs) and inner area programmes (IAPs) have since their inception in 1977 proved an important policy arena for the study of central–local relationships. Both sought to deal with the problem of 'inner city deprivation', following a long line of such initiatives that began with the Urban Programme in 1968.[1]

ICPs and IAPs possessed characteristics which set them apart from their predecessors. First, there was a new conception of the *nature of the problem*, which emphasized the economic roots of inner city deprivation, although this did not at the time result in the designation of an exclusively 'economic' programme to deal with the perceived problem. Secondly, there was a level of *ministerial commitment* in terms both of resources and time, [2] which had not existed before. Thirdly, there was the setting up, particularly in the chosen partnership areas, of *an elaborate inter- organizational and departmental structure* which brought together central and local government in a novel way. Fourthly, there was the use of a *new policy instrument* – the policy planning [4] system (or PPS) – which structured the interaction between the centre and the localities in a way which had occurred previously only in the policy sector of transportation. ICPs and IAPs, therefore, raised a number of interesting issues about central–local relationships.

This chapter provides a review of the progress of inner city policy between 1977 and 1983.[2] Three distinct phases in the history of ICPs and IAPs are identified; we then discuss their implications for central–local relations; and finally, our interpretation draws upon a more conceptual approach to the study of central–local relations.

THE THREE PHASES OF POLICY FOR THE INNER CITY

The Policy Launch and Its Aftermath: 1977–9
This first period was characterized by a high level of political commitment; problem analysis and programme compilation by central–local working parties; a spirit of 'partnership' between the DoE and the local authorities concerned, and much confusion as to what the drawing-up of an inner area programme involved.

The policy launch came from Labour Minister, Peter Shore, with his own constituency roots in a deprived inner city area.[3] Responsibility for the seven ICPs and fifteen IAPs set up[4] was shared between four DoE ministers, including Shore. Until the change of government in 1979 there were regular meetings between local councillors and the relevant DoE ministers, sometimes including junior ministers from the DES, DHSS, or the Home Office. The initiative was welcomed by the favoured local authorities, primarily because of the extra financial resources made available, but also because of government commitment to the problems of their areas. Thus the partnership label was not inappropriate in the first two years as the needs and interests of both central and local politicians were furthered by the initiative.

The Change in Emphasis and Routinization of Inner City Policy: 1979–81
The change of government in 1979 occurred at a time when the implementation of the first inner city programmes was just beginning. Initially there was considerable doubt as to whether the Conservatives would continue the initiative: the Prime Minister and the Secretary of State for Industry expressing strong reservations.[5] Nevertheless, the policy survived,[6] although there were important modifications which had the effect of both *routinizing* and *centralizing* policy. The 'streamlining' of inner city policy at ministerial level was seen to be desirable. This meant fewer partnership meetings and working groups, less concern with analysis and strategy and an increasing focus on the content of ICPs submitted. These programmes became 'bid' documents for government resources constrained by centrally imposed rules about acceptable practice. This entailed the extraordinary phenomenon of ministerial scrutiny of local bids, involving the checking of hundreds of schemes item by item![7] The greater restrictiveness of the new rules – which were in fact operated informally via Regional Offices and were not available in published form until July 1981 – represented a marked change from the previous atmosphere of *laissez-faire*.[8] In February 1981 a

long-standing review confirmed that ICPs and IAPs would survive albeit on a much more routinized basis.[9]

The Inner City Riots of 1981 and the Revival of Interest in Inner City Policy
The third phase was signalled by the rioting which took place in many inner city areas during the summer of 1981, but most spectacularly in Brixton, Toxteth (Liverpool) and Moss Side (Manchester). The government's response was mediated through the Home Office (in view of the implication for social order) and the DoE.

The riots re-established the importance of inner city policy and questioned the existing agenda. This impact was short-lived. Although in 1982 there was the first real increase in ICP/IAP resources since 1977, and although eight new programme authorities were designated in 1983,[10] later that year pressure from the Treasury to cut the programme began once more. For a time fears of further rioting influenced the DoE to move from an exclusive concern with 'economic and environmental projects' to accept projects geared to the needs of ethnic minorities. When further riots failed to materialize, however, inner city policy was restored to its routine, programmatic 'economic' base.

THE CHANGING PATTERN OF CENTRAL–LOCAL RELATIONS IN INNER CITY POLICY

What does this experience tell us about the nature of central–local relations? The inner city policy initiative introduced new ideas about the nature of inner city problems and their potential solution, together with organizational procedural and financial mechanisms for dealing with them.

Conceptions of *the inner city problem* have changed since 1977 from the general idea of 'multiple deprivation' to the much more specific notion of 'economic decline'. These ideas implied different programmes. Multiple deprivation implies a programme of action with economic, environmental and social elements, and with the precise balance varying, depending on the particular circumstances of different inner city areas. 'Economic decline' implies a much more specific programme directed at economic regeneration. While the first batch of programmes (1979–82) revealed significant differences in the allocation of resources to economic, environmental and social projects respectively between the different localities,[11] the choice since then has become much more circumscribed. Although programmes still to some extent exhibit some variation, these now reflect 'historical' priorities and ongoing commitments which have flowed from them rather than current priorities. It has since 1979 been very difficult for ICP and IAP authorities to get new 'social' projects accepted, particularly if revenue expenditure is involved. ICPs and IAPs are now about encouraging economic regeneration by financial inducement, infrastructure provision and environmental improvements, using a predominantly capital programme. They are only incidentally about improving the lot of inner city *residents* through the topping-up of social welfare provision in deprived areas.

It is important for our understanding of central–local relations to emphasize that this *switch of problem definition has been a centrally imposed one*. While some local authorities accepted the new 'economic' emphasis, many did not and said so. By then, however, it was clear that inner city policy was no longer a 'partnership', with the centre and localities jointly identifying problems and agreeing joint action. It had become a centrally dominated policy initiative, with the centre defining the rules and responding to the bids made by local authorities, in the light of these rules. In a subject-specific policy planning system with a specific grant attached it is always possible for central government unilaterally to change the conditions of approval of local submissions and indeed the whole climate of interaction, in this case from 'partnership' to a 'bidding system incorporating central government priorities'. Although in principle it would be possible for an aggrieved local authority to withdraw, in practice given the additional resources involved, and the context of a hard financial climate, none has done so.

The new problem definition received a brief challenge in the aftermath of the inner city riots of 1981. On the surface there was a concern displayed at Westminster about the living conditions of those in inner city areas, epitomized by Heseltine's bid for a major additional allocation of resources for housing improvements in Liverpool.[12] Certain types of 'social' project (for example, special facilities for ethnic minorities) began to appear in ICP and IAP bids and to receive more sympathetic treatment. However, hopes of a major reassessment of the direction of ICPs were not to be fulfilled.

Two features of the *organizational* aspects of central–local relations are worthy of emphasis: first, the problems of developing a genuinely corporate approach and innovatory capacity to complex problems such as 'inner city deprivation'; and secondly, the increasing significance of the regional arm of the DoE in

Dept. of Environ

mediating between central and local government in this particular policy sector.

The new approach in 1977 created unusual organizational demands in the wide range of central and local government departments as well as other local institutions who were involved. In a typical ICP there was a formal involvement in the partnership machinery by the DoE, DHSS, DES, Home Office, Department of Employment, MSC, Department of Transport, the relevant county and district(s), and the local AHA. Informally the local Chamber of Commerce and Council of Voluntary Service would also normally be involved.[13] Indeed, the commitment of other central government departments was essential to the DoE if the aim of persuading local authorities to 'bend their main programme'[14] in favour of the inner city was to appear credible. If central departments could not organize themselves corporately, how could local authorities be reasonably expected to?

Hence in 1977 ICPs provided an intriguing opportunity for joint planning and programming between a range of central government departments and selected local authorities. The various levels of working – Partnership Committees, Officer Steering Group and Topic Working Groups – all provided opportunities in different ways for inter-organizational co-operation. Certainly for two years this machinery 'worked' in so far as the various levels met regularly in each locality, generating prolific studies which informed the formal submissions. However, beneath the surface, problems were emerging. The DoE as lead department was coming to recognize the competing demands, on the one hand 'a serious analysis of inner city problems', and on the other the need with an election looming in 1979 'to demonstrate tangible results'. Furthermore, questions were being raised about the commitment of central government departments other than the DoE.

The eloquently expressed desire of 'Policy for the inner cities' for a comprehensive and integrated strategy for each inner city area was swiftly overtaken by the political constraint of demonstrating the impact of the policy. Precedents were set early on by the making available of central resources for the intermediate period between the policy launch and the operation of the first programme (April 1979). The money from the Inner City Construction Package[15] and the enhanced Urban Programme[16] in 1978–9 encouraged local authorities to submit projects, which already existed in departments' capital programmes. This process was repeated in the first ICP and IAP formal submissions, as in many areas was the practice of assembling *separate* packages of projects from the county, the district(s) and the AHA respectively, following an initial allocation of resources among these bodies. Consideration of strategy and main programme-bending faded into the background in such circumstances. It is hardly surprising therefore that, as one commentator on the first set of inner city programmes noted, 'in general, the connection between analysis and expenditure is thin or non-existent'.[17]

As this emphasis became apparent the processes of departmentalism inherent in the operation of central government (and indeed in many local authorities) soon re-established themselves. Departments other than the DoE had been carried along superficially in the wake of the Cabinet commitment. It soon became clear that their major concern was twofold; to avoid outside interference with their own departmental priorities and paradigms; and to pick up as many extra projects as possible from the new initiative, preferably items already in the pipeline. In other words, the commitment to inter-corporate planning and innovatory joint projects was limited to the DoE, and a few local authorities which contained strategically placed officers and units with a belief in that kind of approach. As the threat of detailed examination of main programmes receded, so the concern of the major central government departments (other than the DoE) waned, their attendance at partnerships meetings became more infrequent (and at a less senior level), and ICPs and IAPs became for them an increasingly peripheral activity.

Following the change in power in 1979 all pretence that commitment to the initiative was an *inter-departmental* one at central government level disappeared and the other central government departments faded further into the background.[18] The programme had become a DoE programme, with an economic regeneration emphasis, attached to a specific grant. In these circumstances the elaborate organizational arrangements set up by Shore became redundant. The lesser degree of political salience was also reflected in the relative infrequency of partnership meetings.

There is no doubt that as far as ICPs and IPPs are concerned the role of the DoE regional office has become increasingly important. They enjoyed a pivotal position in the flow of information between on the one hand local authorities (and other local agencies), and on the other the Inner Cities Directorate (ICD)[19] and the relevant DoE ministers. They played an important role in interpreting the requirements of the centre to the locality, which was particularly important in the periods when little in the way of published guidance or requirements was available, and in interpreting the particular problems of the locality to the centre.

Their role in briefing ministers directly for partnership meetings and on programme documents made them an important potential ally for local authorities. It seems clear that policy instruments such as ICPs and IAPs which are selective in their areas of operation, and/or which require detailed local knowledge, are bound to enhance the position of the regional office which, given their greater accessibility as far as local authorities are concerned, may in some instances shift the balance of influence.

Finally, there is the issue of the extent to which the nature of the selected policy instrument – *the policy planning system* – affected central–local relations. Policy planning systems are discussed in detail elsewhere in this book.[20] All that needs to be emphasized here is their enbodiment of the principles of 'rational' policy-making and planning. Two features of the PPS in the inner city policy sector were notable; the uncertainty surrounding its operation and its scope for manipulation. The conflict between the implications of the operation of a PPS and the dead hand of the Treasury-inspired financial procedures is also important.

The PPS with its emphasis on such features as clarity of objectives, considerable data collection, strategy development, links between strategy and the programme, monitoring, and so on, is an extremely demanding policy instrument. It was suggested to ministers as the most appropriate device to use by civil servants on the basis of recent experience with transportation policies and plans (TPPs) and suggestions from academics.[21] The use of the simple submission of a shopping list of projects by individual ICP and IAP authorities would have undermined the credibility of the initiative as a 'co-ordinated strategic attack on the problems of inner city deprivation'. However, once imposed, no one really knew how to deal with it. The problems and confusions surrounding the formulation and implementation of 'strategy' have been well documented in the field of metropolitan housing by Young and Kramer (1978) and Wildavsky's (1969) comments about PPBS, which bears a distinct family resemblance to PPSs, are also relevant: 'the main problem with it is that no one knows how to do it; or rather many know what PPBS should be like in general, but no one knows what it should be like in any one case'.[22] Advice from the ICD as to what to do was extremely vague. It is perhaps not surprising, particularly in the light of political pressure for quick and visible results, that all concerned evaded the demanding requirements of the PPS concept[23] and operated a whole range of simplifying devices, in order to make progress, while at the same time paying lip-service to the procedural requirements. What followed from this was that, for the first two years, the policy instrument adopted proved infinitely flexible, particularly for the local authorities. Their skill in assembling packages of projects which 'looked right' and prefacing these by a weighty statement of the awfulness of their inner city problems, meant that extremely few projects were rejected in the first submissions. Once the idea of the rationality based PPS was informally discarded in 1979, the detailed critical evaluation by the centre of local authorities' list of projects in terms of its own priorities soon established itself as the new norm.

A further factor inhibiting creativity, innovation and inter-agency co-operation was the set of procedural rules imposed by the Treasury upon the expenditure of the partnership and programme allocations. One example was the requirement that for each individual project, however small, the sponsoring authority had to submit a quite detailed application form for grant, even though the project had been given prior approval in principle by the relevant partnership committee, or in the IAP submission. Another was the fact that ICP and IAP authorities had to spend their UP allocation for a given year within that year. No carry-over of expenditure was allowed. This generated in most authorities a frantic search for 'replacement' projects upon which to spend the money in the last two to three months of the financial year. The general effect of these requirements was to generate a mass of unproductive paper-work and to take up time of local authority (and regional DoE) officials which could have been used to better effect.

INNER CITY POLICY, 1977–83: AN INTERPRETATION

The first phase of inner city policy (1977–9) was heralded as a 'partnership' between central and local government, and for once that concept fits much of the activity that took place. Minister and council leaders sat together on partnership committees; civil servants and local authority officers puzzled over inner city problems in topic working groups; DoE regional offices and newly set up inner city units performed an important mediation and reticulation role. True, the centre retained powers of veto on specific projects[24] and on access to the organizational machinery,[25] but these were rarely used. The concepts of 'mutual inter-dependence', 'games' and 'strategies' developed by Crozier and Thoenig (1976), Rhodes (1980) and Jones (1978) are helpful in explaining much of the central–local behaviour in this policy sector during this period. The centre needed the local authorities to implement its vision of regenerated inner city areas, and local authorities needed the extra resources (albeit with strings attached) and legislation[26] from the centre, to overcome the problems of competing claims on local expenditure in a period when 'growth' could no longer be assumed.[27] Local authorities and other agencies manipulated the procedures and the vagueness of the rules to try to ensure that the content of the inner area programmes reflected their own priorities. The centre attempted, less successfully, to do likewise. Regional offices of the DoE strengthened their position by proving invaluable to ministers and local authorities alike. Indeed, it is possible and useful to analyse the stances and strategies of the various participants in the new policy initiative by using Benson's (1976, 1980) model of inter-organizational relations.

What was not realized at the time was that this was an 'equilibrium' situation which could be disrupted by a change in perspective at the centre. This change occured in 1979. The new government's attitude to the inner city policy sector demonstrates that underlying superficial and temporary 'partnership' is the ability of one partner (the centre) to redefine the rules in a way not available to the other partner (the local authorities). Although the word 'partnership' remained, the nature of the relationship changed fundamentally. First, one of the specific 'partnerships' was disbanded (against the wishes of its members) and replaced by an 'urban development corporation' whose accountability was solely to central government.[28] Secondly, the rules were changed – at first informally and only later in formal terms – to enable the centre to impose its concept of the problem/solution on the local authorities involved. Certain kinds of problem definition (social need) and solution (revenue expenditure on social problems) were now excluded,[29] again against the wishes of many of the local authorities involved. The policy sector was restructured in less than a year from an emphasis on the idea of partnership to a centrally dominated process whereby local authorities submitted bids, on the basis of centrally decided criteria, and had their bids assessed in detail, and if necessary modified on the basis of such criteria.

Of course, areas of mutual interdependence and scope for manipulation remained. Central government had of necessity to rely on the local authorities to submit 'good imaginative projects' and a certain amount of bending of the rules was used to 'encourage' recalcitrant authorities or to reward those which did so.[30] Local authorities continued to develop skills in 'dressing up' projects, so that they appeared to be acceptable, and to juggle categorization procedures, so that the 'balance' of the submission was satisfactory. DoE regional offices could sometimes be used to persuade the centre of 'local' arguments which did not quite fit with central priorities. However, it is essential to stress that all this 'game playing' was going on within a new centrally defined set of rules which had quite transformed the 'nature of the game'.

Local authorities could, of course, have opted out of this particular game. The fact that none of them have yet done so is perhaps hardly surprising in the light of the change in financial climate since 1977. A partnership authority will currently receive around £25 million in allocation, of which 75 per cent is central government grant, and a typical programme authority around £5 million. These sums are not insubstantial in relation to overall local authority budgets. The local authorities concerned have come to be increasingly dependent on this 'cheap money' at a time when RSG levels are dropping steadily. Indeed, this juxtaposition of increasing 'urban programme' grant and decreasing RSG support reflects a major anomaly in the centre's position. Many of the ICP and IAP authorities are among what are currently viewed as the 'overspenders'. The message they are receiving from the centre with regard to expenditure in general is 'spend much less'; the message they are receiving with regard to inner city projects is 'continue to spend'. The fact that in most authorities concerned projects in the latter category are viewed as of significantly lower priority than those at risk in the 'main programmes' illustrates the way in which the centre has introduced a 'bias' into expenditure priorities in such authorities. Indeed, a further anomaly stems from the way in which until recently IAP and ICP authorities have had their level of overspending calculated on the basis of expenditure, which *included* their 25 per cent contribution to their inner city programme.

The underlying process at work here is a growing rediscovery in Whitehall that it is much easier to attach strings to a *specific* grant (and hence more directly implement central government priorities) than it is to a general grant.[31] The more this process continues, the more the dismissal of the 'agent' concept of central–local relations so prevalent in the 1960s and 1970s will have to be reassessed.

NOTES: CHAPTER 8

1   It included the Community Development Projects, the Inner Area Studies and the Comprehensive Community Programme. See Edwards and Batley, 1978, and Lawless, 1979, for useful general reviews.

2 Detailed narrative descriptions are available elsewhere: see Hambleton *et al.*, 1980; Stewart and Underwood, 1983; Nabarro, 1980; Lawless, 1980; Parkinson and Wilks, 1983.

3 See Wicks, 1980.

4 The inner city partnerships were located in Liverpool, Manchester/Salford, Newcastle/Gateshead, Birmingham, Lambeth, Hackney/Islington and London Docklands. The programme authorities were Hammersmith and Fulham, Leicester, Nottingham, Hull, Leeds, Bradford, Sheffield, Sunderland, North Tyneside, South Tyneside, Bolton, Oldham, Wirral, Wolverhampton and Middlesbrough.

5 Interview with DoE officials, 3 November 1980, and 10 February 1981.

6 See, for example, DoE press notice 254, 'Michael Heseltine to visit Liverpool', 26 June 1979.

7 Interviews with DoE officials, 10 February 1981, and officials of the Hackney/Islington Inner City Unit.

8 The only items which were disallowed in the first programmes were items which were seen as being appropriate to 'main programmes'.

9 See DoE press notice 59, 'Review of inner city policy', 9 February 1981.

10 In Brent, Wandsworth, Tower Hamlets, Coventry, Sandwell, Rochdale, Blackburn and Knowsley.

11 See Hall, 1978; Nabarro, 1980.

12 See report in the *Guardian*, 'Heseltine's scheme watered down', 10 October 1981.

13 The National Council for Voluntary Service pressed in the London partnerships for formal 'partner status'. This was turned down by Peter Shore.

14 The term 'bending of main programmes' was a major element in the government's philosophy and was used by Peter Shore to argue that far more than the £100 million of 'enhanced urban programme funds' would be directed to the inner city. The term means the favouring, through reallocation of resources, of inner city areas in the programme of local authority and central government departments.

15 A special sum of money made available by the Chancellor for 1978–9 for capital projects, and concentrated predominantly in ICP and IAP areas.

16 A similar 'interim increase' in funding through the traditional urban programme, to enable ICP and IAP authorities to top up expenditure in the inner city in 1978–9.

17 See Nabarro, 1980, p. 34.

18 There were one or two exceptions; for example, non-DoE ministers who developed a personal interest in a particular ICP (Sir George Young in Hackney/Islington) and central government departments which found an involvement to be to their benefit (the MSC).

19 The Inner Cities Directorate is the unit in Marsham Street with the overall responsibility for co-ordinating inner city policy; it is headed by an under-secretary.

20 See the chapters by Bob Hinings and Chris Skelcher respectively, in this volume.

21 For example, the INLOGOV Report on Urban Deprivation to the Home Office: see Stewart *et al.*, 1976.

22 See Wildavsky, 1969, p. 193.

23 There were differences in the extent to which ICPs and IAPs attempted to take this process seriously. Leicester and Hackney/Islington were among the more imaginative examples.

24 Especially on the more palpable 'main programme' items submitted.

25 For example, in their opposition to pressures from umbrella voluntary organizations to appear at Partnership Committee meetings as of right.
26 For example, the Inner Urban Areas Act 1978.
27 Rate support grant had been cut back from 1975–6 onwards by the Labour government, although it was claimed that inner city authorities had been protected.
28 The London Docklands Development Corporation, set up in 1980; a similar UDC was also set up in the Liverpool Docklands area, but the Liverpool Inner City Partnership continued to exist.
29 Apart from 'special pleading' via personal links between councils leaders and ministers, or via DoE regional officers, and expenditure on such problems already in the programme.
30 The Regional Office had powers from 1981 to vary resource allocations between inner city authorities 'at the margins'.
31 We are seeing similar changes in the field of education, where for the first time a proportion of the education grant which would normally be distributed on RSG has been 'held back' to finance a specific grant-based scheme for the 16–19 age group.

REFERENCES: CHAPTER 8

Benson, J. K. (1976), 'The interorganisational network as a political economy', *Administrative Science Quarterly*, vol. 20, pp. 229–49.
Benson, J. K. (1980), *Interorganisational Networks and Policy Sectors*, University of Missouri, Columbia (mimeo).
Crozier, M., and Thoenig, J.-C. (1976), 'The regulation of complex organised systems', *Administrative Science Quarterly*, vol. 21, pp. 547–70.
Edwards, J., and Batley, R. (1978), *The Politics of Positive Discrimination: An Evaluation of the Urban Programme, 1967–1977* (London: Tavistock).
Hall, P. (1978), 'Spending priorities in the inner city', *New Society*, vol. 46, nos 846/847, pp. 698–9.
Hambleton, R., Stewart, M., and Underwood, J. (1980), *Inner Cities: Management and Resources*, School for Advanced Urban Studies, University of Bristol (Working Paper No. 13).
Jones, G. (1978), 'Central–local relations, finance and the law', *Urban Law and Policy*, vol. 2, pp. 25–46.
Lawless, P. (1979), *Urban Deprivation and Government Initiative* (London: Faber and Faber).
Lawless, P. (1980), 'Partnerships: a critical evaluation', *Local Government Studies* (New Series), vol. 6, no. 3, pp. 17–31.
Nabarro, R. (1980), 'Inner city partnerships: An assessment of the first programmes', *Town Planning Review*, vol. 51, no. 1, pp. 25–38.
Parkinson, M., and Wilks, S. (1983), 'Managing urban decline: the case of the inner city', *Local Government Studies*, vol. 9, no. 5, pp. 23–40.
Rhodes, R. (1980), 'Some myths in central–local relations', *Town Planning Review*, vol. 51, pp. 270–85.
Stewart, M., and Underwood, J. (1983), 'New relationships in the inner city', in K. Young and C. Mason (eds), *Urban Economic Development: New Roles and Relationships* (London: Macmillan).
Stewart, J. D., Spencer, K. M., and Webster, B. A. (1976), *Local Government Approaches to Urban Deprivation*, Home Office, Urban Deprivation Unit (Occasional Paper No. 1).

Wildavsky, A. (1969), 'Rescuing policy analysis from PPBS', *Public Administration Review*, vol. 29, no. 2, pp. 189–202.

Wicks, M. (1980), 'Urban deprivation', in N. Bosenquet and P. Townsend (eds), *Labour and Equality* (London: Heinemann).

9

Transportation

CHRIS SKELCHER

The combination of a Thatcherite central government and Labour local authorities is a certain recipe for excitement in centre–local relations in transport, as in a number of other policy sectors. During the period since the 1981 local elections we have seen a struggle by central government to contain the cheap fares policies of the metropolitan county councils and GLC. For those authorities keeping local transport local has been a major symbol in their strategy to resist pressure from the centre, and also to building support for a tier of local government whose very existence is threatened.

This chapter explores the relationship between central and local government in the transport field, and the way it has changed and developed over the last two decades. The chapter is divided into three main sections. First, we discuss the emergence of a local transport policy sector during the 1960s, and the implications that this had for the financial and supervisory linkages between centre and locality. Secondly, we analyse the transport policies and programmes/transport supplementary grant (TPP/TSG) system which formalized the overall relationship between the two levels of government. The chapter concludes by exploring current developments, especially the move towards greater control of local public transport in metropolitan areas.

THE EMERGING POLICY SECTOR

During the 1960s local transport began to emerge as a distinct policy sector, particularly as a result of Colin Buchanan's report, *Traffic in Towns* (1964). This study expounded the view that land use and transport were part of an integrated system, and needed to be planned as related rather than separate elements.

An important consequence of the systems perspective was the

attempt to develop integrated transport plans for urban areas. The Transport Act 1968 empowered the minister to request local authorities in larger towns to prepare and submit traffic and transport plans, setting out how they envisaged resolving the transport problems of their areas. The Act also created Passenger Transport Authorities in four conurbations outside London, which were to promote an integrated public transport system to meet the needs of the area.

Underlying the traffic and transport plans was the rational model of planning, the belief that decisions should be made in a certain way – by specifying objectives, identifying alternatives, choosing the optimum solution, implementing and monitoring. The rational model formed the basis for the plethora of planning systems created by government in this period, and in the transportation field informed the structure of the traffic and transport plans (1968–74) and subsequent transport policies and programmes (1974 to date).

Implications for Centre and Locality
What implications did the emergence of a local transport policy sector have for the respective roles of central and local government? Before local government reorganization in 1974, the structure of transport planning at local authority level was complex and fragmented. There were over 800 highway authorities, nearly 400 traffic authorities and over 100 parking authorities. There were eighty municipal transport services – although mergers after the creation of PTAs in 1968 reduced this number.[1] Highways were traditionally the focus of local authority transport activity, although the responsibility for planning, design and construction varied between centre and locality according to the 'class' of road, as did the level of central government grant aid.

Besides creating PTAs, simplifying the road grant system and relaxing detailed ministerial control of traffic management, the 1968 Act strengthened the transport planning role of the local authority. This was based on three principles:

> First, the basic planning of local public transport must clearly be a function of local rather than central government . . . Secondly, all the transport matters for which local authorities are to be responsible . . . must be focused on an integrated transport plan . . . Thirdly, investment in local public transport must be grant-aided by central government. (Ministry of Transport, 1967, p. 2)

While the 1968 Act can be interpreted as a measure designed to strengthen the role of the locality in managing local transport, it also reinforced central government's financial and non-financial controls. The main sources of financial control were the specific grants distributed by central government. Following the 1968 Act there were four specific grants. Those for roads and public transport capital expenditure entailed control on a project-by-project basis, while new bus grants and rural public transport subsidy were awarded within conditions specified by the minister. The traffic and transport plans established under the 1968 Act provided a separate non-financial device for monitoring local authorities' management of local transport.

In their status and role the traffic and transport plans are the direct forerunners of the TPPs; for example, 'These plans will have a considerable bearing on the attitude of the Minister of Transport to applications for capital grants towards the cost of highways improvements and transport facilities'.[2]

A System of Confused Principles

The 1968 Act, therefore, extended the scope and complexity of the centre–local relationship. It widened the relationship beyond road construction and traffic management into other transport issues, and began to move towards a system of central strategic control of local transport policy and investment. Yet the central financing system for local authorities' transport responsibilities did not match this newly defined policy sector. The specific and fragmented form of the grant system, while giving a high degree of central control over specific projects, was at odds with the notion of comprehensive and integrated transport planning and the strategic role of the centre. The next major step was to change the financial relationship between central and local government and, at the same time, to formalize the rules and regulations for gaining access to central grant aid for local transport.

During 1972 the Expenditure Committee of the House of Commons undertook an investigation on urban transport planning, and in his evidence Professor Foster provided a substantial critique of the specific grant system, arguing that it biased investment decisions towards capital over current expenditure and tended to encourage misallocation and waste of resources. In its evidence the Department of the Environment expressed sympathy with this view.[3]

Political questions, however, underlay both economic and operational considerations. The issue at stake was the respective roles and responsibilities of central and local government in managing local transport policy, and the relationship between these two levels of authority. The need to clarify the relationship was given an added impetus by the impending reorganization of local government, for the Local Government Act 1972 gave county councils the major new duty 'to develop policies which will promote the provision of a coordinated and efficient system of public passenger transport to meet the needs of the county' and the power to support such activities financially. The solution was the TPP/TSG system.

THE NEW PLANNING SYSTEM

During 1972 the Department of the Environment announced that it was to scrap the existing specific grant system, and introduce a new block grant to aid local transportation expenditure – the transport supplementary grant (TSG). This grant would be allocated to each county on the basis of central government's appraisal of the authority's annually submitted transport policies and programme (TPP) document, and in the light of available national resources.

Critical to the new system was a desire to change the nature of central control over local transport policy. The TPP/TSG system was designed both to reduce central government's detailed project control and to increase its strategic control of resources and policy. The reduction of detailed control and increase in strategic control were presented as complementary:

> The intention underlying [the new system] is to try to change the nature of the control. When a Government Department is paying a specific grant directly related to the expenditure of some other authority it has to impose some fairly detailed controls over the project, and some of these can appear, certainly to local authorities who complain bitterly about them [to] leave too little discretion . . . Local authorities would [now] have resources available in order to meet the level of expenditure expected but we would not have to police this in the same degree of detail. (House of Commons Expenditure Committee, 1972–3, p. 458)

But:

> At the same time the Department has a responsibility to ensure that the overall level and distribution of resources devoted to transport are justified and that national considerations are

brought to bear where appropriate in the preparation and execution of programmes. The requirement is therefore for a system which enables the Department to exercise these responsibilities at the strategic, overall programme rather than individual scheme levels. (ibid., p. 550)

A Rational Route to Central Grant?

Local authorities gained access to the new TSG block grant by preparing an annual statement of transport policies and a costed programme for giving effect to them – the TPP. In the early years of the system local authorities set up elaborate organizational structures and processes for producing and monitoring TPPs, but after the initial burst of enthusiasm had given way to a more pragmatic view of the TPP/TSG system, many of these structures either decayed or were incorporated into simpler designs.

An important influence on this change of attitude by county councils was that their expectations of the system failed to be matched by the behaviour of central government. In the brave new planning world of the early 1970s there was a belief in local government that central government grant could be released by the exercise of logical argument. By presenting local transport problems and needs in a rational manner – supported by facts and figures – central government would respond and provide sufficient resources; or at least this would improve the level of resources the authority was likely to receive. In the early TPP rounds, therefore, many county councils played the game of bidding up their resource requirements to try to maximize grant from central government.

This attitude of local authorities originated to a large extent, and was certainly supported by, the statements of central government. Early TPP circulars emphasized the rational planning process TPPs were expected to demonstrate. As we have argued elsewhere,[4] central government at this time had a strong promotional role in relation to the process of local authority transport planning, and both circulars and decision letters (announcing the grant to be allocated to each county council) contained a critique of that year's TPP submissions on the grounds of their adherence to a logical and rational structure.

But when local authorities did try to follow central guidance on the form of the TPP and the transport planning process which produced it, they could see no reward from central government in terms of allocation of grant. The link between the form and content of an authority's TPP and the grant it received was not clear. A survey of county councils' reactions to the first year of the new system revealed that

A number of local authorities, believing that the new system is fundamentally sound, have had their expectations dashed by the way it has operated in this first round. This derives not from disappointment at the amount of TSG, but rather from a feeling that at national level decisions have been taken arbitrarily. The view has been expressed that there is little point in local authorities getting to grips with a more systematic, rigorous approach to integrated transportation policies when a matching system, rigour or coherent expressions of policy appear not to exist at national level. ('An inter-round commentary on the first TPPs', 20 September 1984)

This view has certainly been evident in the subsequent years of the TPP system and led local authorities to question the effort put into preparing the TPP. The TPP document itself, therefore, places a logical rational veneer over a system of grant allocation which is influenced and shaped by other factors and which rests on criteria other than local transport needs and policies.

Determining National Transport Expenditure

We need, therefore, to explore the other planning systems and decisions which intertwine with the TPP/TSG system. The Department of Transport (DTP) is at the focus of a series of processes which link counties' transport expenditure and policy with central government economic and public expenditure decisions. Of particular importance is the public expenditure survey (PES) process, the annual round of public expenditure planning in central government.

The key decisions that the DTP is required to make are twofold. First, in the PES process, to set planning totals for local transport expenditure, including its distribution between sectors (committed and new capital, revenue support and highway maintenance) and types of authority (GLC, metropolitan and shire counties). These decisions will also establish the scale of public expenditure available for local transport; and then a second set of decisions about managing the demand for resources as expressed by local authorities in their TPPs. This involves matching local authorities' expenditure intentions to central government planning totals as a basis for allocation of TSG and capital authorization (previously loan sanction). Critical here is the decision on how much of an authority's TPP bid to accept for grant purposes, that is, how to ration the available grant.

The main way in which local government is involved is through the Consultative Council on Local Government Finance, principally the Transport Expenditure Steering Group of senior local authority officers and civil servants, and its subgroup of specialist technical staff again drawn from central and local government.[5] During the spring this group explores the implications of planned local authority transport expenditure for public expenditure planning totals from the previous PES round and for central government political priorities. Thus, for example, the group may assess the implications for highway maintenance of illustrative levels of expenditure reductions. Such work provides an important and private forum for expressing local authorities' view to representatives from DTP and the Treasury. Because the DTP is a spending department, in some circumstances a strategic alliance may evolve between it and local government.

The results of the Transport Expenditure Group's work goes via the Consultative Council to become one input in the Cabinet's review of economic policy and public expenditure during the autumn. It is at this point that ministers and civil servants at the Department of Transport will be involved in a series of bi-lateral meetings with their opposite numbers from the Treasury, negotiating the size and distribution of public expenditure on transport. These decisions are ultimately published in the White Paper on Public Expenditure.

In parallel with the Expenditure Group's work DTP officials are beginning to identify possible objectives for the next TSG settlement. The work of the Expenditure Group, estimates of available public expenditure, political preferences and policy statements all feed into the discussions between DTP ministers and their civil servants. As the TPPs arrive during the summer they too will influence the process, as will the appraisal of each county council's TPP by DTP regional offices and the observations of policy divisions (for example, highway maintenance and public transport) and finance division at DTP headquarters.

By the autumn ministers and civil servants in the DTP are exploring options for the TSG settlement, covering distribution between sectors of expenditure or types of authority, or for particular issues (for example, GLC fares policy, maintenance problems arising from a severe winter, and so on). By late autumn/early winter the size of public expenditure and aggregate TSG for the following year will be becoming clear (subject to any late cuts negotiated by the Treasury). Ministers will have agreed the strategic allocation between expenditure sectors and authority types, and determined the principles to be used in the detailed allocation to counties.

The annual process concludes with the announcement by the Secretary of State for Transport of the TSG settlement, on the same day as the RSG settlement is made public; TSG is paid at the rate of 70 per cent on that proportion of an authority's accepted expenditure which falls above a population-based threshold. The threshold (which in 1982–3 was £21·10 per capita) is set so as just to use up total available TSG and is, therefore, a device for rationing the aggregate call on grant. However, the grant entitlement of *individual* authorities is limited by the decision on what proportion of their TPP bid to accept for grant purposes.

In the decision on accepted expenditure the concern about rationing aggregate TSG resources shades off into the specific political and technical assessment of a county's bid. Two main criteria appear to be used. The first criterion is *reasonableness*, an assessment of an authority's ability to achieve its expenditure programme. In other words, has it spent its budget in previous years? Is any planned increase in expenditure justified, and will it be able to achieve a higher level of spending? The notion of realistic expenditure bids was strongly emphasized in early TPP circulars, particularly because of overbidding by English counties in year 1, but also to combat the problem of underspending by local authorities. Reasonableness is a key factor, provided a local authority keeps within policy limits acceptable to central government; *policy* is the second decision criteria. In evidence to the House of Commons Expenditure Committee, Conservative Secretary of State Peter Walker stated:

> The important thing is to have a close dialogue with [local authorities] and try and agree on a rational distribution of the resources available, and if there are some differences [between centre and locality] I think these should be allowed.
>
> If there are fundamental differences which we judge to be exceedingly damaging then we have considerable financial powers ... under the new block grant system to influence them to come to a different decision. (House of Commons Expenditure Committee, 1972–3, p. 508)

This view was put into practice by William Rodgers, the Labour Secretary of State for Transport, who in the 1977–8 settlement took the unique step of refusing to accept a substantial part of South Yorkshire County Council's TPP bid because of that authority's refusal to reduce its high level of subsidy for public transport.[6] Two years later Oxfordshire was also penalized through the grant system, but in this case for its failure to increase subsidy in line with central government policy on rural bus services. In neither case did a change of local authority policy result because of the strength of political commitment by the majority group on the two authorities and the relative insignificance of the grant loss in terms of their overall budget.

More recently David Howell, Conservative Secretary of State for Transport, decided in the 1982–3 settlement to accept only part of the public transport revenue support bids from those Labour authorities committed to cheap fares policies. Howell was less severe than he might have been, since he accepted what he saw as a reasonable level of expenditure, 'which assumes that fares are increased realistically in line with costs, and services are run efficiently'.[7]

The TPP/TSG system thus has three dimensions. At one level it offers the possibility for a rational allocation of national resources to meet local transport needs. At a second level it enables central government to manage the spending of local authorities by ensuring that reasonable and historically based patterns of expenditure are maintained. And at a third level it provides central government with a means of influence and penalty, by enabling the secretary of state to limit grant to county councils whose policies are at variance with those of the centre.

THE LIMITS OF CENTRAL CONTROL

Where local political and financial resources are strong, TSG as a means of central influence breaks down. This is what has happened in the period since Labour gained control of the metropolitan county councils in May 1981, and in a number of these authorities began to implement cheap fares policies using its power to make revenue support payments to the public transport operators. Following court cases against the Greater London Council and Merseyside County Council there was confusion about the legal position of revenue support. The government partially clarified the position in the Transport Act 1983. Under this Act the Secretary of State for Transport issues annual revenue support guidance figures for each metropolitan county which 'relate the Government's view of what can be afforded nationally to the particular circumstances in each area'. The White Paper goes on to comment:

legal challenge to the reasonableness of the subsidy on transport grounds is unlikely to succeed where . . . the subsidy is within the level indicated by the Secretary of State. Whilst it will not necessarily be unlawful for an Authority to pay a subsidy in excess of the indicated level, if they do they will not have the protection of the new provisions. The councillors will know they run the risk of surcharge. (Department of Transport, 1982, pp. 6–7)

Revenue support expenditure up to a certain level is legal. Expenditure above that level may or may not be. Central government avoids the political problem of being seen to limit revenue support and increase bus fares by leaving the decision to the courts.

Three Phases in Centre–Local Relations

The recent history of central–local relations in transport thus has three main phases. Initially there were attempts to clarify and simplify the specific grant system which had grown up over the years, and to introduce some form of local transport planning through the traffic and transport plans. The second phase involved the wholesale restructuring of the linkages between centre and locality with the introduction of the TPP/TSG system of annually produced local transport strategies and expenditure programmes and subsequent allocation of block grant by central government. Until recently it appeared that the TPP/TSG system could serve the interests of both centre and locality – the centre for some means of managing the distribution of national resources, and the locality for greater freedom from central interference than had existed under the specific grant system.

We are now in the third stage of central–local relations in transport. The combination of high-spending Labour authorities and a Conservative central government committed to reducing public expenditure has shown that the TPP/TSG system does not have enough purchase on local transport policy. In order to regain advantage the centre has weakened the local authorities' legal resource to make revenue support payments.

The trend in this third stage is towards greater central control of local transport, especially of public transport in the metropolitan areas. The Conservative Party manifesto for the 1983 general election contained a specific commitment to abolish the metropolitan county councils, and the subsequent White Paper envisages responsibility for public transport being transferred to a joint board composed of councillors from the metropolitan district councils in each county area.[8] Central government control over public transport in metropolitan areas would be increased not only because of the competing political, institutional and geographical interests on each joint board, but also because the centre would be responsible for approving the budget and staffing levels of joint boards. Because of this authoritative restructuring of the political, legal and financial basis of public transport in metropolitan areas, the crucial decisions will in future pass to central government.

NOTES: CHAPTER 9

This chapter is based on research on policy planning systems in central–local relations supported by a grant from the Social Science Research Council.
1 See Starkie, 1973.
2 See Ministry of Transport, 1968.
3 See House of Commons Expenditure Committee, 1972–3, pp. 158–278, 548–51.
4 See Skelcher *et al.*, 1983, pp. 419–34.
5 See Taylor, 1979, pp. 7–35.
6 See Gyford and Mari, 1983.
7 Department of Transport press notice 378, 'Transport supplementary grant settlement 1982/83', 21 December 1981.
8 Department of Transport, 1982, pp. 6–7.
9 See DoE, 1983.

REFERENCES: CHAPTER 9

Buchanan, C. (1964), *Traffic in Towns* (Harmondsworth: Penguin).
Department of the Environment (1983), *Streamlining the Cities: Government Proposals for Re-organising Local Government in Greater London and the Metropolitan Counties,* Cmnd 9063 (London: HMSO).
Department of Transport (1982), *Public Transport Subsidy in Cities,* Cmnd 8735 (London: HMSO).
Gyford, John, and James, Mari (1983), *National Parties and Local Politics* (London: Allen & Unwin).
House of Commons Expenditure Committee (1972–3), *Urban Transport Planning. Second Report,* HC57 (London: HMSO).
Ministry of Transport (1967), *Public Transport and Traffic,* Cmnd 3481 (London: HMSO).
Ministry of Transport (1968), *Traffic and Transport Plans,* Circular 1/68 (London: Ministry of Transport).
Skelcher, Chris, Hinings, Bob, Leach, Steve, and Ranson, Stewart (1983), 'Centre–local linkages: the impact of policy planning systems', *Journal of Public Policy,* vol. 3, no. 4, pp. 419–34.
Starkie, David (1973), *Transportation Planning and Public Policy,* Progress in Planning series (Oxford: Pergamon).
Taylor, John A. (1979), 'The consultative council on local government finance', *Local Government Studies,* vol. 5, no. 3, pp. 7–35.

10

Housing

VALERIE KARN

Housing in Britain has always been a very decentralized service. In the past even in housing production, over which there has been most central control, government has usually had the power only to veto not enforce activity. So in housing local authorities have been used to a degree of autonomy not enjoyed in other services. In recent years, however, this autonomy has been severely eroded.

We can identify three phases of increasing centralization. The first is the period of *laissez-faire* from 1919 to the 1960s. At that time there was scarcely a national housing policy except in the limited sense of having a policy 'to get enough houses of acceptable standard' (Sharp, 1969, p. 70). As Griffith described the situation in the early 1960s, 'The Department do not at present assume a national responsibility for housebuilding; do not assume the function of ensuring that local authorities are fulfilling their statutory obligations to provide housing accommodation to the extent that it is needed' (Griffith, 1966, p. 289). Though central government gave subsidies to help meet the costs of certain activities, the local authorities were left to decide the nature and extent of local housing need and how far (if at all) it was to be met (ibid., p. 519). As Dame Evelyn Sharp (1969, p. 70) has put it, 'the basic conviction that housing is a private responsibility has remained'. There was, however, gradual change over the period, so that by the late 1960s central government had come closer to having a 'national housing policy'. However, this development had been piecemeal, almost accidental, and

certainly not in the pursuit of any deliberate philosophy. Until recently there has been, indeed, little discussion about the philosophy of housing: of the proper roles of public and private enterprise: of what kinds of tenure best suit people's needs and wishes, or the social and economic policies of the country, of how best to help families that must be helped. Equally there have been few deliberate decisions on these questions. (loc. cit.)

From the middle to late 1960s central government increasingly intervened in housing policy and practice, seeking to broaden the definition of a local authority housing service and to achieve higher standards of management. The 'comprehensive housing service' was advocated, with local authorities being urged to become involved with urban renewal and home-ownership as well as public sector construction. Housing associations were launched as an alternative and more directly manageable agency of housing policy and, most crucially, public expenditure cuts became a reality. So this second period is typified by a more interventionist, centralized interest both in the quality and scope of the housing service, and in restraining the cost of that service. Control of service quality and of its costs were closely linked, as we will see later.

The late 1960s and early 1970s were marked not just in housing, but in most services, by a declining willingness of central government to accept local diversity of policy, when that meant dissent from its own policy. The main argument for uniformity was territorial justice; an individual in one part of the country should have the same service and opportunities as an individual in another. Or at a more limited level there should be a guaranteed minimum service. Central government's interest in territorial justice grew, irrespective of party, as the need for public expenditure control grew. To justify expenditure ceilings and to gain their acceptance central government become more and more heavily involved in producing formulas to measure local housing needs, costs and resources and in devising detailed systems, based on these formulas, for controlling service levels and expenditure. The two trends towards greater public expenditure control and greater uniformity of service were, therefore, inextricably intertwined in a third trend, namely, an increasing stress on nationalism in planning and the allocation of scarce resources, which has tended to undermine local political autonomy and disguise central political control as technical control.

The election of the Thatcher government in 1979 marked the beginning of a distinctive third period. This has been characterized by a narrower definition of the housing responsibilities of local and central government; enforced privatization of the public sector stock; draconian cuts in housing expenditure; and, in particular, a style of control of expenditure which has moved from general spending targets and controls to targets and controls set for each individual local authority. This last shift has altered the nature of central control over local housing activities.

Of all the services, housing has experienced the heaviest burden of cuts. In the Conservative government's White Paper on Government Expenditure Plans 1980–1 expenditure on housing was planned to drop by 48 per cent between 1980–1 and 1983–4, compared with a total public expenditure cut of 4 per cent; housing accounted for three-quarters of all public expenditure savings. By 1983–4 housing accounted for only 4 per cent of public expenditure, compared with 10 per cent in 1974–5 (Malpass and Murie, 1982, p. 73). Further cuts between 1983–4 and 1984–5 will bring local authority housing investment to only 60 per cent of its 1979–80 level and little more than one-third of its 1974–5 level, that is, about 3 per cent of public expenditure (Cowan, 1984, pp. 19–21).

There has also been a marked change of style in policies towards the role of the state in housing since 1979. For many years Labour and Conservative governments had an agreement to differ about the relative importance of public and private provision, but a common recognition that each had an important role. In contrast, the present government has sought to achieve a major shift towards a market economy in housing, by privatizing the existing council stock. Unlike the earlier policies of central control which aimed to *increase* public sector activity, a central policy of compulsory privatization and cuts threatens local government officers' jobs as well as levels of public services. In housing the largest body of staff is involved in the management and maintenance of properties, and those jobs are at risk.

Although the recent combination of financial cuts, privatization and increased centralization has produced a highly visible impact, the Thatcher government, as we have seen, is not the first or only administration to have eroded local authority autonomy in the interests of achieving implementation of its policies. Previous Conservative and Labour governments laid the ground for recent, more rapid changes. The present government has made some changes in the opposite direction, relaxing central control over the areas of activity which it does not see as a central government responsibility or where past legislation does not accord with present government philosophy. For example, there have been revisions of the Code of Guidance on the Housing (Homeless Persons) Act 1977, the relaxation of Parker Morris housing standards and withdrawal from an advisory role on housing management. But these moves are in keeping with the present government's policy aims and show that a government may use central control or local autonomy to achieve the same ends, depending on whether it expects resistance or consent. Relaxation of the Code of Guidance is expected to produce a harsher attitude to 'intentional homelessness' and so is supported. Relaxation of the 'right to buy' would, however, be expected to produce less sales and would thus be strongly resisted.

The present confrontation between central and local government over autonomy covers all aspects of the housing service, but this chapter concentrates on the major issues, namely, rents and subsidies, capital programmes and the sale, management and allocation of public sector housing.

HOUSING RENTS AND SUBSIDIES

Housing rents and subsidies reveal the greatest and most crucial erosion of local autonomy. The changes need to be set in historical context.

In line with central government's policy of encouraging housing production, from the 1920s until 1967 housing subsidies were paid on the basis of a flat rate per dwelling produced. Subsidies varied in generosity over time, and in the purposes to which they were attached, for instance, general needs building or slum clearance. After 1935, subsidies were pooled into a single housing revenue account. Pooling became increasingly used to subsidize the rising costs of new construction by raising the rents on the old properties. However, as costs rose with inflation in the 1960s, it became more and more difficult for many authorities – particularly those with the most active building programmes – to afford new construction with only flat rate subsidies; so in 1967 a new type of development subsidy, related to increases in interest rates, was introduced. It was only through this mechanism that building continued into the inflationary period of the late 1960s.

But in terms of territorial justice and economy in public expenditure the new subsidies still had defects. Some local authorities which did not have new building programmes were able to break even on their housing revenue accounts while being able to leave rents at a low level, and yet still received subsidies; others, mostly the large towns, were forced despite subsidies to impose large increases in rents and rate fund contributions to help meet the costs of new construction. Inflation was also producing an escalation of Exchequer expenditure on housing subsidies. So central government needed to find methods both to focus expenditure more effectively and to reduce the total cost. The mechanisms proposed were: to raise the general level of rents, to introduce a rent rebate scheme which would target subsidies to those 'in need', and to focus subsidies on those authorities least able to meet development and management costs themselves. To introduce these changes would mean a total restructuring of housing finance in the public sector.

Rent rebate schemes were first specifically recommended in 1930 when the Labour government was encouraging local authorities to take up slum clearance and reduce rents for lower-income families from the slums. From then onwards central government continued to urge rebate schemes. In 1956 the Conservative government tried to create greater response from local authorities by giving a financial incentive, namely, the removal of the statutory obligation on local authorities to pay a fixed contribution from the rates into the Housing Revenue Account. It was hoped by this means to encourage authorities to 'adopt realistic rent policies' (quoted in Merrett, 1979, p. 179), that is, to raise rents and adopt rebate schemes. A different type of inducement was offered in Labour's Prices and Incomes Act 1968, which required that rent increases be approved by the minister: 'It was made clear that introduction or extension of a [rebate] scheme would be accepted as a justification for a rent increase under the prices and incomes policy' (ibid., p. 187).

However, neither the advice nor the financial incentives had much effect on local authorities. On the whole they resisted rebate schemes. As Merrett says,

> With many councils it was doubtless a question of political principle, the unwillingness to convert a subsidy to the working class as a whole into a welfare benefit. With other councils it was a matter of political pragmatism: subsidy concentration inevitably led to a rise in average standard rents and this might weaken the position of the party in power at the next election. (ibid., p. 175)

However, possibly the most important reason was that the National Assistance Board (later the Supplementary Benefits Commission) was already meeting the rents of the poorest tenants (21 per cent of the total in 1967) (loc. cit.). Authorities had also evolved a system of allocating the cheapest houses to the poorest tenants. Those who suffered were tenants with low incomes but with no rights to welfare benefits, who were either excluded from council housing by rent levels or allocated the worst, cheapest property.

If the local authorities appear at first sight to be the villains of the rent rebate debate, it is right to recall, as Merrett does, the 'hypocrisy' of both political parties at central government level in arguing the case for rebates: 'For the government . . . the function of rent rebate systems was to diminish the total public revenue expenditure required to stimulate the scale of municipal house-building which the centre wished to see achieved' (ibid., p. 174). Arguments were presented in terms of 'fairness' between tenants but nothing was said about the system of tax reliefs to owner-occupiers, which benefited higher-income owners most. In effect economic rather than moral motives were to be the reason why rebates become statutorily enforced on local authorities in 1972.

The Housing Finance Act 1972 introduced the changes desired by central government, namely, reduced subsidies, raised rents, statutory rebates and the channelling of subsidies to needy authorities. The approach adopted was to raise rents nationally through the 'fair rent' formula and hence to raise the revenue coming into the Housing Revenue Account. The subsidy structure was simultaneously changed, so that local authorities would continue to receive subsidy only as long as expenditure within the Housing Revenue Account (accepted as 'reckonable' for subsidy purposes) was greater than rent income (McCulloch, 1982, p. 97). For the first time profits could be made on the Housing Revenue Account, though they had to be returned to the Exchequer. This Act also introduced a national rent rebate scheme, which meant that general rent levels could be raised without excluding the poorest from council housing.

Because of the fear that some authorities would refuse to implement the rent increases required by the fair rent formula, the Act provided for Housing Commissioners to be appointed to do so. Following a bitter campaign of defiance by a small number of local authorities a commissioner was appointed to administer housing at Clay Cross, setting a precedent for such central action (Skair, 1976). Nationally enforced rent increases and the use of surpluses on council tenants' rents to subsidize the Exchequer were generally unpopular. None the less, the 1974 Labour government, like its Conservative predecessor, was concerned to do something about the rising cost of subsidies, and about inequity of subsidies between areas and people. Thus, though the new Labour government carried out its commitment to repeal the fair rent clauses of the Housing Finance Act, and to reinstate the right of local authorities to fix rents subject to a 'no profit' rule, it retained rent rebates. It also introduced a new Act (the Housing Rents and Subsidies Act 1975) which was designed to target special help towards authorities with the highest development costs and worst financial position on their Housing Revenue Account (HRA). Concern that all authorities should be encouraged to build and improve their property was, however, reflected in producer subsidies which were paid irrespective of the financial position of the housing authority.

The Housing Rents and Subsidies Act 1975 was seen as only an interim arrangement pending the outcome of the Housing Policy Review. The 1979 Housing Bill, a product of this review, was designed to introduce deficit financing but was lost in the 1979 general election. When the Conservatives returned, they introduced a subsidy system under the Housing Act 1980 which was essentially the same as the proposals of the failed Bill. As Bramley *et al.* say of the 1980 Act,

> the system is one which gives the government great flexibility in determining the level of subsidy to HRAs (Housing Revenue Accounts) and in varying this from year to year in response to changing circumstances. As such its appeal to central government is universal (Bramley *et al.*, 1981, p. 3)

Under this Act central government gained more control and flexibility in future budgeting for housing subsidies; local government lost autonomy and gained financial uncertainty, which also further eroded planning capacity and autonomous action. It was not intransigent local authority behaviour or housing policy which indicated such legislation, but the requirements of central government currency strategies and, in particular, short-term control of public expenditure.

THE 1980 ACT AND BLOCK GRANT

To understand the recent shift that has occurred in the relationship between central and local government over housing finance we need to consider the housing subsidies and rent arrangements introduced in the 1980 Act, the way in which these have been operated and the interaction of these with the block grant system. One of the marked changes that has occurred since 1980 is that housing finance is no longer a separate entity, but is inextricably interwoven with local government finance in general.

The 1980 Housing Act subsidies differ from those in the 1975 Act, in that there is no longer a producer subsidy as of right. An authority that is deemed to be 'in surplus' receives no general housing subsidy of any sort, not even for new construction or modernization. For such authorities, there is now no central government financial incentive to produce housing. There may indeed be a local financial penalty, namely, the need to raise rents or rates to meet the costs of production and subsequent management. The sharp decline in council housing construction must partly be attributed to this withdrawal of production subsidy as well as to insecurity about future levels of subsidies and capital receipts from sales. The characteristic of the Housing Act 1980 which most erodes local autonomy is the ability of central government to determine what rent levels the local authority should be charging. It has been possible for central government effectively to eliminate subsidy through central rent increase decisions (McCulloch, 1982, p. 102). Each year the secretary of state decides how much he expects local authorities to increase their local contribution to the Housing Revenue Account ('the local contribution differential'). This effectively means the level of rent increases expected. The increases actually required in 1981–2 (£2·95 per dwelling per week), in 1982–3 (£2·50) and in 1983–4 (£0·83p) have been in excess of the rate of inflation. The increases have been based on strategies to cut public expenditure and increase demand for council house sales rather than any national rent policy based on costs of management, maintenance and debt servicing.

The effect of these raised rents and the drop in building activity has been to eliminate general exchequer housing subsidy from all but a few local authorities. However, it should be stressed that this does not mean that all these authorities even if they charged the rent increases required by government would break even on their Housing Revenue Account. The subsidies have not been designed as a fully fledged deficit subsidy in the sense that they meet the full difference between even 'reckonable income' and 'reckonable expenditure'.

For the few authorities whose notional deficits on the Housing Revenue Account still qualify them for subsidy, there is still the question of whether they should raise rents by the amount expected by government or whether they should use rate fund contributions instead. For those without subsidy, there may appear no motive for raising rents at all and, therefore, no mechanism for central control. However, this is not the case. For both types of authority, there may be severe financial penalties for not raising rents. These penalties are not part of housing subsidies, but a product of the block grant system introduced in 1981–2 and the subsequent spending 'targets' superimposed on the block grant system (see Chapters 3 and 4).

The system of block grants has been designed to ensure that a local authority, whether or not it receives housing subsidy, has every incentive to raise its rents to make a contribution to the rate fund. By this means, it was hoped to achieve the three aims of rent equity, fair grant distribution and public expenditure savings. The actual scheme has not worked out in this way as political expediency and an emphasis on penalizing the heaviest-spending (Labour) authorities, rather than necessarily reducing the total level of expenditure, have overridden questions of need, resources and equity.

For housing the GREA measure used is that of rate fund contributions to the Housing Revenue Account, not the money contributions but the notional amount needed to meet a notional Housing Revenue Account deficit. The calculation is not the same as that for subsidy purposes. It is based on the so-called E7 formula, into which penalties are built to help enforce central government policies. These relate, for instance, to high-spending authorities with lower than average rents, and to authorities with higher than average voids or lower than average sales (McCulloch, 1982, p. 101).

The E7 formula produced many authorities with negative GREAs, which would have meant commensurate reductions in block grant. However, many of these were Conservative authorities, so for political reasons it was decided from 1982–3 onwards to make all negative values 0. By doing this, the government destroyed the territorial justice of the formula. The authorities with least need and most resources, according to the government's own formula, benefited and authorities with most need received a smaller share of the total grant. (The total grant was not increased to take account of the reformulation.)

The overall effect of the housing subsidy and block grant system is that low-spending, affluent authorities retain a greater share of government grant than their needs would predict and the high-spending urban authorities with bad housing receive a relatively smaller share. Similarly, rent levels in the affluent authorities can remain lower than in the less affluent. In some authorities large surpluses from rents are being spent via the Rates Fund on people who are far better off than the tenants paying those rents, and who are themselves in receipt of owner-occupier tax subsidies. The financial pressures are such that authorities have little alternative but to use rent profits in this way. Those that defy the pressures and raise rates rather than rents are now to be the subject of further controls through 'rate-capping' measures. So two of the faults of the old system, inequity between areas and inequity between tenants, have been retained and three more added – complexity, a disincentive to build and further erosion of local autonomy. All that has been achieved is a massive reduction in housing expenditure.

CONTROL OF BORROWING AND CAPITAL EXPENDITURE

Controls on rents and subsidies are only part of the financial mechanisms open to central government: in addition, there is the system of control of borrowing and capital expenditure. Here too central control has increased as governments have become more concerned to reduce public expenditure.

Up to the mid-1970s local authorities were broadly free to set their own capital programmes in housing. Central government's loan sanction had to be obtained but was normally readily given. Even during the public expenditure cuts after 1967 loan sanction applications by individual local authorities seldom had to be refused on the ground of economy because local authorities as a whole were voluntarily cutting back as much as central government required (Malpass and Murie, 1982, p. 71).

However, after the mid-1970s the picture changed. Since then successive governments have set maximum limits on the capital expenditure of individual local authorities. These limits began under the Housing Act 1974 for improvement expenditure and were extended to all capital spending for housing after 1976. The new system, called housing investment programmes (HIPs), brought together the forward planning of local housing policies and programmes with the allocation and control of investment resources by central government (see Bramley *et al.*, 1981).

Originally the HIPs system was advocated on the grounds that it would control public expenditure, help national allocation of resources and 'increase local discretion by putting greater responsibility for deciding the right mix of investment on the local authorities' (Department of the Environment, 1977, p. 77). It was also hoped to make housing authorities programmes more cost effective and flexible and to make them aware of the needs of the private sector. However, as Malpass and Murie say,

> Although presented as an increase in local autonomy, and generally welcomed as such, it has become clear in practice that

the HIPs system in fact represents an extension of central control which has been used to bring about substantial cuts in investment right across the country . . . the decision about the appropriate level of investment locally has been taken over by Whitehall. (Malpass and Murie, 1982, p. 72)

The process of capital allocations has two stages. The first is the programme of spending that the local authority submits through HIPs to the Department of the Environment. The second is the response to this submission, the system through which the Department of the Environment decides how much to allocate to each local authority. The latter process pays very little regard to the former and is divided into three stages: the national, regional and local allocations. The national allocation of capital for local authorities 'takes no account of bids under HIPs. It is an arbitrary figure in relation to need', being based on national economic policy aims (West Midlands County Council, 1983, p. 118). In putting limits on what may be borrowed as opposed to spent government also makes the assumption that local authority capital receipts will be used to the maximum to supplement borrowing. At the regional level too the allocation system (via the general needs index, GNI) no longer bears any relationship to the expenditure programmes of authorities under HIPs. Until 1982–3 the formula included an element – 50 per cent of the total – which was based on committed expenditure under HIPs. At the local level of allocation more account is taken of HIPs in the GNI but allocations are also based on an element called 'the locally determined element'. The formula for this is not released, but it probably relates to local needs, committed expenditure, ability to spend previous allocations and a willingness to pursue preferred central government policies such as low-cost home-ownership schemes (ibid., p. 122).

This description shows the very detailed level of control being imposed on the capital expenditure plans of local authorities and, in particular, the very small part that the authority's own spending proposals play in the determination of its own allocation. Once the allocation has been made, an authority still has a further decision as to whether it will borrow to carry out its programme or use cash receipts. Here again central government is using financial incentives to press its policy of selling housing and land. These incentives have two purposes. The first is to increase private sector developments as a substitute for the public sector. (Whether the private sector can and will substitute in this way is ignored.) The second aim is to use cash receipts to reduce public sector borrowing. Local authorities are not required to use cash receipts for this purpose. However, this has become almost the only possible option since the financing of loans has become so expensive – because of withdrawal of subsidy, and because interest rates have become high relative to the rate of inflation.

Local authorities are finding that their ability to plan for local needs and to execute those plans is being impeded by the present system. They can safeguard their highest priority activities by using cash receipts but the unsubsidized cost of borrowing has drastically affected HIP proposals. In addition, the annual or even more frequent revisions of expenditure limits are totally inappropriate to a flow of production of new dwellings. Insecurity is producing underperformance and underspending on programmes. While from a central government point of view the HIPs and capital allocation system may seem a success in preventing 'overspend', they direct priority towards capital projects with the minimum of revenue consequences, whether or not they meet needs best, and they contribute to a tendency for authorities to underspend and not make the maximum use of resources.

The use of the HIPs system as a mechanism of financial control has eroded its merits as a system of planning to meet local needs. As with the housing subsidy system, it is the use to which HIPs have been put rather than the intrinsic system itself which causes the problems. But the powers were put into the legislation to be used as government saw fit, and when central government provides itself with a useful tool for control it will use it, not necessarily in the way originally intended or originally announced.

PROJECT CONTROL

Apart from its control of overall local authority capital expenditure, the Department of the Environment also operates a system of individual project control. Until 1981 the system was the housing cost yardstick, or systems similar to that, under which professional DoE staff inspected design, standards and costs before approval would be given. Since 1981 this system has been relaxed. Parker Morris standards are no longer required, there is less scrutiny of design and market value has been introduced as the basic criterion of benefit, but with some recognition of wider social benefit. As Bramley *et al.* (n.d., p. 49) comment, 'This is one of the few, if not the only, areas of housing finance where there is indeed greater local autonomy'.

However, local autonomy is by no means totally restored. The system still makes sure that the privatization aims of government are met, in that land acquisition and municipalization plans are still subject to case-by-case control. Also even on other types of projects local authorities are not being allowed to take their own decisions as consistently as the description of the system suggests. As John Mills commented recently,

> Pressure is being brought to bear on authorities to provide small units regardless of local needs . . . There have been indications that Ministers have been getting involved in making decisions on individual projects right down to the level of rehabilitation of single dwellings. This level of involvement can only lead to delays and inefficiency just at a time when Ministers are urging authorities to speed things up. (Mills, 1983, p. 5)

More crucial, perhaps, in the long run is the dubious relevance of cost–value ratios as a measure of the suitability of a public sector housing scheme. Local authorities often need to make types of provision and investment which would be unprofitable for the private sector (Bramley *et al.*, n.d., p. 50). Yet again central and local priorities are likely to conflict.

HOUSING MANAGEMENT AND ALLOCATION

The management and allocation of the public sector housing stock has traditionally been the area of housing policy in which local authorities have had almost complete autonomy. However, a number of factors have led to the erosion of this autonomy, notably concern over the protection of public assets in the form of housing (CHAC, 1959, para. 138), the rent and rebate policies described earlier and, indirectly, the decline and in some places almost disappearance of the private rented sector. When there was a large supply of privately rented housing, people who failed to obtain a council house could still rent. The fact that some authorities disbarred particular types of applicants was, therefore, easier for them to justify. However, as the private rental sector declined, so central government started to be more anxious about the adverse effects of particularly residential qualifications on people recently arrived within a local authority area. This worry was partly on grounds of humanity and equity but there was also a concern about labour mobility and that nationally subsidized housing should be allocated with maximum efficiency. The latter concern was the same as that which led to statutory rent rebates, namely, that in state-owned housing resources should be targeted on those people most urgently in need. As the private rental sector shrank there developed the additional embarrassment of visibly rising numbers of homeless people.

Through the Central Housing Advisory Committee (CHAC), set up in 1936, government pressed local authorities to improve arrangements for mobility in housing by reducing or eradicating residential qualifications, and by improving transfers and exchanges; advocated better training for housing managers; and offered advice on estate management generally (see CHAC, 1945, 1949, 1955, 1959, 1969).

Local government resisted change in residential qualifications for applicants because it was primarily concerned with being seen to satisfy the housing needs of the local electorate. Even so, central government did not legislate to enforce changes in the allocation rules. In 1969 a CHAC subcommittee chaired by Professor J. B. Cullingworth recommended that authorities should be placed under a statutory duty to maintain open waiting-lists (CHAC, 1969). This was not followed up by the government. Other than that recommendation the Cullingworth Report rejected increasing central control over local authorities, notably on the ground that local authorities were in the best position to identify the needs of their area. However, in order to raise what it considered to be very uneven standards of housing management the Cullingworth Committee recommended strengthening the housing management advisory functions of the ministry. By this time CHAC had become virtually inactive but it was not finally wound up until 1974. Cullingworth's recommendations to strengthen the housing management advisory role were not followed up until 1976, when the Housing Services Advisory Group (HSAG) was appointed for an initial period of two years to review what central government saw to be the key housing management issues and make recommendations to the secretary of state. The list of topics HSAG was to review were those with which central government was most concerned at the time, notably training, tenancy conditions, hard-to-let estates, repairs and maintenance, assessment of needs and security on estates. The emphasis was particularly on protection of the publicly owned asset of housing, through improved management and maintenance.

The HSAG was somewhat resented and distrusted among local government elected members, particularly the local authority associations. Even after government set up a formal Housing Consultative Council (HCC) in 1977, fears were expressed that the

HSAG was being used to by-pass the formal discussions of the HCC whose members consisted of representatives of the local government organizations. Local government representatives also criticized the HSAG as being the mouthpiece of central government, advocating practices that had central government's seal of approval. On their side some of the HSAG members felt that housing issues became lost in the politics of the HCC. Both criticisms had some force. Another objection voiced from the voluntary sector was that neither the Housing Corporation nor the National Federation of Housing Associations was represented on the Consultative Committee.

After the HSAG had been set up, the Labour government produced the potentially more important part of its housing management advisory structure, the Housing Services Advisory Unit (HSAU), to be staffed ultimately by three housing professionals. Full staffing was achieved, however, only just before the 1979 election after which a new style of housing policy was introduced with much less central government interest in the management of the public sector. The HSAU was never allowed to develop in the way originally intended, as a clearing house for good practice. The HSAG was disbanded.

HOMELESSNESS

Although governments had been unwilling to intervene over residential qualifications, growing public concern over homelessness did lead the Labour government to act more forcefully in this area. Controversy about the level of homelessness, particularly in London, had been building up since the mid-1960s. Spearheaded by Shelter, the voluntary housing groups were pressing hard for a change in legislation. Some housing officers also favoured legislation partly because they saw it as the only way to obtain more equal treatment between authorities, but partly also because the more liberal authorities were afraid of being swamped with applicants.

The Labour government of the time was interventionist in style, particularly on consumer issues (it had set up the National Consumers' Council in 1975). Faced with pressure on the issue of treatment of homeless families, it ultimately designed and supported a Private Member's Bill which became after amendment the Housing (Homeless Persons) Act 1977. It represented a massive erosion of the autonomy in allocations that local authorities had enjoyed up to that time. Under the Act local authorities were for the first time given a statutory duty to house certain categories of homeless people. For the first time a group of people had a 'right' to housing. The homeless legislation was hotly contested, particularly by Conservative local authorities. Because of this opposition, an element of discretion was allowed to local authorities to decide whether they would or would not rehouse people who were 'intentionally homeless'. This loophole has been used extensively by local authorities opposed to the legislation, as a means of minimizing their compliance with it.

The Labour government's intention was to follow up the homelessness legislation by enforcing open waiting-lists and a statutory, national mobility scheme. Clauses to this effect were inserted in the 'tenants' charter' section of the 1979 Housing Bill, despite strong opposition by the local authority associations. However, when the 'tenants' charter' was reintroduced by the Conservative government in the Housing Act 1980 these clauses were left out. The Conservatives *were* interested in mobility though, and as a *quid pro quo* for the statutory scheme being dropped, the local authority associations had to produce their own voluntary national mobility scheme. This scheme now includes most housing authorities but is at such a minimal level that it makes little difference to allocations. Even now only a minority of local authorities maintains open waiting-lists, so access to council housing still remains a matter about which a future, more left-wing government might legislate, removing yet another area of autonomy from local government.

The homelessness legislation highlights the point that central–local relations cannot be seen as just a two-way relationship. Successful appeals to central government by pressure groups may result in loss of autonomy by local government, though probably only if the legislation does not run counter to the interests of the central administration of the time. The introduction of change in this way may, however, lead to less than rigorous enforcement of the legislation. Both Labour and Conservative administrations have very much left the enforcement of the homelessness legislation to the initiative of Shelter, and to individuals taking cases to the courts. This low-profile monitoring is in marked contrast to the persistent administrative pressure on local authorities which government maintains over the implementation of the 'right to buy' (see p. 179).

The homelessness legislation and the abortive clauses in the 'tenants' charter' were a reaction to the processes going on in the housing market at the time. With the decline of private renting, households had fewer alternatives to council housing. The Shelter lobby and the Labour government were, therefore, aiming to open up access to council housing for those in immediate need. But it is also possible to see the Act as reinforcing another trend, namely, the shift of council housing towards a more 'welfare' role, with owner occupation as the 'normal' tenure. Much of central government's interest in homelessness, allocations and council housing management in the 1960s and 1970s stemmed from the view that council housing should be more directed towards the poorest households. This view was shared by both Labour and the Conservatives. Though the Labour left saw council housing as also maintaining a wider role as a general rental sector, the tide was running heavily in the opposite direction. Both Labour and Conservative governments were coming out in favour of owner occupation as the 'normal' tenure, while the tax system together with inflation was giving the average worker an increasing incentive to buy.

The 1977 Act can, therefore, be seen simultaneously as a protective measure for the poor and a step towards a more 'welfare' role for council housing. The homelessness legislation is not after all inconsistent with the present government's policy of reducing public services, such as council housing, to a 'safety net'. Giving homeless families priority for rehousing helps, for instance, to disguise the growing crisis of mortgage default caused by the recession and marital break-up and so helps to legitimate the privatization strategy of government.

Though the 1977 Act and the 'right to buy' under the 1980 Act both eroded local authority autonomy, their effects on local government have been very different. The homelessness legislation was aimed at giving local authorities greater responsibility, albeit for housing poorer people, and was therefore opposed mainly by Tory councils. The right to buy removed not only the right to allocate housing, but also the public ownership of it. Therefore, it was mainly (but not exclusively) opposed by Labour authorities. Also as in the Housing Finance Act 1972 legislative provision was made for commissioners to be appointed to enforce the 'right to buy'. This has actually been done in the case of Norwich District Council. Though similar in the sense that both the 'right to buy' legislation and the 1977 Act give 'rights' to a set of individuals, the former is a much more powerful weapon against local authorities. Its strength lies in the fact that it makes its appeals to a much larger body of public opinion. Although in effect it grants financial privileges to a select group, it is couched in terms of giving everyone the chance to be a home-owner. Surveys show that ownership is now an almost universal aspiration (Building Societies Association, 1983), a fact which disarms opposition. Local authorities who oppose sales are easily labelled as part of an unfeeling bureaucracy, denying rights to tenants which many officers and councillors enjoy themselves. Unlike the authorities that evade the homeless legislation, authorities cannot fall back on the argument that buyers are outsiders taking homes from local people.

To conclude this section on central government intervention in housing management we need to discuss the other elements of the 'tenants' charter' in the Housing Act 1980, namely, the right to security of tenure, the right to consultation and the right to information. All these measures had been carried over, though in modified form, from Labour's 1979 Housing Bill. Labour had, belatedly, come to see a 'tenants' charter' as an attractive vote-winner, in competition with the Conservative sales policy. Sales, it was felt, could only be resisted on the basis of a changed style of management of council housing which took greater account of tenant opinion. To achieve this rapidly, or the promise of it, seemed to require government action to shake local housing authorities out of their lethargy. When Labour lost the election, the new government had far less interest in a 'tenants' charter'. It appears to have retained it more to make a point about the inadequacies of local authority housing management than out of zeal for its enforcement. Thus in contrast to its attitude towards the 'right to buy', we find central government showing little interest in whether or not local authorities have implemented the 'tenants' charter' requirements of the Act (see, for example, Cooper, 1983, p. 13).

CENTRAL CONTROL, LOCAL AUTONOMY, OR INDIVIDUAL RIGHTS?

The loss of autonomy suffered by local government in the management and allocation of its houses has mainly been achieved through a single mechanism, the granting of rights to individuals which effectively allow central government to by-pass the local authority. The first example of the use of this type of mechanism in housing was in 1959 with the introduction of standard grants to force local authorities to give improvement grants. Rent rebates in 1972 were the next major example, followed by the homelessness legislation and then the 'right to buy' and the 'tenants' charter'.

This mechanism, adopted as we have seen by the right and the left, has the effect of disarming opposition by appealing directly to the local electorate. The more popular the 'right', the harder it is for the opposition to mount an effective campaign. The ability to appeal to the public directly, in face of local authority opposition, especially on the 'right to buy', has been much facilitated by the 'low public esteem of local government' in general (Raine, 1981), and of council housing in particular. Local government has to accept considerable responsibility for the loss of public esteem. Had housing authorities shown more sensitivity to the housing problems of their own areas and adopted a less bureaucratic and sometimes hostile management style, they would have retained more public support. But it is also true to say that adverse public attitudes have been reinforced and fuelled by central government itself. Attacks by central government on local government have been most strident under the Conservative administration but, in the area of housing management, we find a continuous thread of dissatisfaction emanating from the Department of the Environment and its predecessors, the Ministries of Housing and Health.

The criticism has, at its most intense, led to arguments in favour of removing housing from local government control and setting up a central housing organization along the lines of the National Health Service (see, for example, Sharp, 1970; Foot, 1973, pp. 69–71) or the Northern Ireland Housing Executive. Whether from the right or the left, the reasons for such proposals are the same, namely, the desire to be able to plan housing provision nationally, or regionally to produce greater uniformity in the standard of housing services and to be able to implement policy changes rapidly with the minimum of resistance. During the last decade or so the desire to control public expenditure can be added to these motives.

But even for those most in favour of centralized services, the developments particularly of the last three years have made proposals for a central government housing agency almost redundant. First, local authority autonomy is so reduced that there must be little remaining purpose in transferring its housing powers to a quango. Secondly, government has developed in parallel with local authority housing a set of housing agencies which are more easily controlled by central government, namely, the housing associations and the Housing Corporation. Increasingly housing resources are channelled through these, rather than through the local authorities. And through greater reliance on housing associations central government has made itself less dependent on local government for the implementation of its housing policies.

This has also changed the housing association movement from a small, independent movement to a large one, implementing central government policies with central government funds.

Housing associations are attractive to central government because they can be very minutely controlled and present no party political opposition. In the last few years they have shown themselves willing to switch to whichever activity they are offered money to enter, rehabilitation for sale or rent, or new construction for sale or rent. It is not surprising that they are used in this direct way by central government to by-pass local authorities since this is precisely what both ends of the political spectrum wanted them to do, but for different reasons.

So over the last two decades central government has used a combination of financial controls, legislation on individual rights and development of the housing association movement as a directly funded 'third arm' of housing to loosen local government control of the housing service. These trends derive not just from economic exigencies, but from central governments' view of the world. For central government, reduction of local authority autonomy is often seen as increasing individual autonomy or community autonomy. (Housing associations, despite their metamorphosis, are constantly referred to as 'community-based' associations; local authorities are not seen as 'community-based'.) It is one of the constant features of central–local relations that each level tends to see itself as protecting the public from the excesses of the other. This is particularly the case if there are differences of political control. In fact both do have a claim to such a function; neither has a monopoly of it. The problem is that so great is the imbalance of power between the two that central government, if it chooses to do so, can deprive local government of any power to operate its protective role. This is what is happening in housing at the present time.

The crucial dilemma is that, if those in power believe in the need to defend local government as a safeguard of democracy, they have to accept the right of a local authority to adopt policies and practices with which they do not agree and which may harm the interests of those whom they want to protect. On the other hand, if they sacrifice local autonomy and diversity to the need to defend the interests of minorities, there is always the risk that a change of control at the central government level will destroy those interests much more effectively on a national scale. The difficulty is how to recognize when the balance is in danger of swinging too far in either direction.

REFERENCES: CHAPTER 10

Birkenshaw, P. (1982), 'Homelessness and the law – the effects and responses to legislation', *Urban Law and Policy*, vol. 5, pp. 255–95.

Bramley, G., Leather, P., and Hill, M. (1981), *Developments in Housing Finance*, Working Paper No. 24 (Bristol: Bristol University School for Advanced Urban Studies).

Bramley, G., Leather, P., and Murie, A. (n.d.), *Housing Strategies and Investment Programmes*, Working Paper No. 7 (Bristol: Bristol University School for Advanced Urban Studies).

Building Societies Association (1983), *Housing Tenure* (London: BSA).

Central Housing Advisory Committee (CHAC) (1945), *Management of Municipal Housing Estates* (London: HMSO).

CHAC (1949), *Selection of Tenants and Transfers and Exchanges. Third Report of the Housing Management Sub-Committee* (London: HMSO).

CHAC (1955), *Residential Qualifications. Fifth Report of the Housing Management Sub-Committee* (London: HMSO).

CHAC (1959), *Councils and Their Houses. Report of the Management Sub-Committee* (London: HMSO).

CHAC (1969), *Council Housing, Purposes, Procedures and Priorities. Ninth Report of the Housing Management Sub-Committee* (London: HMSO).

Chester, D. N. (1951), *Central and Local Government* (London: Macmillan).

Cooper, P. (1983), 'Making the most of tenants' handbooks', *Housing*, vol. 19, no. 4 (April), pp. 12–14.

Cowan, R. (1984), 'Where the cuts hurt', *Roof*, vol. 9, no. 1, pp. 19–21.

Davies, E. M. (ed.) (1983), *GREAs – Where They Came From and Where They Are Going* (Birmingham: INLOGOV, University of Birmingham).

Department of the Environment (1977), *Housing Policy. A Consultative Document*, Cmnd 6851 (London: HMSO).

Foot, M. (1973), *Aneurin Bevan. A Biography. Vol. 2, 1945–1960* (London: Davis Poynter).

Forrest, R., and Murie, A. (1983), 'Residualization and council housing: aspects of the changing social relations of housing tenure', *Journal of Social Policy*, vol. 12, no. 4, pp. 453–68.

Gibson, J. G. (1981), *The New Housing Subsidy System and its Interaction with the Block Grant* (Birmingham: INLOGOV, University of Birmingham).

Gibson, J. G. (1982), 'The block (and target) grant system and local authority expenditure – theory and evidence', *Local Government Studies*, vol. 8, no. 3 (May–June), pp. 15–31.

Griffith, J. A. G. (1966), *Central Departments and Local Authorities* (London: Allen & Unwin).

Laffin, M. (1979), *Professionalism in Central/Local Relations* (London: Tavistock Institute for Human Relations).

Malpass, P., and Murie, A. (1982), *Housing Policy and Practice* (London: Macmillan).

McCulloch, D. (1982), 'The new housing finance system', *Local Government Studies*, vol. 8, no. 3 (May–June), pp. 97–104.

Merrett, S. (1979), *State Housing in Britain* (London: Routledge & Kegan Paul).

Mills, J. (1983), 'Asset-stripping says AMA', *Housing*, vol. 19, no. 5, p. 5.

Raine, J. (ed.) (1981), *In Defence of Local Government* (Birmingham: INLOGOV, University of Birmingham).

Sharp, E. (1969), *The Ministry of Housing and Local Government* (London: Allen & Unwin).

Sharp, E. (1970), *Housing in Britain – Successes, Failures and the Future*, Bellman Memorial Lecture (London: Abbey National Building Society).

Skair, L. (1976), 'The struggle against the Housing Finance Act', in R. Miliband and J. Saville (eds), *Socialist Register, 1975* (London: Merlin Press), pp. 250–92.

West Midlands County Council (1983), *West Midlands County Structure Plan. Proposals for Alternations* (Birmingham: West Midlands CC).

II Services

11

Education

STEWART RANSON

As the keystone of public policy-making and social reform at times during the postwar period, education has been expected to fuel economic growth, facilitate equality of opportunity and afford some social justice to the deprived: to educate has been to bring a new world out of the old. To accomplish this burdensome collective vision education has managed a disparate network of relationships. Indeed, the Education Act 1944 intentionally created a complex division of powers and responsibilities between 'partners' to the service with central government, for example, being charged with the duty to 'promote' education, while local authorities retained responsibilities for providing schools and the curriculum.

There has been much discussion in the literature about the balance of power and influence between the partners (cf. Fowler *et al.*, 1973; Kogan, 1975; Griffiths, 1966; Regan, 1977; OECD, 1975). A number of studies support the view that ministers and the department have remained the determinant power in postwar educational decision-making. I have argued elsewhere (Ranson, 1984) that the balance of power has varied over time and that three approximate periods of dominant influence can be identified: an early postwar period until the mid-1950s specifies a time of central dominance; a middle period until the early 1970s identifies a time of local dominance; while the present period witnesses forces which are accelerating the growth both of centralization and decentralization.

This chapter explores the changing relationship between central and local government in education since the mid-1970s. It focuses upon the policies of successive governments to support the effective management of contracting school rolls and financial resources by rationalizing educational provision. The chapter describes the instruments of persuasion, pressure and control which have been used to implement policy. Finally, analysis unravels the implications of the changing controls for centre–local relations in education and thus for the opportunities of young people in a period of social, economic and political restructuring. In the context of declining school rolls and constrained resources the department and successive governments have believed rationalization to be essential to the management of education in a period of contraction. An early consultative paper on the 16–18 group suggested that because of the problem of limited resources, physical, human and financial, 'objectives must be set in some order or priority, and care must be taken that resources are efficiently used' (DES, 1971). The need for rationalization was, however, most clearly expressed by the Macfarlane Committee on education for 16–19 year-olds which convened government and local authority association representatives to examine systematically 'the problems of rationalisation and cost-effectiveness' in education (Macfarlane Report, 1980). That overriding policy of rationalization has, however, embraced three interrelated forms of rationalization, some more clearly and publicly expressed than others: first, the efficient use of resources through the elimination of surplus capacity; secondly, the integration, post-16, of school and college to facilitate the vocational redirection of education; and thirdly, the systematizing of access and opportunity.

RATIONALIZING INSTITUTIONS FOR RESOURCE EFFICIENCY

In a period of contracting numbers the financial resources governments have argued that there are important educational as well as financial benefits to be gained by closing or amalgamating schools and thus adjusting the scale of institutional provision to reduced school rolls. The effective management of scarce resources was emphasized by the Macfarlane Committee but had its most forceful expression in Circular 2/81, which set out the financial case for removing surplus capacity of accommodation:

> The precise savings to be realised will vary according to local factors. But they will include reductions in heating, lighting and maintenance costs, as well as – for whole schools – teaching, administrative and caretaking costs. Every 100,000 surplus places taken out of use should on average yield savings approaching £10 million – excluding any savings on teachers' salaries. (DES, 1981, p. 5)

Not to make such financial savings could only be at the expense of much-needed teachers, books and other educational resources. Indeed, the circular stressed educational arguments: 'a reduction in the number of permanent places can bring substantial educational benefits.' In secondary schools closure and amalgamation would protect the curriculum and staffing – the HMI (in *Aspects of Secondary Education*) have demonstrated the way the range of subjects becomes restricted when forms of entry fall to three or four forms, while particular subjects such as science and languages are especially vulnerable. Post-16 the disadvantages of small teaching group sizes become especially acute, and attempts to staff a full range of curricula opportunities is often achieved at the expense of provision in the lower school. There are, the circular maintained, 'powerful arguments in favour of educating 16–19 year olds in fairly large groups' (ibid., p. 4).

RATIONALIZING SCHOOL AND COLLEGE

The process of rationalizing resources to ensure greater effectiveness of educational provision, especially for 16–19 year-olds, required the focus to shift beyond the closure or amalgamation of schools to the relationship between schools and further education colleges. Rationalization of provision across the education sectors could eliminate waste and duplication of resources, introduce much-needed flexibility in the use of institutions and manpower and, most important, facilitate the new objective of developing a vocationally oriented curriculum by breaking down barriers between education and training.

These policy intentions were made clear in a series of consultative documents. In *Providing Educational Opportunities for 16–18 Year Olds* (1979, p. 3) the Labour government expressed concern at the unplanned overlap in provision between the sectors: 'commonly both school and FE sectors are concerned with providing for the 16–18s and often there is overlap between them ... much duplication has undoubtedly occurred because of uncoordinated growth amongst institutions'. The pressures upon resources and the need to make effective use of plant and teachers, and the requirements of students and employers, all 'demand flexibility in structures and institutions' and suggest, in particular, that 'it may be necessary to ask whether the present boundaries between school and college are the right ones'.

LEAs, as Macfarlane proposed, should review the totality of institutional provision in the 16–19 group; and consider the scope for extended collaboration between school and college or seek to create new integrated institutions for 16–19 year-olds.

The educational as much as the economic argument for rationalizing school and college provision was given significant emphasis. The changing world of employment and the pressing demands of employers suggested a rationalization and redirection of the post-16 curriculum offering. Traditional distinctions between training (specific vocational tasks) and education (the general development of knowledge, moral values and understanding) were now outmoded. The rationalization of the curriculum as between school and college would allow 'the well recognised national need for more vocational education of a high standard in the face of major changes in the nature of employment' and enable the country to produce 'the skilled and versatile workforce needed for the future'.

RATIONALIZATION OF OPPORTUNITIES

It was well understood, however, that rationalizing provision really presupposes qualitative policy decisions about educational opportunities, that is, about systematizing access to educational routes and thus to the labour market. The rationalization of resources presupposes a rationalization of educational offerings and opportunities. As the Treasury official insisted at an Expenditure Steering Group (ESGE) 16–19 subcommittee in 1979, for the members of the committee to determine how to rationalize educational resources, they must first attend to the issue of *how much* opportunity, choice and access is to be allowed *to which* groups of young people. First define desirable levels of participation for the whole age group, and then the separate 16–19 'client groups'. The Macfarlane Report (1980) incorporated these arguments about the need to rationalize educational opportunities: what was offered in the past may now be unreasonable in cost as well as being unsuited to the nation's needs. The aspirations of young people must be realistic and rationalized from now on: 'that a range of opportunities is available of a quality that meets the realistic aspirations of young people, parents and society at a cost which the nation judges it right to pay.' The Macfarlane Committee believed that it was appropriate to define more clearly than hitherto what should count as a reasonable or suitable range of opportunities for 16–19 year-olds. Opportunities, they argued, should be seen in relation to the educational and training (or the vocational) needs of different 'client groups'. The Committee classified these groups as comprising the different routes taken by young people at 16: for example, those who enter employment, those who are without work or the prospect of work, those who pursue A-level courses, those who seek specifically vocational qualifications in TEC and BEC and the 'new sixth', who return to education without any clear vocational or educational objective. Distinct groups, therefore, could be distinguished and differentiated in educational needs and opportunities – 'it is right that young people should branch out at the age of 16, each according to his or her abilities, aptitudes and career intentions'. The Macfarlane Committee was concerned to erase status distinctions between these different vocational routes and thus to promote 'even-handedness of treatments' and 'parity of esteem' between them.

The policy of rationalization of educational provision, therefore, comprised a number of dimensions. At the most obvious level rationalization meant reducing surplus capacity in school accommodation and thus promoting the efficient use of resources. The efficient rationalization of resources taken a stage further embraced colleges as well as schools since the department wished to systematize the use of resources as between school and college, so as to prevent duplication and waste. Rationalizing the relationship between school and college, however, was designed more to accomplish the integration of education and training provision than just the efficient use of resources. The economic objectives were a means to achieve educational policy objectives and to improve the relevance of education to the world of work. At this point the more complete rationalization plan is disclosed. Effective rationalization presupposes a tightening of the relationship between educational 'outputs' and the needs of society and economy through the systematizing of access and opportunity. Much of the success of rationalizing resources, offerings and opportunities would depend, however, upon the preferred pattern of institutional reorganization.

INSTITUTIONAL ALTERNATIVES AND PREFERENCES

A number of options are available to LEAs to rationalize their institutional arrangements. Schools and colleges can be encouraged to enter 'consortia' agreements to share pupils and staff, in order to ensure economic use of resources and an adequate range of educational opportunities. The problems involved in achieving the necessary degree of co-operation has persuaded most LEAs that this is the weakest solution to the management of contraction. Some LEAs have chosen to retain their existing pattern of schools and colleges but to propose closure or amalgamation of some schools as the best means of protecting effective provision. A few LEAs have chosen the 'mushroom system', which seeks to concentrate academic sixth-form courses on a few 11–18 schools; in the remaining schools senior pupils feed into a neighbouring sixth form or further education college at 16. An increasingly popular strategy for many LEAs has been the option of creating new institutions for 16–19 year-olds: all pupils cease school at 16 and enter sixth-form or tertiary colleges. This pattern of reorganization encourages the integration of traditional academic and vocational courses as well as offering economies of scale. The commitment among LEAs to creating post-16 colleges is a commitment to protect and extend the principle of comprehensive education and the equalizing of opportunities available to all young people.

At the centre both Labour and Conservative governments as well as the DES have acknowledged that a national policy for rationalizing institutional provision should allow LEAs flexibility to accommodate diverse local circumstances. Nevertheless, governments have formed a view about which institutional strategy would best implement their policies of rationalizing resources, curricula and educational opportunities.

Two general strategies have dominated the centre's policy on institutional rationalization since the mid-1970s. Common to each has been a view about the relationship between institutions and the curriculum, in particular, a view about those institutional arrangements which would facilitate a more vocational curriculum while, at the same time, differentiating 'abilities' and opportunities. At the heart of both strategies are assumptions about the ethos and significance of the traditional school sixth form. The two strategies are as follows.

Common Institution and Differentiated Curriculum
LEAs should create a framework where school finishes at 16 and young people move into post-16 colleges. The trend towards common institutions open to all is retained but then great emphasis is placed (by government) upon the structure of the curriculum, first, to provide a more vocational bias to courses, and yet secondly, to differentiate young people according to ability and aptitude. This can be achieved because the citadel of the academic tradition – the school sixth form – has been removed, allowing a more vocational ethos to the post-16 college and also in the last

years of secondary schooling, where courses must be oriented to those beyond school-leaving.

This strategy of rationalizing provision was the preferred solution of the dominant faction within the DES, of the Labour administration under Shirley Williams from 1976 to 1979 and of the Conservative administration under Mark Carlisle. The view of the DES was expressed[1] by a senior official:

> there will be increasing differentiation of routes at 16, the academic A-level route will become more intensively academic, and a jolly good thing too. Within each stream there will be different but intensive provision. There will be some switching of courses – about as much as there was between the secondary moderns and the grammar schools.

Mr Carlisle published the report of the Macfarlane Committee which developed this DES argument. It encouraged the view that post-16 colleges would be the best solution educationally and financially for many LEAs as well as arguing that young people should become more differentiated at 16, although there would need to be 'parity of esteem' between the different curriculum tracks. The language of tripartite education – a parity of esteem between modern, technical and grammar sectors – having been almost eliminated from institutions in the secondary sector would reappear within the curriculum of the tertiary sector.

Differentiated Institutions for a Differentiated Curriculum

This argument proposes that because institutions create a distinctive ethos that will shape students' experience and performance, different institutions must be created to fulfil different purposes. If the post-16 college is successful in creating a more vocational emphasis, the quality of academic courses may be threatened. The sixth form, so it is proposed, is indeed the nursery of academic virtues, for the lower school as much as for older pupils, and needs therefore to be retained – in *some* schools. The implementation of this policy would encourage the 'mushroom' (11–16/11–18) solution or closures and amalgamations which ensure efficient use of resources while protecting institutional diversity.

These arguments gained the support of two of the four Education Ministers while the Macfarlane Committee sat and were responsible for the moderation of its tertiary recommendations. In the second Conservative administration Sir Keith Joseph's team comprised arguably the victorious remnant of the previous ministerial team: that is, those ministers who were committed to schools rather than colleges, to the virtues of the traditional sixth form and to giving parents as much scope as possible to choose between the different institutions, believing that the quality of schooling is much improved if made responsive to consumer preferences.

The scale and quality of a school's sixth form was made the defining characteristic of the 'worth' of a school and a key principle in planning reorganizations:[2]

> The secretary of state regards it as essential that when local education authorities consider the educational and financial factors they should bear prominently in mind the need to retain what is best and has proved its worth within their existing system of secondary education. He will not normally approve proposals which have as their consequence the closure or significant change of character of schools which, by demonstrating their success in the provision they make for sixth-form education have already proved their worth under existing arrangements and in his judgement can continue to do so.

The implication of commitment to consumer preferences together with the policy on sixth forms favoured a mixed rather than uniform strategy on institutional reorganization. That is, parents should be given the opportunity of sending their children to schools as well as colleges, and to schools different in kind. As rationalization proposals are being submitted to the secretary of state for approval his judgements will reflect, wherever possible, the values of maximizing parental choice and institutional diversity.

INSTRUMENTS OF CHANGE

The centre has drawn upon a variety of strategies and instruments to implement its policies. These strategies include: persuasion (promotion, planning and advice), pressure (information, finance and parental preferences) and control (legislation and regulation).

Persuasion

The centre has tried to persuade LEAs, through a number of processes and channels, of the soundness of its claims and the urgency for action. Persuasion has embraced promotion, planning and advice.

Promotion. Policies which begin to emerge and acquire definition need promotion if they are to be effective across the educational network. A major policy initiative began in 1977 to persuade LEAs of the need to rationalize their institutional arrangements. A series of speeches and statements by senior ministers and officials provided a remarkable illustration of a policy launch: the secretary of state spoke at the north of England conference in January and was followed within a fortnight by the permanent secretary speaking to the Society of Education Officers. The message was reinforced by statements in Parliament and by subsequent speeches to professional conferences. The policy launch was given wide and sympathetic coverage in the education media and the timely publication of research operated to reinforce the claims for institutional reorganization and rationalization.[3]

Policy planning. Persuasion has more chance if grounded in cumulative analysis which has equally been supported by and has involved key representatives of the education partners. To this end, between 1977 and 1981, a series of centre–local committees were formed to study and review the issues surrounding 16–19 institutional rationalization. Professional teams were gathered together first, as subgroups of ESGE, to work at clarifying the issues and to prepare papers and agendas. This largely professional phase of discussions was followed by a political phase with the establishment of the Macfarlane Committee.

The centre believed these phases of joint policy planning to be an essential part of the process of persuading and co-opting the educational network. Thus a DES official on the reasons for the Macfarlane Committee after a year or more of discussions: 'Macfarlane was needed because it was an elected-member body. There are limits to meetings of officials, who in the end say they cannot take discussions further because they need political instructions.'[4] Another official concurred: 'We wanted Macfarlane because we wanted to carry the LEAs with us politically as well as professionally. This engagement of the LEAs is very critical.'

Procedural advice. The centre sought further to persuade LEAs by preparing practical advice for them about the methods and procedures of reorganizing institutions: 'the task of the DES and Macfarlane is to confront LEAs with the severity of the situation. We must identify options for them, tell them how to approach the problem methodologically – by identifying the client groups, etc., by identifying the options and courses which they should be providing, etc. We aim to give practical advice to LEAs: they will need a practical handbook informing them how to go about the cost rationalization.'[5] The main thrust of DES advice was contained in the manual, 'Costing educational provision for the 16–19 age group', prepared for the Macfarlane Committee by Arthur Young management consultants. This manual suggested that sixth-form or tertiary colleges tended to be a cheaper solution than amalgamation of 11–18 schools.

Pressure
The government, as well as persuading LEAs, sought to bring more direct pressure to bear upon them by requesting information, by applying financial constraints, and by encouraging parental preferences.

Information.   Circular 2/81 asked LEAs for information about surplus places and their plans to remove them: 'the Secretary of State . . . asks every LEA to inform the Department by 31 December 1981 (and if possible earlier) about the expected number of surplus school places up to 1986 and their plans for taking out of use, by supplying the following information in the format suggested in the Annex.'

The request for information was conceived by the centre as a means of placing pressure upon LEAs to begin the process of rationalization:[6]

knowledge about the education service is a source of power and influence to the DES. The extent to which knowledge is accumulated raises, of itself, the issue of LEA discretion. If ministers wish to extend their influence, they could in certain circumstances do so by calling for more information about the education service as an alternative to, rather than as a concomitant of, other initiatives.

The DES hoped that information about surplus capacity in LEAs could become a potential source of influence when attached to rate support grant negotiations.

Finance.   The DES hoped that expenditure cuts would constrain LEAs to rationalize schools in order to ensure the more efficient use of resources:[7]

the biggest incentive is cash limits: LEAs which keep all their schools despite falling rolls are doubly penalising themselves because they are using resources inefficiently and they are losing resources because they are inefficient. GREs are now calculated on the basis of surplus capacity being withdrawn. This is a very real issue. The White Paper plans assume that closures have in fact taken place. The savings therefore have already been taken away and if the LEAs do not rationalise places cuts will have to be made in other parts of their budgets which can only affect the quality of education in the authority.

Pressure, therefore, could be brought to bear upon LEAs directly from the centre through the financial cuts. The centre was equally aware that pressure upon LEAs could be increased from below – from parents.

Parental preferences. One of the primary purposes of the Education Act 1980 was to provide parents with the capacity to express a preference about the schools to which they wished their children to be admitted. The Act reflected the Conservative government's belief that the education service, as much as other services, should be more accountable and responsive to consumer interests.

DES officials, no less than ministers, were in no doubt about the significance of such policies for the rationalization of institutions. A little 'healthy' competitive pressure would further constrain LEAs to reorganize their pattern of provision since 'unpopular' schools – as expressed in parental preferences – became more expensive to staff and maintain an adequate curriculum:[8]

the 1980 Act gives the centre powers to control information. It is an indirect power seeking to influence parents directly and LEAs indirectly. For example . . . shire, a county of small towns and few comprehensives. The county has used a parental choice system in which 90% of parents gain their first choices. The county will use the choice system as a means of managing falling school rolls by letting popular schools expand (become over-subscribed) and the others wither away (become under-subscribed). If . . . shire has the choice of sharing out numbers between schools or closing schools they will choose to close the less popular (and least successful?) schools. This policy may not be popular with those local residents who want a local school nearby but schools must be taken out of the system. (DES official)

The 1980 Act sought to generalize that policy. Squeezed between financial constraint and market forces, the centre hoped to create the conditions that would encourage LEAs to rationalize their schools.

Control
The most important instrument in the possession of the centre is the capacity to legislate in order to facilitate policy objectives. During the period which provides the focus of this chapter (1977–83) both Labour and Conservative administrations prepared to reorganize institutions. The 1979 election cut short Labour's plans.

The 1980 Act incorporated clauses which the government believed would speed up the rationalization of institutions. Section 12-16 related directly to the issues of institutional change developing section 13 of the Education Act 1944. Section 13 stated that if an LEA wished to open or 'establish' (or discontinue or significantly change) a school, then the LEA should submit its proposals to ministers and, at the same time, publish notices of the proposals in the local community. If within three months members of the public objected to the LEA's plans, then it was up to the minister to make such modifications to the proposals 'if any, as appear to him to be desirable'. This was a procedure where the LEAs initiated, the public disputed (if they wished) and the ministers arbitrated: 'Section 13 is a mechanism by which the LEAs [re]organize their schools, taking into account and involving local opinion [through the statutory means of objection rather than consultation] with the minister acting as long-stop judge' (DES official).[9]

The powers conferred on the centre by section 13 are powers of approval. Such a power can seem considerable but is more limited in reality, setting a framework for transactions between partners:

These legal powers of central government are familiar and appear frequently in the text books, creating an impression of a powerful central government with a formidable battery of controls. Yet when one scrutinises the legal provisions it seems that what is provided for the centre is a general legal framework in which more specific administrative and political pressures can operate. (Jones, 1979, p. 30)

Sections 12–13 of the 1980 Act appear to grant more discretion to LEAs to close or to change the nature of their schools. LEAs will not necessarily have to seek the approval of the secretary of state: if having published notices there are no objections to the reorganization proposals, the changes can be implemented automatically. Unless, that is, the secretary of state states that *he* wishes to modify the proposals. The government has retained the right to call in proposals and to veto them in the interests of national policy even if there is a consensus locally about the value of the changes proposed. (All voluntary school proposals still require the approval of the secretary of state.)

Circular 2/80 elaborated the procedures relating to section 12-16. Proposals would be called in by the secretary of state only sparingly and then on grounds of implication for national policy. He may accept, reject, or modify proposals, although he cannot modify 'to such an extent as to change them in substance' (see Circular 2/80, p. 6). The possibility of modification is an additional power for the secretary of state – under section 13 he could only accept or reject. The case of *Legg* v. *ILEA* has established the precedent that the secretary of state's modification should not be able to change the intentions of the proposals. Judge McGarry's judgment stated that the proposal must remain essentially the same. It was the opinion of a senior DES official, however, that although modification may therefore be a limited power for the centre, it could nevertheless be a significant one: 'we could still do quite a lot. Most LEAs will have to put up proposals to the centre because of the constraints of contraction and this will place the Secretary of State in a powerful position to intervene, shape and modify' (DES official).[10]

IMPLICATIONS FOR CENTRAL–LOCAL RELATIONS

The centre has created a set of policy objectives to rationalize schools and colleges, in order to improve the financial and educational effectiveness of provision. It has sought to implement its policies of rationalization by developing a collection of strategies that have embraced persuasion, pressure and control.

These strategies have been contradictory in their effects upon the established postwar partnership between central and local government which made local authorities pivotal in the planning and provision of education. The intention has been to weaken the position of the LEA (thereby reasserting the authority of the department based upon the authority of section 1 of the Education Act 1944, which expects the secretary of state to control and direct the education service) through a strategy of centralizing and decentralizing influence and control. The centre has made significant directive policy interventions, for example, into the reorganization proposals of Manchester (breaking up the tertiary scheme) and Haringey (to raise the admission limits to allow more parental movement), while the resubmitted Birmingham scheme established the new canonical form of institutional diversity.

While the centre has been seeking to centralize its powers at the expense of the LEAs, it has also pursued a policy of influence to the consumer of the service through the Education Act 1980. One senior chief education officer believes that the legislation is designed to shift the balance of influence in favour of the individual against the LEA. Caroline Benn has been more explicit about the consequences of such legislation; it would seriously undermine the capacity of LEAs to plan and maintain a comprehensive education system:

> the legislation will make it far harder for local authorities to maintain the balance between preference, neighbourhood and continuity which is the essence of a successful admissions system for comprehensive education, for it is legislation designed to stimulate imbalance not to keep the needs of all schools and all pupils in equal consideration. It is designed deliberately to enhance the advantage of a minority of parents and a minority of schools. It forces authorities, whether they wish it or not, to run secondary education systems with parent against parent and school against school in a consumerist free for all. (Benn, 1980, pp. 36–40)

Schools are to be placed in the market-place and their account-ability mediated by the test of consumer preference.

The centre is strengthening the principle of hierarchy and encouraging the assumption of market values to undermine the LEA:[11]

> the 1980 Education Act, the block grant system, the school curriculum initiative and the planned reductions in the Government's financial support for education represent when taken together, an actual or potential diminution of LEA discretion which substantially outweighs the combined effects of the measures taken in a contrary sense. Looking at the education service as a whole, it seems that the DES acting on its own initiative and in the context of more general Government policies, is now in the process of expanding its power and influence at the expense of LEAs. (DES official)

As one senior education officer remarked, what the centre is in the process of creating is a new contract between state and citizen that will erode the middle-level planning function.

The centre is rationalizing institutions and opportunities which it seeks to accomplish by redistributing the balance of influence. Relations within the education partnership are being reordered. The centre is embodying these policies and relations in organizational procedures and rules. Rules can condense purposes and relations and thus selectiveness in effect upon policy (cf. Offe, 1974; Lukes, 1974). This structuring of purpose and power through rules is nicely illustrated in the procedures of institutional reorganization. Those who wish to reorganize schools so as to enlarge and equalize educational opportunities will typically propose a development plan (or scheme) for all schools, embracing admissions policies, catchment areas, staffing, etc. Comprehensive education presupposes a design for an authority as a whole. Those, on the other hand, who wish to select and differentiate young people will typically be oriented to support and protect the interests of particular schools. Section 11 of the Education Act 1944, Circular 10/65 and the Education Act 1976 all reinforce the development plan principle. Section 13 of the 1944 Act and section 12 of the 1980 Act focus upon individual schools. The different procedures operate selectively upon policy and relations of influence.

Circular 10/65, for example, initiated a new two-stage planning procedure for institutional reorganization. LEAs produced 'schemes' of reorganization for all schools which were submitted to and vetted by DES officials, who visited the LEAs to discuss the schemes' implementation. Schemes were then put up to ministers for comment and approval. All was entirely non-statutory and based only upon a circular. The process of approval was internal and unofficial, based upon private discussions between the centre and the LEAs. Only when it came to implementing the approved schemes were the section 13 procedures formally activated, as if there had been no prior consultations, discussions, or planning. Notices proposing changes were then published about individual schools and parents were allowed to object, but only about particular schools. The planning system initiated by Circular 10/65 and formalized by the Education Act 1976 established the importance of the secretary of state and the LEA as the principal actors in the reorganization of schools. Although the processes of submission and approval under Circular 10/65 allowed the secretary of state to amend schemes as he wished, the influence of the centre was on reinforcing the principles underlying reorganization, while the LEA became the central planning authority.

The formal argument against the Circular 10/65 planning arrangements was that it was unconstitutional. When Mrs Thatcher became secretary of state in 1970, she argued that she did not want to receive unstatutory schemes of reorganization. Proposals for reorganization should be presented statutorily school by school. This stress on individual schools reasserted the paramount importance of section 13 allowing for public objections at the planning stage.

The effect of placing section 13(12) at the centre of the reorganization stage is to reduce the status of the LEA and establish a closer alliance between the secretary of state and parents. The powers of the secretary of state under section 13 when compared to those provided by Circular 10/65 and the 1976 Act appear considerably to be reduced, the former providing powers only to reject proposals rather than to amend or to modify. On the other hand, whereas Circular 10/65 made it difficult for a secretary of state to discriminate between schools or areas of an LEA, reorganizing on a school-by-school basis using section 13 alone allowed a secretary of state to apply different principles to the reorganization of schools and thus undermine the comprehensiveness of individual schools and the overall system of schools. David discusses the consequences of Circular 10/70:

> One of the first actions of the Tory government in 1970 was to change, by what appeared to be minor emendments, the pattern of comprehensive education. This dramatically altered the relationship between parents and the State. The government rescinded circular 10/65 and replaced it with circular 10/70 which set out the new procedures for the approval of plans for the reorganisation of secondary education. The basic change was that plans would not be considered LEA by LEA but school by school . . . This Tory change of procedure therefore allowed parents to compete with each other over the system of local schooling. (David, 1980, p. 188)

The Education Act 1980 reinforced this process by consolidating the importance of section 12 as against development plan procedures, and thus the importance of individual schools above the system of schools. The influence of the state and parents have been reinforced against the LEA. The new purposes and power relations were enacted in Manchester, where the secretary of state, grounding his argument in the claims of parental pressure groups, decided that the LEA must retain sixth forms in three (neo-grammar) 11–18 schools in the more middle-class sector of the city, leaving the authority to introduce its 'comprehensive' tertiary system for the remaining areas.

CONCLUSION

The centre is reordering the balance of influence and power in the 'partnership' between central and local government to facilitate its policy of rationalizing institutional provision. The intention is to differentiate schools (and colleges) to allow parents to express their consumer preferences. Underlying this policy, however, are deeper commitments (to which the previous administration were also committed) of rationalizing curricular experiences and educational opportunities. The policies are directed to stratifying young people by rationalizing provision.

It has been well understood by DES and Treasury policy planners since the late 1970s that the question of rationalization really presupposed qualitative decisions about educational provision. The resource question is in essence an opportunity question about the educational offering with which young people should be provided. The means of limiting opportunities is being determined through more sharply differentiated institutional and curricular experiences. The strategy is, first, to identify separate 'client groups' who are claimed to possess significant differences in ability, attainment, aptitude and maturity. Such different groups are then defined as possessing alternative 'needs' which clearly require different provision. The age group, it is increasingly argued by the state, should be classified and differentiated at 16. The stratifying language of tripartite education – parity of esteem between modern, technical and grammar sectors – having been almost eliminated from the secondary sector is reappearing in the tertiary (16–19) sector (cf. Ranson, 1984, 1985).

The institutional and curricular changes are being designed by the state, as one chief education officer has notably argued, to 'facilitate social control as much as encourage manpower planning'. The simple economic argument, therefore, that education is producing differentiated skills for a stratified labour market is incomplete. It must be complemented and rounded out with a more developed argument about the social and political order. Both Labour and Conservative governments seemed concerned as much about the social consequences of an over-supply of highly educated young people in a period of contracting job opportunities as they were about ostensible shortages of certain industrial skills. Writers such as Boudon (1974) and Hirsch (1977) have noted the tendency of oversupply in education to produce not only queuing, but also frustration, disappointment and disillusionment. The consequences have not been lost on the state's policy-makers:

(1)   by making continued full-time education the norm, we may be encouraging unrealistic career aspirations among young people (Labour minister, reported in *Education*, 18 March 1977).
(2)   to offer young people advanced education but not thereafter the work opportunities to match their career aspirations is to offer them a false prospectus (DES senior official).[12]
(3)   there has to be selection because we are beginning to create aspirations which increasingly society cannot match. In some ways this points to the success of education in contrast to the public mythology which has been created. When young people drop off the education production line and cannot find work at all, or work which meets their abilities or expectations, then we are only creating frustration with perhaps disturbing social consequences. We have to select: to ration the educational opportunities to meet the job opportunities, so that society can cope with the output of education (ESGE 16–19 subgroup representative).[13]
(4)   we are in a period of considerable social change. There may be social unrest, but we can cope with the Toxteths. But if we have a highly educated and idle population, we may possibly anticipate more serious social conflict. People must be educated once more to know their place (DES official).[14]

The motivating concern here is about the nature of the polity as much as the economy. The impending structural changes to the economy are raising issues about the distribution of work and thus of wealth and power in society. Citizenship has probably closer ties with involvement in the productive economy rather than the formal political franchise. How education is structured will result in different responses to these critical social issues and thus the nature of the political order. The lineages of the current restructuring of education, however, seem unmistakably clear. The state is developing modes of control in education which permit closer scrutiny and direction of the social order.

NOTES: CHAPTER 11

1 Interview; the undated interview material in this chapter draws on research undertaken as part of the SSRC centre–local policy planning project.
2 Interview.
3 Interview.
4 Interview.
5 Interview.
6 Interview.
7 Interview.
8 Interview.
9 Interview.
10 Interview.
11 Interview.
12 Interview.
13 Interview.
14 Interview.

REFERENCES: CHAPTER 11

Benn, C. (1980), 'A new 11-plus for the old divided system', *Forum*, vol. 22, no. 2, pp. 36–40.
Boudon, R. (1974), *Education, Opportunity and Social Inequality* (London and New York: Wiley).
Briault, E. (1976), 'A distributed system of educational administration; an international viewpoint', *International Review of Education*, vol. 22, no. 4, pp. 429–39.
David, M. E. (1977), *Reform, Reaction and Resources: The 3Rs of Educational Planning* (London: National Foundation for Educational Research).
David, M. E. (1980), *The State, Family and Education* (London: National Foundation for Educational Research).
Department of Education and Science (DES) (1971), *16–18: A Consultative Paper* (London: DES), February.
DES (1981), *Falling Rolls and Surplus Places*, Circular 2/81 (London: DES), 16 June.
Fowler, G., Morris, V., and Ozga, J. (eds) (1973), *Decision-Making in British Education* (London: Heinemann).
Glatter, R. (1979), *An Introduction to the Control of Education in Britain* (Milton Keynes: The Open University).
Griffiths, J. A. G. (1966), *Central Departments and Local Authorities* (London: Allen & Unwin).
Halsey, A. H., Heath, A. F., and Ridge, J. M. (1980), *Origins and Destinations* (Oxford: Oxford University Press).
Hirsch, F. (1977), *Social Limits to Growth* (London: Routledge & Kegan Paul).
Her Majesty's Inspectorate (HMI) (1979), *Aspects of Secondary Education in England* (London: HMSO).
James, P. H. (1980), *The Reorganisation of Secondary Education* (London: National Foundation for Educational Research).
Jones, G. W. (1979), 'Central–local relations, finance and the law', *Urban Law and Policy*, vol. 2, no. 1, pp. 25–46.
Kogan, M. (1975), *Educational Policy Making* (London: Allen & Unwin).

Lukes, S. (1974), *Power: A Radical View* (London: Macmillan).

Macfarlane Report (1980), *Education for 16–19 Year Olds* (London: DES).

OECD (1975), *Educational Development Strategy in England and Wales* (Paris: OECD).

Offe, C. (1974), 'Structural problems of the capitalist state', in K. von Beyme (ed.), *German Political Studies* (London: Sage), Vol. 1.

Pattison, M. (1979), 'Intergovernmental relations and the limitations of central control: reconstructing the politics of comprehensive education', *Oxford Review of Education*, vol. 6, no. 1, pp. 63–89.

Ranson, S. (1984), 'Towards a tertiary tripartism: new codes of social control and the 17+', in P. Broadfoot (ed.), *Selection, Certification and Control* (London: Falmer Press), pp. 221–44.

Ranson, S. (1985), 'Contradictions in the government of educational change', *Political Studies*, vol. 33, no. 1 (March).

Regan, D. (1977), *Local Government and Education* (London: Allen & Unwin).

Saran, R. (1973), *Policy-Making in Secondary Education* (Oxford: Clarendon Press).

Weaver, T. (1976), *Policy-Making in the DES: Tenth Report from the Expenditure Committee 1975–76* (London: HMSO), p. 379.

12

Social Services

ADRIAN WEBB AND GERALD WISTOW

INTRODUCTION

The complexity and interactive nature of central–local relations in the personal social services (PSS) is exacerbated by the very nature of these services: by the close and intentional interlocking of policies for the PSS with those in the National Health Service (NHS); by the importance of voluntary provision and of informal care within the family; and by the rapid growth of private provision. While the relationship between central government and local government remains vital, it is only one element of the much wider issue of the impact of central government on local communities and on the services available to them (Abrams, 1977; Webb and Wistow, 1982b).

A practical implication for central government of these characteristics of central–local relations is that changes in direction at the local level are not simple to achieve. There are levers to pull, but their individual – and especially their combined – effects in localities are difficult to predict or guarantee. Nevertheless, central government has opportunities for effecting specific and intended changes in local policies and practices, provided the overall effects of different elements of central–local relations are systematically taken into account. The extent of central influence on the way in which services develop depends heavily upon the successful co-ordination of different policy strands and of the communications flowing through the various channels which collectively constitute central–local relations. In the past attempts have been made to achieve this co-ordination through elaborate forward planning. There is now a different approach, that of centrally structured financial incentives. It is a potentially powerful, albeit selective, means by which central government can exercise influence in the face of complexity and uncertainty. Nevertheless, it may be doubted whether there is sufficient understanding within central government of its impact on local policy-making and implementation to ensure that such selective approaches are used successfully.

THE NATURE OF THE PSS

The statutory core of the PSS in England and Wales consists of 116 local authority Social Services Departments (SSDs). Central government oversight rests in the Department of Health and Social Security (DHSS) and the Welsh Office. Arrangements in Scotland and Northern Ireland are significantly different and cannot be covered in this chapter.

Non-statutory provision has long been a substantial and integral part of the whole (Wolfenden Committee, 1977). It comprises three primary elements: informal care; voluntary and volunteer services; and provision by private entrepreneurs. In particular, informal care – by the family, friends and neighbours, for dependent people such as the frail elderly, the mentally handicapped, the physically handicapped and chronically sick – accounts for a very substantial proportion of all care. While statutory policy is heavily dependent on the level and dependability of informal care, many social forces are potentially hostile to it (for example, high female participation rates in paid employment, demographic change and changing patterns of family life). Governments can hope to exercise some impact through the manipulation of the cash benefits system, but beyond that they can only hope to influence the values and norms which govern family life and neighbourliness. In addition to informal care, voluntary organizations and volunteer workers provide many services. There is also much private provision especially of a residential kind. Any coherent central government policy towards the PSS must take these providers into account, but opportunities for direct influence are again comparatively limited. Powers to inspect, approve and advise local non-statutory services – as well as to fund them from public moneys – rest primarily with local authorities and district health authorities, not with central government.

This 'mixed economy of welfare' underlines the importance of relationships not merely between central government and local government, but also between government and all those providers of care – organizations and individuals alike – to be found in any particular locality.

The other critical feature of the PSS is that they are closely aligned with the NHS (Pinker, 1978; Webb and Wistow, 1982b; Wistow, 1982). Policy in the DHSS has for a long time linked developments in these two fields not merely because they constitute a programme area for expenditure purposes, but also because much of the health service is directly influenced by the adequacy and method of operation of the PSS. For example, the capacity of local authority services and of care within the community largely determines whether hospital beds will become 'silted up' by old people who cannot be rehabilitated, and this is true of all hospital wards in which old people feature in significant numbers – not merely geriatric wards. The need to link NHS and PSS policy is, therefore, inescapable (though it too readily over-shadows crucial relationships with other services such as housing). The crucial fact for central–local relations is that while the PSS exist within the system of political decentralization (local government), the NHS is an example of field decentralization (central government). Consequently, local–local relations between the NHS and local authorities assume great importance, not least because of this direct accountability of the NHS, in principle, to the DHSS.

CENTRAL GOVERNMENT AND THE PSS

Central government has three primary interests in the PSS: the overall responsibility for PSS 'policy' and for standards exercised through the Secretary of State for Social Services; the co-ordination of NHS and PSS policy; and the control of overall levels of local government expenditure – of which PSS expenditure is a significant, and has been a rapidly growing, element (Ferlie and Judge, 1983). While the first and second are essentially matters for DHSS and, in part, the Treasury, the Treasury and the Department of the Environment are central to the third.

The DHSS involvement in PSS 'policy' is largely expressed through four channels of articulation. The first, the Social Work Service, is best described as a professional inspectorate though its formal inspectoral role has not been emphasized until recently (Utting, 1979; Barclay, 1982). Its central task has been to relay and interpret policy and practice standards and to provide advice locally, while collating and forwarding information and ideas of value to the central policy-making role. The Service is, in principle, well suited to a broad involvement in policy formation and implementation; it 'faces both ways' through regionally based teams which work to the headquarters team in DHSS. The regional teams are in direct contact with the SSDs (and other providing agencies) within their territories. The professional contribution to policy debate in DHSS can, therefore, be grounded in local experience and be sensitive to local issues.

The second channel is the Service Development Group in the DHSS which includes the key client group teams (for example, for children, the elderly, and so on). These teams are multi-professional, bringing together the social work and medical professions though they pivot upon generalist civil servants. Their role is to construct client group policy for both the health and personal social services. The contributions of the client group teams are expressed through legislation, through policy documents and through their role as a point of interaction for professional, academic and political opinions of policy issues. In addition, there are three 'strategy groups' designed to take a policy overview and to monitor the relationship between the 'two sides' of the DHSS: health and personal social services, and income maintenance.

There was until recent years a Local Authority Social Services (LASS) Division which provided a further channel for such communication. Its *raison d'être* was that while DHSS policy for the NHS could be directly transmitted through the managerial structure, the independence of local authorities required something different – a focal point for administrative and broad policy issues. When detailed forward planning was in fashion, the LASS division had a major role to play in central–local relations. With reduced emphasis on planning and reductions in civil service staff, however, LASS functions have been absorbed into the Community Services Division. Issues of finance, focused through the Finance Divisions, constitute a fourth stream of articulation.

This multiplicity of channels, combined with the heterogeneity of local agencies and service providers, results in the conditional and unpredictable nature of central influence. Policy formation is the outcome of diverse forces, but so also is policy implementation. Many of these forces, in both cases, flow through the maze of central–local relations. One strategy open to central government is to attempt to co-ordinate action in as many of these arenas and channels as possible. This would be the rational response of a government wishing to adopt what has elsewhere been called the 'direct' approach to policy implementation (Webb and Wistow, 1980). However, there is always the possibility of adopting a more 'indirect' approach involving greater reliance on the climate of opinion to facilitate movement in the desired direction. This process of modifying assumptive worlds would give greater prominence to the political and professional networks and correspondingly less to administrative networks.

POLICY IN THE PERSONAL SOCIAL SERVICES

The fractionalized nature of central–local relations underlines the problems of achieving co-ordinated action. It is also necessary to think of potentially autonomous, disparate and mutually contradictory *streams of policy*. The problem of achieving a desired impact through central–local relations, from the government viewpoint, is then more clearly seen as one of ensuring that the combined effect of these different streams influences local actors to act in appropriate ways.

The most obvious sense in which streams of quasi-autonomous policies are institutionalized is in functional specializations, which are often reinforced by organizational and professional boundaries. Co-ordination of policies across these functional divisions is the holy grail of administration: it persistently eludes both routine pursuit and more heroic, but periodic, crusades such as the Joint Approach to Social Policy (CPRS, 1975). But functional divisions are not the only, or necessarily the most crucial, examples of institutionalized policy streams. While it can crucially affect outcomes, it is no longer unusual to note that service policies – those which constitute the common-sense meaning of 'policy' in the social services – often exist alongside quite contradictory policies about resource use and allocation. It is only infrequently, however, that governance policies – such as the recent emphasis on minimal central guidance and direction – can be seen to be a potentially lively and disruptive influence in relation to other policy objectives (Webb and Wistow, 1982b). Governments can have valued but essentially autonomous and deeply conflictual policies within each of these three streams; if policies are mutually reinforcing, it is likely to be the product of a pragmatic and hard-won move towards a reasonably coherent strategy. One of the most interesting issues is precisely that of whether, and if so how, central–local relations are structured to achieve this end.

The PSS yield an excellent example of how central government attempts to structure central–local relations to a particular long-term end can change over time. The end is that of co-ordinating policy towards high-dependency groups (the elderly, mentally ill and mentally handicapped) across the NHS and PSS. The task has been to achieve this co-ordination of policies in related fields by, in turn, co-ordinating service and resource policies. For several decades the slowly advanced solution was to establish and improve a system of long-term planning. It seemed to be well suited to the co-ordinative task. However, it began to be undermined in the mid-1970s, though not decisively, by unanticipated constraints on public expenditure. Since 1979 it has been further undermined by an ideological shift which, in governance terms, requires a move away from a large and active role for the state in both service provision and in centralized planning. Two sets of adjustments have, therefore, had to be made over recent years: adjustments to increasing disequilibrium in the balance between service and resource policies; and fundamental changes in the way that central government perceives and attempts to fulfil its role. The remainder of this chapter will be devoted to a case study of these changes and responses.

LOCAL–LOCAL RELATIONSHIPS IN THE 1970s: CENTRAL–LOCAL ARTICULATION THROUGH THE NHS

Central government objectives for the NHS cannot be met without local authority co-operation and most particularly that of the SSDs. The broad thrust of these objectives has been to secure the development of alternatives to hospital provision, especially for the elderly, mentally ill and mentally handicapped. By adjusting the balance of care in this direction, the DHSS seeks both to create a pattern of services more appropriate to individual need and to achieve a more cost-effective utilization of resources within the NHS and across the health and PSS system as a whole (DHSS, 1976a, 1977a, 1981a).

Two aspects of the interlocking nature of health and the PSS are especially relevant. First, the DHSS cannot afford to adopt a neutral stance towards the actions of local authorities (Social Services Committee, 1980). Their decisions about levels of spending and the structure of services within the PSS have important implications for the NHS. The present government, for example, intervened in Solihull, when the council proposed to withdraw all hospital social work services and cut other fieldwork services (Jenkin, 1981). Secondly, the objective of shifting the balance of care away from hospital provision implies not only an increase in overall levels of spending within the PSS, but also the structuring of service developments in ways which complement and support the DHSS objectives for the NHS. The implementation of central government policy is dependent, therefore, on the extent to which local authorities are able and willing to meet DHSS and health authority priorities for the expansion and development of their personal social services. Yet the implementation of these (NHS-determined) objectives are not the only demand made upon PSS resources, even by central government. Other demands include the prevention and 'treatment' of delinquency, the provision of support to families under stress and the growth of need in the community among DHSS priority groups. In recent years all these demands have had to be met against a background of reductions in expenditure growth imposed by central government (Webb and Wistow, 1983) and substantial shortfalls in existing service stocks (ADSS, 1981). Moreover, SSDs have themselves sought to secure a shift in their own balance of care, away from residential services. This readjustment has been dictated by considerations of cost effectiveness and by professional concern about the institutionalization of residents. As a result, while the DHSS has advocated the expansion of substitutes – often residential – for hospital care, many SSDs have been attempting to develop domiciliary and day services as alternatives to their own traditional patterns of residential care.

The task for central government has been to achieve a co-ordinated shift in the pattern of health and PSS outputs in this context of conflicting pressures and competing priorities. Local authority autonomy largely precludes a top-down authoritative route to such co-ordination. Consequently, the key issue for the DHSS has been how to shape local–local relations to secure the desired shift in the balance of care across the system as a whole. In practice the implementation strategy adopted has been to seek to recreate locally, through the medium of collaboration between the NHS and local authorities, the system-wide perspective adopted at the centre. Until the late 1970s the strategy relied upon four principal elements, as follows.

Centrally Co-ordinated Planning
Systematic attempts at co-ordinating forward planning across the health and personal social services, begun in the early 1960s, were strengthened in the early 1970s. These planning developments gave shape and promise to the long-standing but ill-developed policy of community care (Titmuss, 1968; Walker, 1982). However, the public expenditure squeeze of the mid-1970s precipitated the need to establish clear priorities. Expenditure growth, now very limited, was forecast and 'allocated' in national aggregate terms between competing uses across the health and

social services (DHSS, 1976a, 1977a). These priority exercises, though subject to criticism (PSSC, 1977), were highly influential. They acknowledged the necessity of a minimum 2 per cent rate of growth in the PSS, in order to meet increasing need (arising especially from demographic trends) and to distribute this limited growth differentially between client groups. At the very least, local authorities were given a framework against which to devise their own strategies, and the framework reminded them of the need for interaction with the NHS.

Although long-term planning in the PSS did not survive the resource shock of the mid-1970s, the belief in forward planning did survive. However, simply to co-ordinate a system of 'parallel planning' between the NHS and PSS was not enough; the DHSS needed to create an environment which was strongly conducive to local collaborative planning.

Enabling Structures and a Legal Mandate
An important theme in the simultaneous reorganization in 1974 of local government and the NHS was the need to base both systems upon common boundaries, in order to facilitate inter-authority co-operation. The NHS Reorganization Act 1973 also laid upon both types of authority a duty to collaborate with each other. The emphasis was upon collaboration for 'shared populations' through the mechanism of Joint Consultative Committees (JCCs). In retrospect 1974 may be seen as the high-water mark of the approach which sought to achieve co-ordination both 'horizontally' and 'vertically' through structural reorganization. There was, though, growing appreciation that the reordering of structures did not eliminate problems of co-ordination; the emphasis on structure came to be increasingly accompanied by a concern for process.

Joint Planning
By 1976 'joint planning' – between health and local authorities – had become the principal catchword in the DHSS litany. The NHS planning system was designed as the mechanism through which national priorities and guidelines would be passed down through the new administrative structure and plans for their implementation passed up for approval. But the initial statement of objectives highlighted the inability of the NHS alone to achieve them and thus underlined the need for joint as well as NHS planning (DHSS, 1972b). Consequently, the publication of an NHS planning manual (DHSS, 1976b) was accompanied by a consultative circular setting out a framework for joint planning

(DHSS, 1976c). A definitive circular followed (DHSS, 1977b).
Three features of the joint planning initiative are significant.

First, it emphasized the role of joint planning as an instrument
for securing the priorities and objectives of the centre: 'effective
joint planning is vital to the Government's overall strategy of
developing community-based services to the fullest extent
practicable so that people are kept out of hospitals and other
institutions and supported within the community' (DHSS, 1976c).

Secondly, the mechanisms were clearly designed to establish
joint planning as an integral part of the NHS planning system. The
DHSS appeared to be locking the PSS into planning processes
devised for the centrally administered NHS. The *raison d'être* of
such planning was to bring decentralized resource allocation
processes into alignment with department objectives. The PSS
objectives – even community care – were not necessarily
congruent with those of DHSS for the NHS. Yet the approach
advanced by the department in the circulars appeared to imply
either the pre-existence of local consensus around national
objectives or that local compliance with central government
strategy could be secured. However, from a different viewpoint,
this approach threatened the autonomy of local authorities in
general, and the SSDs in particular, and could all too easily be
characterized as the offloading of centrally funded responsibilities
on to local ratepayers. In addition, it failed sufficiently to take into
account the corporate dimension of local authority planning, a
point emphasized by local authorities in their response to the 1976
priorities document (DHSS, 1977a).

An imperfect appreciation by the centre of the nature of the
local policy environment was also evident in the third feature: the
planning circulars and the planning process which they
prescribed. Joint planning was to be based on a model of
comprehensive rationality. Authorities were enjoined to integrate
their activities throughout the planning process, which was
described as one in which 'each authority contributes to all stages
of the other's planning from the first step in developing common
policies and strategies to the production of operational plans to
carry them out' (DHSS, 1976c).

What was missing was evidence of any systematic understanding
of the conditions which would have to be fulfilled if local actors
were to give effect to this vision. Those conditions may be briefly
stated as the existence of a systems-wide perception of needs and
service interdependencies; a developed analytical capacity;
consensus on the nature of need and on the best ways of meeting it;
and the presence of organizational and professional altruism – a

willingness to surrender resources and authority in order to achieve a systems-wide objective (Webb, 1982). These are highly demanding and atypical conditions (Lindblom, 1965; Benson, 1975; Schmidt and Kochan, 1977). Empirical research suggests that the experience of joint planning fell far short of DHSS prescriptions (Barnard *et al.*, 1979; Booth, 1981; Norton and Rogers, 1981; Glennester, 1983). The questions to be answered, therefore, are:

(1)   whether any progress in inter-corporate rationality has been made at all;
(2)   what lessons the centre may learn from the joint planning initiative.

A national survey conducted in 1982 found a considerable increase in planning machinery, especially for DHSS priority groups (Wistow and Fuller, 1983); the centre had been successful in securing a basic framework for joint planning and an increase in the extent of interaction between the NHS and PSS. The effectiveness of such interaction is a more difficult issue. There has, however, been a growth of inter-authority learning and of systems-wide thinking, and even occasionally of organizational altruism (Webb, 1982). Significantly the greatest progress seems to have been made when planning time and capacities were concentrated on selected client groups rather than spread across the whole field of NHS and PSS interaction.

Conflicts about objectives and about needs and priorities as well as sectional interests did, however, constrain the intensive and productive interaction which the DHSS prescriptions for joint planning assumed. Effectiveness in joint planning is more likely to be promoted if the centre operates not on the assumption that rationality is its own reward, but on the principle that incentives are necessary to generate and sustain inter-authority planning. The DHSS built a financial incentive – joint finance – into the joint planning framework in 1976.

Joint Finance
Joint finance is a relatively small allocation of NHS funds earmarked for expenditure by the SSDs and the voluntary sector for purposes approved by health authorities. It was explicitly designed to provide an incentive for health and local authorities to develop and operate the joint planning machinery (Castle, 1975). However, funds were available for only a limited period (initially five and subsequently seven years) and could be used to support

the full cost of PSS projects for a maximum of three years, after which NHS contributions began to taper off. Joint finance only primed the pump. The schemes represented a future claim on SSD budgets, which was of significance because PSS growth rates fell from almost 20 per cent in 1973–4 to under 3 per cent in 1976–7, the year in which joint finance was introduced (Webb and Wistow, 1982a).

The continuing restriction of PSS growth had two consequences. First, joint finance increasingly appeared to be a mechanism by which the centre – through the NHS – might determine the limited development programmes available to SSDs. Secondly, the relative scarcity of other sources of funds constituted a powerful incentive for SSDs to seek to utilize joint finance to serve their own, rather than NHS or systems-wide, policies and priorities. To succeed in this objective, however, SSDs would have to exercise a critical influence over the distribution of joint finance. In the early years the SSDs secured this with little resistance from health authorities, primarily because unspent joint finance funds had to be carried forward to the next financial year. Since health authorities were permitted to carry forward only 1 per cent of their revenue allocation, under-spendings on the joint finance programme could result in their losing part of their main revenue allocation in the following year. Thus the operation of the carry-forward rule encouraged health authorities to accept whatever proposals SSDs brought forward for joint finance, rather than negotiate projects of maximum benefit to the NHS. The administrative costs of seeking to exercise a positive influence over the selection of joint finance projects were also high. Consequently, SSDs were able to make the running, and health authorities were left without the ability or inclination to do other than approve their proposals (Wistow, 1983). A potential Trojan horse had been turned to the advantage of SSDs and central control remained comparatively weak – at least in the early years of joint finance.

CENTRAL–LOCAL RELATIONS SINCE 1979

The philosophy of the present Conservative government had two immediate implications for the PSS. The first was that a shift was sought in the mixed economy of welfare towards an expanded role for non-statutory provision. The second, paradoxically, was that this potentially radical change was to be accompanied by a shift away from centralized planning and control. The new governance strategy made it difficult to implement the new policies for service development. In practice, the problem was real but the response was to retreat only selectively from the direct approach to policy implementation. On the resource side central control over local authorities has been vigorously enhanced. It is only in the service stream that direct implementation has withered on the vine. In the NHS the process of decentralizing control has resulted in further structural changes: the abolition of Area Health Authorities has significantly reduced the coterminosity with local authorities which was achieved in 1974.

This partial withdrawal from central co-ordination has generated two problems. As earlier service goals in the PSS have not been renounced but resource controls have become more stringent, the task of reconciling these two policy streams has been exacerbated (Webb and Wistow, 1982b). Similarly, the ideal of collaboration through joint planning has been reaffirmed, but the structural base for it has been attenuated. As Patrick Jenkin noted in his introduction to *Care in Action*,

> I want to see as close a collaboration between health authorities and local government as possible. Increased freedom from central government is a main theme of our policies towards both local government and the health service. It will be for you and your opposite workers in the health service to decide in the light of local circumstances how this collaboration is achieved. (DHSS, 1981b)

The dilemmas have been decentralized.

A NEW APPROACH TO FINANCIAL INCENTIVES

The interaction between health and personal social services is one area in which the decentralization of dilemma has been accompanied by a real attempt to continue to exert central influence over local policies. The importance of selective financial incentives and of financial arrangements more generally has been underlined. However, developments in this field do suggest that the central government approach lacks coherence and may fail because selective attempts to develop service provision are counteracted by the overall impact of central policies on local authorities, and on the PSS in particular.

The simple lesson for central government which emerged from the early years of the joint finance initiative was the need to build an appropriate balance of power, resources and incentives into such mechanisms. Both parties (NHS and SSDs) need an incentive to interact, and a sufficient degree of influence over the other's actions. The DHSS has recently amended the joint finance rules (DHSS, 1983b) with the intention of increasing NHS influence over the PSS. This amendment results, in part, from a refocusing of service policy objectives in which the transfer of long-stay patients from hospital to local authority care has become the first priority in the community care field. Joint finance is seen as having been successful in preventing admissions to hospital but not in securing patient transfers, due in large measure to the use of joint finance by SSDs to meet demand from their own communities rather than from the NHS. At the same time, however, the local authorities have been seeking improvements in the terms on which joint finance is available to them, arguing that continuing constraints on their budgets have made it increasingly difficult to sustain joint finance projects as NHS support tapers off. There is survey evidence to suggest that this is not merely a case of special pleading (Wistow and Head, 1981).

The DHSS response has been to combine these two pressures and to facilitate new developments. Joint finance is now available to support the full cost of schemes for ten years, and for a further three at tapering rates. However, this amendment applies only to expenditure which permits the direct transfer of patients from hospital to the community. The price the PSS must now pay for improved terms is the implementation of DHSS community care objectives rather than their own. In addition, constraints on a wider transfer of resources from the NHS to local authorities are being removed. The intention is to enable health authorities to achieve economies by closing wards and hospitals devoted to long-stay patients, so that the moneys saved can be channelled into local authority (and voluntary) support services. These resource transfers are intended to operate alongside, and to be fostered by, the new joint finance arrangements.

However, the earlier failure of the patient transfer route to community care arose, in part, from resistance to the closure of hospitals, and the commitment in the NHS to a medico-nursing model of care. The new arrangements do not appear to create any added incentive for health authorities to tackle these issues. A symmetrical pattern of incentives remains to be established (Wistow, 1981). It is, therefore, more appropriate to see the new arrangements as an enabling measure which suffers from the same deficiency as the original joint planning prescriptions: the DHSS approach continues to assume considerable consensus at the local level and implies that the role of the centre is merely to develop mechanisms which facilitate the implementation of locally agreed policy objectives, which would otherwise be unnecessarily impeded by administrative barriers and financial constraints. This presumption of consensus, in turn, rests upon an assumption that local authorities should attach priority to need arising from the health service and that this objective – as well as the meeting of community-based need – can be fulfilled within existing resources.

While joint finance has been – and remains – a flawed mechanism, its operation illustrates the value of a centrally created financial incentive in bringing together agencies which might otherwise have remained apart. The existence of joint finance makes it worth while for SSD managers to be involved in such planning machinery albeit at varying levels of commitment. The experience of working together has helped to foster the degree of mutual awareness, learning and confidence which were necessary preconditions for joint working on a broader front. Whether closer collaboration will result from the recent initiatives remains to be seen, but past experience suggests that central government has structured a new local environment in which conflicting objectives are exacerbated by resource pressures, and which therefore will only imperfectly stimulate the kinds of collaborative planning which is desired. A new approach to social planning – and central–local relations – has been developed, but with insufficient attention to the lessons to be learned from past approaches.

The Wider Context
It may, however, be argued that the government's policies amount to a coherent approach to central–local relations. Greater reliance upon non-statutory providers of service necessarily means that central control is limited and that an indirect approach to policy implementation is crucial. Local authorities have been placed in a position in which one way of resolving heavy demands on limited resources is precisely to look to an expansion of non-statutory provision. In addition, the pursuit of particular values surrounding the family, private enterprise and self-help have reinforced this indirect approach. In practice, however, the approach to central–local relations has been somewhat more complex and less coherent.

The first element of complexity concerns the non-statutory sector. Governments wishing to extend care within and by 'the family' have three basic options: they can reinforce the sense of obligation felt by family members, reduce services and thereby impose greater responsibilities on families, or enhance the capacity of families to care. The emphasis on 'traditional values' and on public expenditure restraint have been consistent with the first two, but the third exposes the contradictions in the strategy. The capacity of 'the family' to care and to cope tends to depend in reality on the availability of women as carers and on the balance struck between their resources of health, devotion and stamina and the demands made on them by their dependents.

A desire to increase the availability of female carers has certainly emerged in the form of negative attitudes towards women working outside the home, but economic and demographic forces are key and they are not so readily moulded by central government. The real opportunity for influence, therefore, lies in providing services which will support carers and prevent them being overwhelmed by the burden of caring. To do so, however, means extending statutory and voluntary, rather than private, services: growth in the private sector is concentrated in residential provision which is largely a *substitute* for care by the family. However, the first consequence of pressure on public expenditure is that SSDs concentrate resources on 'the most needy' – those without family support. Central policy, then, is producing contradictory trends in different elements of the local service system.

Both the private and voluntary alternatives to statutory provision are profoundly dependent on public policies and public money, and a further consequence of expenditure restraint is that local government is less able to afford to 'buy in' services (especially residential care) from the voluntary and private sectors, or directly to subsidize voluntary organizations. Whether or not as a direct response to this dilemma central government has increased the funds available to local voluntary organizations, and to private provision, in recent years. Additional money for voluntary organizations has flowed through such schemes as the Intermediate Treatment Initiative, Opportunities for Volunteering and various Manpower Services Commission programmes; money for private provision has flowed from the social security system and has enabled elderly and mentally handicapped people, in particular, to be supported in residential settings.

The additional amounts being channelled into the private sector are not known at present; the sum channelled through the voluntary sector is less than 1 per cent of total PSS expenditure (Westland, 1983). Nevertheless, these developments do mean that local authorities are being systematically by-passed and their ability to exercise a strategic influence over local services is probably declining. In some areas the provision of residential care for the elderly, for example, could now be left entirely to the private sector. The significance of these developments depends upon one's perspective. For a convinced adherent of state provision, or of strategic planning, they must represent a real and perhaps conclusive reversal of postwar trends in social policy. For the student of central–local relations, a different message emerges: central government's impact on local communities is exceedingly complex and it cannot be understood by concentrating solely upon its impact on local government.

REFERENCES: CHAPTER 12

Abrams, P. (1977), 'Community care: some research problems and priorities', *Policy and Politics*, vol. 6, no. 1, pp. 125–51.

Association of Directors of Social Services (ADSS) (1981), *Personal Social Services Expenditures, Staffing and Activities: Report of Survey* (Newcastle upon Tyne: ADSS).

Barclay, P. (1982), *Social Workers: Their Role and Tasks*, Report of a Working Party (London: Bedford Square Press).

Bains Report (1972), *The New Local Authorities: Management and Structure* (London: HMSO).

Barnard, K., Lee, K., Mills, A., and Reynolds, J. (1979), *Towards a New Rationality: A Study of Planning in the NHS* (Leeds: University of Leeds).

Benson, J. K. (1975), 'The interorganisational network as a political economy', *Administrative Science Quarterly*, vol. 20 (June), pp. 229–48.

Booth, T. (1981), 'Collaboration between the health and social services', *Policy and Politics*, vol. 9, no. 1, pp. 23–49, and vol. 9, no. 2, pp. 205–26.

Castle, B. (1975), 'Priorities in the social services', speech to Local Authority Associations' Social Services Conference, London, 28 November 1975.

Central Policy Review Staff (CPRS) (1975), *A Joint Approach to Social Policy* (London: HMSO).

Department of Health and Social Security (DHSS) (1972b), *Management Arrangements for the Reorganised National Health Service* (London: HMSO).

DHSS (1976a), *Priorities in the Health and Personal Social Services* (London: HMSO).

DHSS (1976b), *The NHS Planning System* (London: DHSS).

DHSS (1976c), *Joint Care Planning: Health and Local Authorities*, HC (76)18; LAC (76)6 (London: DHSS).

DHSS (1977a), *The Way Forward* (London: HMSO).

DHSS (1977b), *Joint Care Planning: Health and Local Authorities*, HC (77)17; LAC 9(77)10 (London: DHSS).

DHSS (1977c), *Forward Planning of Local Authority Social Services*, LASSL (77)13 (London: HMSO).

DHSS (1981a), *Care in the Community: A Consultative Document on Moving Resources for Care in England* (London: DHSS).

DHSS (1981b), *Care in Action* (London: DHSS).

DHSS (1983a), *The Social Work Service of DHSS: A Consultative Document* (London: DHSS), 14 April.

DHSS (1983b), *Health Service Development: Care in the Community and Joint Finance*, HC (83)6; LAC (83)5 (London: DHSS).

Ferlie, E., and Judge, K. (1983), 'Retrenchment and rationality in the personal social services', *Policy and Politics*, vol. 9, no. 3, pp. 311–30.

Glennester, H. (1983), *Planning for Priority Groups* (Oxford: Martin Robertson).

Jenkin, P. (1981), 'Interview', *Social Work Today*, vol. 12, no. 28, pp. 6–7.

Lindblom, C. E. (1965), *The Intelligence of Democracy* (Glencoe, Ill.: The Free Press).

Norton, A. L., and Rogers, S. (1981), 'The health service and local government services', in G. McLachlan (ed.), *Matters of Moment* (Oxford: Oxford University Press).

Personal Social Services Council (PSSC) (1977), 'Comments by the officers of the Personal Social Services Council: *The Way Forward*', London, PSSC; mimeo.

Pinker, R. (1978), *Research Priorities in the Personal Social Services* (London: Social Science Research Council).

Schmidt, S., and Kochan, T. (1977), 'Inter-organisational relationships: patterns and motivations', *Administrative Science Quarterly*, vol. 22 (June), pp. 220–33.

Sharpe, L. J. (1977), 'Whitehall: structures and people', in D. Kavanagh and Richard Rose (eds.), *New Trends in British Politics: Issues for Research* (London: Sage).

Social Services Committee (1980), *The Government's White Papers on Public Expenditure: The Social Services*, HC 702–1 (London: HMSO).

Titmuss, R. M. (1968), 'Community care – fact or fiction', in R. M. Titmuss (ed.), *Commitment to Welfare* (London: Allen & Unwin).

Utting, W. (1979), *The Social Work Service of DHSS*, Document No. DSWS (79) No. 1 (London: Department of Health and Social Security), January.

Walker, A. (1982), 'The meaning and social division of community care', in A. Walker (ed.), *Community Care* (Oxford: Blackwell/Martin Robertson), pp. 13–39.

Webb, A. (1982), 'Collaboration in planning: a pre-requisite for community care', *Collaboration in Caring: Conference Proceedings* (Birmingham: British Association of Social Workers).

Webb, A., and Wistow, G. (1980), 'Implementation, central–local relations and the personal social services' in G. Jones (ed.), *New Approaches to the Study of Central–Local Government Relationships* (Farnborough: Gower), pp. 69–83.

Webb, A., and Wistow, G. (1982a), 'The personal social services: incrementalism, expediency or systematic social planning?', in A. Walker (ed.), *Public Expenditure and Social Priorities* (London: Heinemann), pp. 137–64.

Webb, A., and Wistow, G. (1982b), *Whither State Welfare?* (London: Royal Institute of Public Administration).

Webb, A., and Wistow, G. (1983), 'Public expenditure and policy implementation: the case of community care', *Public Administration*, vol. 61 (Spring), pp. 21–44.

Westland, P. (1983), 'No sense of direction', *Community Care*, 17 November, pp. 15–17.

Wistow, G. (1981), *Incentives for Financing Community Care*, Working Paper in Social Administration No. 9 (Loughborough: Loughborough University, Department of Social Sciences).

Wistow, G. (1982), 'Collaboration between health and local authorities: why is it necessary?', *Social Policy and Administration*, vol. 16, no. 1, pp. 44–62.

Wistow, G. (1983), 'Joint finance and care in the community: have the incentives worked?', *Public Money*, vol. 3, no. 2, pp. 33–7.

Wistow, G., and Fuller, S. (1983), *Joint Planning in Perspective: The NAHA Survey of Collaboration 1976–1982* (Birmingham: National Association of Health Authorities).

Wistow, G., and Head, S. (1981), 'Joint finance: pump priming programme', *Health and Social Services Journal*, 3 July, pp. 806–7.
Wolfenden Committee (1977), *The Future of Voluntary Organisations* (London: Croom Helm).

13

Health

BRYAN STOTEN

INTRODUCTION: CENTRE–LOCAL DILEMMAS IN THE NHS

For more than thirty years the politicians, civil servants and managers responsible for the National Health Service wrestled with the problem of linking national policy developments to the pattern of local service provision. Over that period a variety of strategies were employed to deal with the frustration most strikingly expressed by Richard Crossman when as secretary of state he said:

> You don't have in the Regional Hospital Boards a number of obedient civil servants carrying out the central orders . . . you have a number of powerful, semi-autonomous boards whose relation to me was much more like the relations of a Persian satrap to a weak Persian emperor. If the emperor tried to enforce his authority too far he lost his throne or at least lost his resources or something broke down. (Crossman, 1972, p. 10)

The ten-year hospital plans, the development of a departmental planning programming and budgeting system, and two structural reorganizations, together with a national health care planning system, variously modified and, more recently, introduced systems of monitoring and review, all represent an apparently unending quest for mechanisms to translate national policies into local practice. The irony of National Health Service policy-making is that possessing, unlike local government, clear lines of command and accountability from government department to operational management, the health service has remained obdurately idiosyncratic in its local practices.

One consequence, as we shall see, is that lacking the ability to direct major policy into operational practice, the central department has fallen back upon 'nit picking pedantry in matters of detail' (Klein, 1983, p. 79).

The cultures of local government and the National Health Service differ greatly in their experience of central direction of policy formulation. The tendency towards centralization so feared by local government arises out of the attempts by central government to constrain aggregate expenditure not from attempts to specify standards of service provision. The NHS, however, has always had its expenditure centrally controlled; the critical problem for the NHS has arisen out of the rationale for its centralized chain of command. The rationale is that health care is so important that inequity in its distribution would be politically intolerable; that technological and professional criteria are more important than local political priorities or consumer preferences and that the scale of resources deployed, especially in certain specialist services, require the strategic planning that only a central governmental body can provide.

However, DHSS direction goes further than strategic planning. Guidance 'goes down to quite detailed guidance on individual buildings and types of buildings and the operational policies one would expect to carry out in those buildings and also broad guidance on design'.[1] The centralist culture of the NHS–DHSS relationship is founded, argues Mackenzie (1979, p. 165), upon the existence of a narrow pyramid of accountability: 'It keeps the span of control at higher levels rather narrow; in so doing it makes possible rather close control of subordinates, and indeed intermediate officials may find themselves short of work if they do not keep themselves busy with such control.' The very existence of a chain of command leads on the one hand to overambitious attempts by the centre to influence the detail of operational practice, and on the other to the existence of so many filters between the promulgation of guidance and its implementation that central guidance is endlessly translated into regional and local 'dialects' of priorities. The effect is both to water down central direction through a system of 'Chinese whispers' while discouraging initiatives at the operational level of the service.

Brown *et al.* (1974) have pointed to the stultifying effect on local initiatives of the unceasing promulgation of DHSS circulars. Yet the financial allocation outcomes, year-on-year, indicate the failure of DHSS to secure their macro-policy objectives of shifting resources towards the elderly, the mentally handicapped and the mentally ill.

A comparison of DHSS and DES communications with local health authorities and local education authorities respectively provides a startling comparison. As the Central Policy Review Staff (1977) point out, central government circulars form 'the main instrument of formal communication with local authorities'. In 1975 the Department of the Environment issued 127 circulars to local authorities, while the Department of Education issued thirteen. The DHSS issued 321 circulars to health authorities in the same year. The impact of this deluge of advice, exhortation and general guidance diminished the capacity of health authorities to take independent initiatives.

Thus while NHS reorganization was intended to encourage, through health care planning teams and joint consultative committees, 'local patterns of practice and decision making to emerge', yet, said the Royal Commission, we find too strong a *sense of inevitability* about the system.[2] Clinical imperatives outweigh national policy priorities but local policy initiatives, squeezed between these upper and nether millstones, rarely emerged let alone influenced the pattern of service provision.

One consequence of the hierarchical chain of command in the NHS has been to encourage dependency and an associated degree of irresponsibility.[3] Brown *et al.* (1974) found in their study of reorganization in Humberside that the service was 'conditioned to think of planning in terms of persuading higher authorities to approve proposals for expansion and therefore to use these authorities as a scapegoat for local inadequacies'. The Royal Commission concluded:

> It seems to us that the fact that the Secretary of State and his chief official are answerable for the NHS in detail distorts the relationship between the NHS and health authorities. It encourages central involvement in matters that would be better left to the authorities. In consequence no clear line is drawn where the Department's involvement ends. (Royal Commission on the NHS, 1978, section 19–23)

But the centre cannot control the execution of policy or the spirit of its application or the processes of admission or discharge; it is, therefore, forced back upon the details of resource provision rather than allocation. In such a way the unity of considerations of efficiency *and* effectiveness is broken and the former overly emphasized, while any grip on the latter is abdicated in favour of the 'executants of policy'.[4]

Thus when fresh DHSS interventions in the management of the NHS occur, they concentrate upon strengthening central control of resources rather than influencing the pattern of health priorities. The DHSS does issue such priority statements, as with the PHPSS, but such statements are necessarily exhortatory; the levers of power available to the DHSS are limited to general resource allocations (now including manpower) rather than specific policy initiatives. As Mackenzie (1979) has it: 'in this area ... the Department's rights are merely those of modern constitutional monarchy.... "to be consulted, to encourage, to warn".'

The development of a national planning system for the NHS was an important outcome of the 1974 reorganization. The system was asked to achieve more than the development of planning, it was to be 'the principal means of achieving accountability between the statutory authorities'.[5] In this attempt the introduction of the NHS planning system marked a new stage in central–local relations in the NHS.

PRE-1974: THE POLICY VACUUM

For twenty-five years after the formation of the NHS policy priorities were set – if they were set at all – at the point of service delivery. As the White Paper on National Health Service Reorganization (1972, p. 6) pointed out: 'There has been no identified authority whose task it has been ... to balance needs and priorities rationally and to plan and provide the right combination of services for the benefit of the public.' The regional hospital boards (RHBs) with block grants from central government were concerned primarily with capital development programmes and particularly with developments in the acute sector. The lack of central direction became particularly evident in the publication of the ten-year hospital plans.[6] Neither central direction nor local circumstances appeared to influence the submissions of regional hospital boards at this time. The assumptions – and even the population projections – of the hospital plan showed no sign of consultation with local authorities preparing the supposedly complementary health and welfare plan.[7]

The RHBs received little direction other than norms of provision (beds per 1,000 population, and so on) from the centre but lacked any formal channels of communication with the local communities they served. Impervious to local political priorities, the NHS reflected the priorities of those who worked in it rather than those to whom it delivered services, or those who represented them.

RESOLVING THE DILEMMA: THE 1974
REORGANIZATION AND THE NHS PLANNING SYSTEM

The 1974 reorganization of the NHS not merely restructured the relationship between primary care, hospital care and community services, it also reshaped the relationship between the DHSS and the local health authorities. It was intended to create a clearer and more effective system of decision-making, delegating authority down the tiers of the service, while matching such delegation with accountability for the achievement of planning goals upward through area and region to the DHSS.[8] However, the tools necessary for such a system were lacking. Without a cadre of health planners or a comprehensive range of output measures or national policy guidelines, the NHS was forced to be more modest in its approach to planning. The early form of the 'NHS planning system', therefore, concentrated upon securing from field authorities clear statements of programme objectives. Strategic statements embodying objectives and priorities were to come later when greater sophistication and expertise might develop. The system was intended to be one from which central government could learn and develop responses to the priorities of those providing services. In consequence, the attention of health planners was initially devoted to the work of the multi-disciplinary Health Care Planning Teams organized on the basis of client groups. Not until 1976 was central government able to contribute its input to this system with the publication of a comprehensive statement of central government priorities: the priorities for health and personal social services (PHPSS).

The impact of PHPSS on individual authorities is illuminating. The general direction of national policy and resource allocation priorities was plainly difficult to apply to specific authorities. None the less, many authorities attempted to apply national programme area targets to their local tier. The confusion caused with many authorities was an indication of the failure of the DHSS to communicate to local health authorities the role of strategic planning. Indeed, not until 1976 was any statement regarding the department's view of the role of strategic planning forthcoming.[9]

The lesson to be drawn from the PHPSS exercise is that while the service had developed a capacity for both national strategic thinking and local programming, the centre still lacked the ability to disaggregate national strategic thinking in ways relevant to particular health authorities.

The frustration created by this impasse lay behind the regional chairmen's inquiry into the workings of the DHSS in relation to the RHA, arguing that 'The NHS must be prepared to stand on its own feet and make a major contribution in policy formulation'.[10] In an attempt to remedy the problem the department issued in the following year *The Way Forward*. This document reflected a change in style. Ham (1982) interprets the new guidelines in terms of a shift:

> away from relatively specific quantitative targets towards broad, qualitative indications of central government's priorities. This move has been associated with a greater emphasis being placed on the local interpretation of national guidelines.

PATIENTS FIRST AND THE 1982 REORGANIZATION

By 1981 with a further reorganization underway the formal planning system had been effectively discarded as a vehicle for central–local strategic planning: 'Overall there is little evidence that the DHSS has used the Planning System as an instrument of central control.'[11] Indeed, in 1981 the Comptroller and Auditor-General argued that the balance 'between the necessary central direction and oversight of the NHS and a system of delegation and discretion appropriate to a locally based and managed service may be moving too far against central control'.[12] The response of the department referred back to its experience with the earlier promulgation of national policy guidelines – which, it argued, could only be indicative because of the wide variety of local factors.

The management ethos of the service had changed from the days of the 'Grey Book' of McKinsey and Brunel's managerial logic. While *Management Arrangements in the Re-organised National Health Service* (DHSS, 1972) laid emphasis upon role definition, monitoring relationships, delegation matched by accountability and ten-year corporate plans, *Patients First* (DHSS, 1979) rejected 'overcomplicated and bureaucratic' planning arrangements. The removal of the area tier and the emphasis upon the hospital as the focus of management and decision-making authority harked back to the pre-1974 pattern of hospital management committees. Such 'decentralization' did not imply less central government involvement in issues affecting the service – despite the language of 'squaring the circle of delegation and accountability' – that had never successfully been achieved. It did, however, mean that such involvement would be more *ad hoc* than pre-1974 and rely on negotiation rather than formula and, through a system of regional and district reviews, formalize the piecemeal, incremental decision-making that had previously been overlaid with the routines, timescales and deadlines of a formal planning system. Planning was to remain as part of an authority's management tool box but it no longer carried the burden of the complex inter-tier management relationships required by the 'Grey Book'.

The hierarchical chain of control had been shortened. In the process directions based upon norms were replaced by negotiations between those responsible for macro-resource allocation and those involved in service delivery. That is not to say central control and intervention was reduced, but merely that its capacity for sensitivity was increased.

THE MACHINERY OF CENTRAL–LOCAL NEGOTIATION: CENTRALIZING TENDENCIES

The chain of accountability is clear in the NHS. Regional and district health authorities are corporate bodies,[13] accountable to the secretary of state and the regional authority respectively. None the less, the introduction in 1983 of a formal review procedure to examine the plans of authorities and their achievement has introduced ambiguity into this apparently defined attribution of responsibilities. The system of reviews primarily involves ministers and individual regional chairmen, with their officers, or regional chairmen and individual district chairmen, again with their officers.

It has been suggested that

there is . . . evidence that commitments are being entered into by chairmen and chief officers of an authority without the prior agreement of, or even without prior consultation with, the authority itself. (NAHA submission to NHS Management Inquiry Team, June 1983, paper 2, para. 3)

One implication is that chairmen of authorities are becoming *de facto* chief executives. This development further reduces the already limited influence of members as a whole.

The National Association of Health Authorities argues:

The trend towards reliance on chairmen rather than the authority is seen as part of an increasingly centralist and authoritarian approach in relation to the management of the Health Service . . . contrary to Parliament's intention to provide for devolution of the management of the health services to local corporate bodies working in collaboration with local authorities and informed by the views of the public expressed through the CHCs. (ibid., paper 2, para. 5)

The analysis of the centralizing tendencies of present NHS planning approaches does not argue that the concept of performance reviews itself is inherently centralizing. Indeed, in principle, effective accountability for the achievement of agreed performance goals, if it could be secured, would free subordinate tiers from detailed supervision over the deployment of resources used to achieve such goals. In practice, however, the absence of operational output measures has forced systems of reviews back upon norms and other measures of input or service delivery rather than the achievement of specified health outputs.

The extent of direct involvement of the centre increased significantly after the first round of regional and district reviews. In September 1983 the secretary of state entered into further negotiations with regional health authorities, in which he laid down specific manpower targets. This represented a significant change from past practice where central government control was secured through the machinery of cash limits. In a revision of cash limits for 1983–4 (published in August 1983!) the secretary of state also stated his intention to set indicative manpower targets for each region representing a cut of between 0·75 and 1 per cent in staffing levels over the year.[14] Within this overall target certain regions and categories of staff were to diminish at different rates. This degree of central involvement in detailed staffing of the service was unprecedented and served to reinforce anxieties about the centralist tendencies of the DHSS.

The response of health authorities to the attempt to impose manpower targets was varied. In one of the most celebrated acts of resistance Brent Health Authority voted to reject the proposed level of cuts communicated to it by the regional health authority. Such defiance was taken up by a number of other authorities. In some cases it was apparent that this was essentially a negotiating stance – only recalcitrant authorities were eligible for further negotiation over their targets.

The response to such defiance is illustrative, however, of the formally clear-cut nature of the relationship between the centre and the locality. In the Brent case the RHA chairwoman wrote[15] to each DHA member threatening to remove from office any members unwilling to sign a pledge to accept the cuts at the next meeting of the authority. (By mistake the chairwoman's letter was also sent to the representatives of the local authority over whom she had no authority. The subsequent apology to them confirmed the long-denied difference in status of local authority DHA members.[16]) In the resulting furore the role of the DHA member as a local agent of the secretary of state – with the exception of the local authority members – rather than as local representative of local needs and conditions was reaffirmed.

In the final analysis national policy overrides local circumstances and priorities. Directives from the DHSS about privatization and the contracting out of laundry and domestic services have been expressed in terms which brooked no opposition. Local health authorities, as agents of the secretary of state, are required to implement such directives when they are promulgated.

Such direct and arbitrary policy interventions by the centre are necessarily crude in their effect and disruptive to the local administration of the service. Although they would once have been regarded as an action of last resort, their increasing use is indicative of a profound, centralizing change in the nature of the relationship between the DHSS and NHS.

It might be argued that such interventions simply reflect more generalized centralizing tendencies within the political system. The absence, however, of any elected authority within the NHS exacerbates the issue. In local government there exists an inherent tension between the will of local politicians and the judgement of professional officers. The tension exists because of the perceived legitimacy of local councillors whose right to determine the pattern of service provision rests upon their elected status. Even where agreement exists between officers and members, that agreement rests upon different bases of legitimacy – the one political, the other professional.

Three main consequences arise from this:

(1) The role of the professional as an 'executant of policy' can be closely monitored by the policy-makers themselves in local government. Indeed, it is through their observation of the impact of services upon the community that councillors comprehend the implications of the policies they adopt.

(2) Negotiation between central government and local authorities is based, in part, upon an acceptance that local values, electorally expressed, have a legitimate right of expression in the form of local service provision chosen.

(3) Local government officers look to their committees and chairpersons for direction and support rather than to a higher

tier authority – a regional principal, for example, of the appropriate central government department.

No such conditions exist in the NHS. Health authority members lack any direct popular support. (The local authority members are themselves nominated, they need not be elected members of local authorities and are, subsequent to their nomination, accountable to no one.) One consequence is that the tension between professional practice, clinical judgement and political priorities is weak because it is mediated through the long hierarchical chain of political control which culminates in the political office of the DHSS. This accounts for the frustration of the centre, promulgating policy yet not securing professional compliance at the point of service delivery.

The absence of an elected system of local health authority members results in the dominance of professional clinical priorities over political ones, while encouraging increasingly detailed attempts by central government to tie the whole NHS into the political priorities of the secretary of state.

MANAGERIAL SOLUTIONS

The increasing recourse to direct interventions in local manage-ment practice has occurred in parallel with the inquiry of a committee under the chairmanship of Roy Griffiths (an executive with the Sainsbury grocery chain), which was given the task of reviewing the NHS management system.

The willingness of ministers to intervene directly in operational management and not merely to confine themselves to strategic policy-making marks a significant break with the management principles of the 'Grey Books' and the 1974 reorganization. Yet doubts must remain as to the effectiveness of such action in changing NHS practice. The interventions remain limited to the peripheral elements of service provision: setting overall manpower targets; drawing up standardized tendering documents for the contracting out of domestic services and specifying services to be privatized.

Such a clear exercise of authority by the centre still fails to touch upon the day-to-day pattern of service delivery. Here change is so difficult for the centre to effect. As the Griffiths Report (1983, p. 12, para. 8) commented: 'the DHS is so structured as to resemble a "mobile": designed to move with any breath of air, but which in fact never changes its position and gives no clear indication of direction'. Against the heightened awareness of the inadequacy of ministerial fiat the Griffiths Report's proposals received an unqualified welcome from central government.

The Griffiths Report proposed the setting up of a Health Services Supervisory Board to be chaired by the secretary of state and to include senior officers and politicians in the DHSS. Such a Board would, together with determining strategic plans and patterns of resource allocation, review performance throughout the service. A Management Board, accountable to the Supervisory Board, would be responsible for implementing strategy and controlling performance. The Griffiths Report envisages that this body would draw heavily upon management capacity developed 'outside the NHS and the Civil Service'. A chain of command through 'general managers' would be introduced to replace the existing 'consensus team management' system. The report goes on to delimit the 'decisions reserved to the Authority meeting itself'.

Most particularly, the Griffiths Report – endorsed by the secretary of state – found that the essence of the problem of securing that central policy priorities are implemented through the local agency of the health authority lies in the weakness of 'a clearly defined general management function ... if Florence Nightingale were carrying her lamp through the corridors of the NHS today she would almost certainly be searching for the people in charge' (ibid., p. 12).

The NHS is entering yet another phase of redesign – this time of organization and process rather than structure. But still the motive force lies in the dilemma of bending a service provided through a multitude of field authorities, each with accumulated culture, history and tradition, and unique demographic and epidemio-logical characteristics, to a central political will. The dilemma is at the heart of central–local relations in the health service. Having rejected for the NHS the local government pattern of elected representatives, central government inexorably is forced into closer and more detailed control. Such control will diminish the roles of the health *authorities*. In sustaining their anomalous status the DHSS has faced failure in securing the objectives of the centre. The formal allocation of responsibility for operational tasks to the district health authorities, while reserving strategic tasks for the DHSS, represented an attempt to find a legitimate and discrete role for both. In the event the dependence of the health authorities upon central government for finance and the inability of the centre to distinguish between policy and practice undermined such a division of roles. In attempting to differentiate between strategic and operational plans the DHSS left the health authorities in the position of 'being swamped with directive without being given direction' (loc. cit.).

The new Boards – introduced as early as April 1984 – will take the NHS closer to the model of the nationalized industries. The extent to which the Management Board attains a degree of separateness from the Supervisory Board under the secretary of state will depend upon both political ideology and the extent to which the financial basis of the service becomes less dependent upon central government funding. The opportunities for radical change now exist.

The weak links in the chain of command lie in the roles of regional and district chairmen. The authority chairmen, at present part-time non-executive amateurs chosen for their political persuasion, will continue to occupy the key interface between one tier of management and the next. Their pivotal roles and the implications of their remunerated status may lead to their eventual incorporation into the officer structure – already achieved, *de facto*, in a minority of authorities where the chairman sits as *ex officio* member of the management team.

Since 1948 the NHS has developed structures and procedures to accommodate the sensitivities of professionals – doctors, nurses and para-medical workers – within the framework of an accountable government bureaucracy. The resultant tensions emerging between centrally formulated priorities and local practice have formed a major part of the backcloth to the subsequent structural and managerial reorganizations.

We may now be seeing in the present changes in management systems an actual reverse for professional interests in the NHS. It is questionable, however, whether what is lost in local influence and variety is outweighed by the gains derived from securing the primacy of socio-political values over those of the health professions.

A NEW POLICY ENVIRONMENT

The effect of two major reorganizations in eight years, continual controversy over resource levels and a major investigation by a Royal Commission, then ignored, has left the NHS demoralized at all levels of the service. Despite the pain, there is little evidence of a resolution of the supposed problems to which such changes have been directed.

As Hunter (1983, p. 134) points out, the insensitivity of the NHS to central political control runs parallel to a remarkable willingness to adopt and encourage clinical initiatives which arise locally. But locally it is clinical imperatives rather than socio-political priorities that hold sway. The clinicians – and the clinical hierarchies of status – determine intra-authority resource allocation and the pattern of service delivery.

In moving towards more centralized political direction the NHS may succeed in 'reining in' the excesses of clinical innovation and practice, but in doing so it may not also be able to replace the priorities of professional interest groups with those responsive to local needs and circumstances. Because there are few direct channels for local political influence to be exerted upon the NHS,[17] the service remains relatively impermeable to local community values.

Political control emanating from the DHSS is necessarily limited in the areas of service delivery to which it can attend. This is partly because of the organizational energy that needs to be mobilized to create a consensus among those affected by a particular service initiative, and partly because holistic policy directives – and the scale of their impact – tend towards marginal changes to historical patterns of service, or require such extensive research and monitoring as to exhaust the centre's ability to appraise more than a limited number of changes.

Paradoxically, then, the more centralist the system becomes, the fewer are the political initiatives that are undertaken. The greater the power of the centre, the greater are the risks involved in employing it. It is one thing to seek to shift the balance of care in favour of the 'Cinderella' services. Once power is taken over the executants of such policies, however, the central department's task becomes infinitely complex and burdensome. Policy paralysis rather than initiation is the most likely outcome.

The local authority system of political control is much less affected by such considerations. A local authority's range of service-delivery points is far more restricted. Feedback, through the political channels, from service recipients is easier and the experience of one authority can be drawn upon by others. The risks of innovation, though still considerable for a single authority, are marginal for the service as a whole. A comparison of developments in post-Seebohm social work and post-Salmon hospital nursing demonstrates the ease with which local authorities have been able to adapt to local circumstances, and to innovate and experiment, compared with their complementary health authorities.

The implication of such an analysis will be unpopular with both the professionals and bureaucrats of the NHS and central government politicians. It is that locally accountable politicians in local health authorities (whether part of existing local authorities or not) offer the best chance of affecting the pattern of service delivery. Furthermore, if the experience of the education service and personal social services is generalizable, then central policy priorities are better communicated and implemented through a structure with locally elected members than through a long hierarchical chain of administration.

Present trends in the NHS, however, will continue to provide observers with the spectacle of Ministers of Health with 'responsibility but not power' – as Bevan indicated at the inauguration of the NHS, that is the prerogative of the martyr.

NOTES: CHAPTER 13

1   Mr G. G. Hulme, deputy secretary of finance, to the Procedure (Finance) Committee, House of Commons, 7 December 1982.
2   Royal Commission on the National Health Service, 1978, p. 227; quoted in Regan, 1980; see also SSRC Study Group on Government Disengagement, 29 February 1980.
3   See, for example, Brown *et al.*, 1974.
4   Klein, 1983, p. 19.
5   See DHSS, 1972, p. 49.
6   See Ministry of Health, 1962.
7   See Ministry of Health, 1963.
8   Mackenzie notes, 'One could give many examples of the use of terms not effectively defined ... the most disastrous of all is the utterly unintelligible proposition that "Delegation downwards should be matched with account-ability upwards" ': Mackenzie, 1979, p. 171.
9   See DHSS, 1976.
10 See Ham, 1982, p. 116.
11 ibid., p. 117.
12 Quoted in Allen, 1982, p. 4.
13 National Association of Health Authorities' submission to the NHS inquiry team (chairman Roy Griffiths), June 1983.
14 HC 83(16), para. 3.
15 On 20 October 1983.
16 See DHSS, 1974.
17 The success of the joint planning arrangements with local authorities appears to depend less on formal systems of collaboration and more on the personal characteristics of the key actors involved: see Norton and Rogers, 1981, pp. 141–4.

REFERENCES: CHAPTER 13

Allen, D. E. (1982), 'Annual reviews', *British Medical Journal*, no. 285 (28 August–4 September), pp. 665–7.

Brown, R. G. S., Haywood, S. C., and Griffiths, J. G. (1974), *Waiting for Guidance* (Hull: University of Hull Press).
Central Policy Review Staff (1977), *Relations between Central Government and Local Authorities* (London: HMSO).
Crossman, R. H. S. (1972), *A Politician's View of Health Service Planning* (Glasgow: University of Glasgow).
Department of Health and Social Security (DHSS) (1972), *National Health Service Reorganisation*, Cmnd 5055 (London: HMSO).
DHSS (1974), *Democracy in the NHS: Membership of Health Authorities* (London: DHSS).
DHSS (1976), *Guide to the NHS Planning System* (London: DHSS).
DHSS (1979), *Patients First* (London: DHSS).
Griffiths Report (1983), *NHS Management Inquiry*, DA (83)38 (London: HMSO).
Ham, C. (1982), *Health Policy in Britain* (London: Macmillan).
Hunter, R. (1983), in K. Young (ed.), *National Interests and Local Government* (London: Heinemann).
Klein, R. (1983), *The Politics of the NHS* (London: Longman).
Mackenzie, W. J. M. (1979), *Power and Responsibility in Health Care* (Oxford: Oxford University Press).
Ministry of Health (1962), *A Hospital Plan for England and Wales*, Cmnd 1604 (London: HMSO).
Ministry of Health (1963), *Health and Welfare – the Development of Community Care*, Cmnd 1973 (London: HMSO).
Norton, A., and Rogers, S. A. (1981), 'The health service and local government services', in G. McLachlan (ed.), *Matters of Moment* (Oxford: Oxford University Press).
Regan, D. (1980), *Devolution in the NHS*, paper prepared for SSRC Study Group on Government Disengagement, 29 February (London: Social Service Research Council).
Regan, D. (1977), *Relations between Central Government and Local Authorities* (London: HMSO).
Royal Commission on the NHS (1978), *The Working of the NHS*, Research Paper 1 (London: HMSO).

14

Police

LEE BRIDGES

During a period in which local government generally has faced massive cuts in its resources and ever-increasing legal, administrative and financial constraints on its activities there is one local agency whose resources (both physical and financial), legal powers and scope for action have all been greatly increased in recent years. Certainly in the wake of the urban rebellions of 1981 the British state has been quick to rearm its police with new weaponry in the form of plastic bullets, CS gas and mobile water cannons in order to quell any further outbreaks of disorder. But these developments are only a part of a more fundamental review of urban policing policy that while dating back over a number of years is now being rapidly pushed forward in the form of the Police and Criminal Evidence Bill and related legislation,[1] which will institutionalize vastly increased legal powers for the police over the citizen, and in the major reorganization of the policing function such as that now taking place under the plan of London's new Metropolitan Police Commissioner, Sir Kenneth Newman, will greatly enhance the local autonomy of the police and extend their influence over the community at large.

Of course, this contrast in the fortunes of local government and of the police is by no means fortuitous. As Stuart Hall predicted in 1979,

> The new laissez-faire doctrine, in which social market values are to predominate ... is not at all inconsistent with a strong, disciplinary state. Indeed, if the state is to stop meddling in the fine-tuning of the economy, in order to let 'social market values' rip, while containing the inevitable fall-out, in terms of social conflict and class polarisation, then a strong, disciplinary regime is a necessary corollary. (Hall, 1979, p. 4)

Five years on, in 1984, the combined effects of the new technology and monetarist policies of enforced inequality have become even more starkly evident, in terms of permanent mass unemployment, growing social polarization and spreading urban decay. Such conditions must inevitably result in the short term in all types of social disintegration, including rising rates of crime, and lead to populist demands (from both the right and the left) for increased policing. But more significantly these developments imply a shift in the qualitative nature of policing, for in order to meet the threat to what Lord Scarman referred to as the 'normal state of society'[2] from the growing ranks of the disaffected among such groups as blacks, women, the unemployed and 'never employed' youth,[3] the state must take extraordinary measures. These include gearing up the police physically, legally and ideologically to control opposition when it surfaces on the streets, in demonstrations and other popular forms of protest. Beyond this, however, there is the need to pre-empt such protest by extending the influence of the police and their tentacles of surveillance ever wider into the community, its schools and social and political institutions, and even the family, instilling 'discipline' and keeping tabs on ever-larger sections of the population.

This extension of police influence has profound implications for local government and other local state agencies. Indeed, if the 1960s and 1970s saw developments, both nationally and locally, towards what many commentators described as a corporatist–managerial state,[4] then recent trends mark not so much a reversal of corporatism (as the ideologues of the New Right would claim), but a shift in its objectives, away from managerialism and towards repression and social control. This raises the issue of what role local government will assume within the emerging corporate-repressive state. Will it follow the populist clamour for 'law and order' and the urgings of senior police spokesmen and central government and be drawn into collaborative programmes of 'community policing' and 'multi-agency crime prevention'? Or will those in local government (and other local statutory and voluntary services), both politicians and officers, recognize the threat to civil liberties posed by such developments and see the need to extend their current defence of local democracy beyond questions of organizational self-preservation to encompass even more basic issues of the fundamental political and civil rights of the citizen?

THE POLITICS OF POLICING

That a new political impetus in defence of civil liberties is required at this time can best be demonstrated by examining the back-ground, contents and underlying purposes of the Police and Criminal Evidence Bill now before Parliament. The government has been anxious to portray this legislation as the product of a rational–technical process of law reform, as marked out by a series of reports beginning with that of the Criminal Law Revision Committee (1972) and extending through to the Report of the Royal Commission on Criminal Procedure (RCCP) (1981), on which the Bill is nominally based. According to this view, the Bill is largely a codifying measure designed to rectify the legal uncertainties and inconsistencies that have grown up over the years regarding the nature and extent of police powers.

In fact beneath the government's rhetoric and the official reports of the past decade there lies a very different political history of policing. This dates back at least to the 1972 miners' strike and widespread popular opposition to the then Tory government's trade union legislation, culminating in the 'battle of Saltley' in which a massed picket of 30,000 miners and other demonstrators successfully blocked the entrance to a coal depot in Birmingham. Following this, steps were taken to establish a Civil Contingency Unit within the Cabinet Office to revise government plans for dealing with such 'emergencies', thus marking a move towards more direct central planning of policing. At the same time, the Association of Chief Police Officers (ACPO) began to emerge as a central co-ordinating body among local police forces and as a corporate link between them and central government, a role paralleling for policing that assumed during this period by the various local authority associations in respect of local government generally. Also a number of measures were being taken locally to 'modernize' police organization and methods. In developments closely associated with Sir Robert Mark's period as Metropolitan Commissioner of Police in London in the early to middle 1970s there was a major shift in urban policing towards a reactive, 'fire-brigade' style of operations, involving a heavy reliance on motorized patrols backed by increasingly specialist centralized police squads and advanced equipment and technology. This latter included the development of sophisticated police computer systems, both nationally and locally, for purposes of 'command and control' over police operations and the storage of wide 'intelligence' information.[5]

This move toward 'fire-brigade' policing was not without its critics. John Alderson, when Chief Constable of Devon and Cornwall, emerged in the late 1970s as the most well-known proponent of 'community policing', and he criticized the way in which police thinking had become seduced into a 'quasi-military reactive concept' of policing in which the 'car, radio and the computer dominate the police scene'.[6] This style of policing would serve, Alderson argued, only to alienate the public, as the police and the people would increasingly tend to meet only in conflict situations. He proposed instead a 'pro-active' model of policing (as distinct from both reactive, 'fire-brigade' policing and preventative policing based on large numbers of officers on the beat), which he defined at the Ditchley Conference on Preventive Policing in March 1977 as containing

> all the elements of preventive policing but [it] goes beyond it. Whereas preventive policing tends to put the system on the defensive, pro-active policing sets out to *penetrate the community in a multitude of ways*. It seeks to reinforce social discipline and mutual trust . . . it serves to activate all possible resources in support of the common good.

He added that the police were probably 'better placed than most other organisations for providing social leadership of this kind', and called for closer links between the police and other local agencies in order to push forward this form of wider social control.

While Alderson's ideas remained unpopular among most urban police commanders during the 1970s, resulting only in a few isolated 'community policing' experiments,[7] he did share with them a recognition of the importance of developing an 'open and trusting' relationship with the media in order to gain wider support for police operations and policies. Again it was Sir Robert Mark who, through his cultivated liaison with the press and politicians, did the most to push the police into a more active political stance, projecting them beyond their traditional role as enforcers of the law and into a position where they might more directly influence the content of the law itself.[8] One outcome of this greater politicization of the police was the setting up of the Royal Commission on Criminal Procedure in 1978 and the pre-emptive evidence presented to it by Sir David McNee, Mark's successor as Metropolitan Commissioner, ACPO and the rank-and-file Police Federation, all demanding extensive increases in police legal powers. The RCCP Report, published in January 1981, went a considerable way towards meeting these police demands for new legal powers.

Of course, the more immediate context of the Police and Criminal Evidence Bill lies in the 1981 'riots' and, more significantly, in the active police campaign that emerged following the Scarman Report, designed to undermine its supposedly liberal conclusions and police critics in the community and among more radical Labour-controlled local authorities. Characteristically this campaign was launched by the Metropolitan Police's carefully stage-managed release in March 1982 of racialized crime statistics purporting to show a dramatic increase in 'muggings' and predominant black involvement in such offences.[9] Viewed in this light the Bill, which in its proposals for extending police powers goes well beyond the RCCP recommendations and reflects more the various police evidences to the Commission, represents an open invitation by the present government to the police to continue their 'post-riot' clampdown on inner city areas and their black populations in particular. Certainly any notion of 'soft' policing that may have emerged following the Scarman Report[10] has been belied by the policing policies pursued in such areas since the 'riots', including saturation foot patrols backed by newly formed Instant Response Units, consisting of local-based squads of specially trained and equipped mobile riot police, used for purposes of carrying out increasingly frequent road blocks and searches.

A BILL OF RIGHTS FOR THE POLICE

Of equal if not greater significance, however, is the capacity the new powers contained in the Bill will give the police to increase their general surveillance of the community and its overall effect in statutorily safeguarding police discretion and the autonomy of local police operations. Just as rates legislation, although nominally directed at a minority of 'high-spending' local authorities, is now widely recognized as more fundamentally eroding established principles of local democracy, so the Police and Criminal Evidence Bill, while presented as a codifying measure and seemingly directed at minority groups in the population, will undermine the traditional concept of civil liberties in this country and thus has far wider implications for future relations between the police and the citizen and society. Historically in Britain civil liberties have been based not on a written Bill of Rights, but on an unwritten constitutional convention that the police operated as 'citizens in uniform', with only very few and strictly delimited powers to interfere in the affairs of their fellow citizens. Of course, there has always been a gap between these theoretical limits on police powers and their actual practices, especially when it has come to the policing of urban working-class areas and, during the past twenty years, the black community. But this gap between theory and practice has created a political space in which trade unionists, civil libertarians and black community defence campaigns supported more recently by radical local authorities have been able to struggle for a wider recognition of their rights and for greater accountability and control over the police. This political space is now being closed and the gap between limits on police powers and their practices transcended by legislation that will effectively enshrine within statute extensive 'rights' for the police to interfere with the citizen in the ordinary course of its daily activities.

Thus the Bill will establish for the first time on a national basis a power for the police forcibly to stop and search persons and vehicles on 'reasonable suspicion' of carrying not only stolen goods (as currently exists in London and a few other localities), but also 'offensive weapons' and articles for use in theft, the legal definition of both of which is open to arbitrary interpretation and widespread abuse by the police. The police will also be empowered to set up roadblocks, sealing off an area for up to seven days, whenever a local police superintendent considers that the 'pattern of crime in that area' justifies it. It has been widely noted that these provisions will give legal sanction to such mass stop and search operations as Swamp 81, in which nearly 1,000 persons were stopped on the streets of Brixton in the days immediately preceding the April 1981 'riot'. Nor should it be overlooked that stop and search and roadblocks have become an increasingly routine part of policing in inner urban areas. The recent Policy Studies Institute Report has confirmed that an estimated 1·5 million stop and searches are carried out in London each year, with blacks and young people discriminatorily subject to frequent police actions of this type,[11] and although fewer than one in twelve stops result in an arrest or summons (let alone a subsequent legal conviction), it would appear that the Metropolitan Police rely on this arbitrary method to achieve a significant proportion of their total arrests. This heavy operational dependence of the police on stop and search, along with the general effect of such operations in harassing and building up intelligence on particular sections of the community, no doubt explains the government's persistence in seeking to extend police powers in this field in the face of strong legal and public criticism of these provisions.

The Bill will also provide the police with extensive statutory powers of arrest and to enter and search premises both of those arrested and other members of the public. It was this new power for the police to conduct general searches for evidence in premises of those not themselves suspected of any crime that attracted wide criticism during the Bill's original passage through Parliament prior to the 1983 general election, especially in its application to confidential records held by professional persons. In an attempt to buy off their critics among the professions and other elite pressure groups, and to isolate them from more popular opposition to the Bill, the government has made concessions supposedly to protect confidential professional records from arbitrary searches.[12] However, this will still leave 'non-professional' advisers and all other individuals and organizations liable under the Bill to general searches of their records and premises on the warrant of a single magistrate. A telling sign of the possible future use of this power may be found in Sir Kenneth Newman's recent outburst against the 'small minority of police watchers' and other 'activists on the Left', whom he accused of a 'campaign of dedicated denigration of the police'.[13] In singling out community-based defence campaigns and local police monitoring groups in this way, and further officially labelling them as a 'destabilising influence and a threat to public order', Newman would appear to have given a clear lead to police efforts to undermine their work, including potentially subjecting them to regular searches of their offices and seizure of files and other documents.

A further area in which the Bill provides the police with extensive new powers is in the detention and interrogation of suspects. The police will be empowered to hold a person without charge in order 'to secure or preserve evidence . . . or to obtain such evidence by questioning him', and they will also be granted increased powers forcibly to search, fingerprint and take body samples from detainees. In most cases such detention can extend for up to thirty-six hours on the police's own authority, during which a detainee may be denied access to a lawyer or relations, and for a further sixty hours on order of a local magistrates' court. Of course, these new powers of detention – paralleling those already in use against the Irish and black communities under the Prevention of Terrorism and the Immigration Acts – will operate alongside the Bill's other provisions giving the police wider scope to gather evidence and intelligence in the community, and they will therefore be in a much stronger position than at present to obtain and use information about detainees or their families and friends in order to induce them into making confessions. And even where it is not possible using the vastly increased powers in the Bill to induce confessions or obtain other evidence upon which to secure a legal conviction, the ability to detain innocent persons over long periods, to subject them to often humiliating searches, and continually to rearrest them on new 'suspicions' will constitute, as the experience in Northern Ireland and among Irish Catholics in mainland Britain has shown, a powerful weapon of summary punishment and intelligence-gathering in the hands of the police.

Apart from these specific new powers, a significant feature of the Bill is the way in which it will entrench police discretion more deeply by giving it statutory backing and serve to further isolate police decision-making from effective external review or control. A good example of this can be found in the concept of a 'serious arrestable offence'. The exercise of various of the more exceptional powers in the Bill is technically restricted to situations involving a 'serious arrestable offence'. Yet, as originally drafted, the Bill defined this in a blatantly self-fulfilling and self-legitimating way as 'an arrestable offence which the person contemplating the exercise of the power considers to be sufficiently serious to justify his exercising it'. In the revised version of the Bill now before Parliament the government has seemingly conceded the need to define 'serious arrestable offence' more precisely, tying it to a list of specific crimes such as murder, rape, and so on. However, the police will still be entitled to treat any of a wide range of other offences as 'serious' if they consider that certain consequences have or will arise from their commission, and these include such vague criteria as 'serious harm ... to public order', 'serious interference with the administration of justice', or 'serious financial loss', the latter to be judged subjectively from the point of view of the person suffering the loss. Even the Law Society, which was brought in initially to assist in the redrafting of the definition of a 'serious arrestable offence', has subsequently complained that these later government additions to the definition will leave the police with a virtually unchallengeable discretion in determining how to employ their considerable new powers. In a similar vein the exercise of various powers of stop, search and arrest in the Bill is supposed to require 'reasonable suspicion' on the part of the police that an offence has been or is about to be committed. Yet the recent Policy Studies Institute Report has confirmed with regard to stop and search that

reasonable suspicion does not act as an effective constraint on police officers in deciding whether to make a stop ... We could see no good reason for the stop in one third of the cases recorded in the course of our observational work. (Smith and Gray, 1983, vol. 4, p. 321)

But if the Bill in conferring extensive powers and a wide statutory discretion in their use on the police effectively places the citizen's traditional liberties in police custody, then what of the statutory 'safeguards' it supposedly provides in return? It should be noted, first of all, that these 'safeguards' will not in themselves limit or restrict police powers, but merely lay down procedures that should technically be followed in exercising these powers. Moreover, when placed in the context of police operations, many of these 'safeguards' will also prove, like the legal concepts of 'serious arrestable offence' and 'reasonable suspicion', either to be ineffective or, even worse, to function in practice as a shield for the police, protecting them from any subsequent exposure of malpractice by officially reducing their actions and the rationale behind them to standardized forms and categories. This point can again be illustrated by reference to stop and search, in relation to which the Bill will require the police, where practicable, to make a written record of each stop and the reasons for it. However, given the mass scale on which this power is already used and the heavy operational reliance of the police upon it, it is likely that the police will continue to treat a large proportion of stops as 'unofficial' and, therefore, make no record of them (it is known that around one-half of all stops currently go unrecorded in police statistics). At the same time, where an official record is made, this undoubtedly will be reduced to a pro forma, with fixed categories for the police to tick giving their reasons for the stop, and as experience of the use of police notebooks in court has shown, it is frequently impossible effectively to probe behind such 'official' records to uncover underlying abuses of power.

TOWARDS THE LOCAL POLICE STATE

Legal powers and discretion, even as extensive as those granted in the Police and Criminal Evidence Bill, do not in themselves make for a police state. It is through the medium of police organization and strategy that legal provisions are translated into instruments of oppression. It is, therefore, important to look at the organizational and inter-governmental context in which these new police powers will be implemented, especially in the light of the current campaign for greater democratic accountability of the police. It is worth noting in this regard that the move outlined above, from the traditional protection of civil liberties through strictly delimited police powers to the granting of extensive legal powers to the police supposedly balanced by new 'safeguards', itself implies an organizational shift from the concept of the legal accountability of the police through the courts to a system of more purely administrative review of their activities. Whatever the short-comings of judicial review of the police in the past, the courts have at least provided an open, public forum for challenging their malpractices. By contrast, the bodies that will be given the function of 'enforcing' the supposed 'safeguards' in the Bill such as the Police Complaints Board or the new 'independent' prosecution service will be entirely administrative in character and likely to be made responsible to central government rather than having any local democratic input or accountability.[14]

What, then, of demands now emanating from some, primarily Labour-controlled local authorities for a strengthening of the direct accountability of the police to local government? The effectiveness of the local police authorities that currently operate outside London is severely restricted by their composition, which includes magistrates as well as elected local councillors (a fact that may partly explain the reluctance of these authorities to exercise even the limited powers they do possess for critical scrutiny of the police), and more so by the narrow range of police activity defined as 'policy' and therefore open to their consideration, as opposed to the much wider 'operational' matters for which chief constables, with central government backing, claim sole responsibility. It has been this limited formal role assigned to them, combined with the fact that it is the Home Secretary who alone acts as the police authority for London wihout local democratic input, that has led local authorities such as the Greater London Council to put forward detailed blueprints for a fully elected local police authority. Under the GLC plan, for example, the local police authority would have control over all matters of police policy and operations (excluding decisions relating to individual cases), including police finance and expenditure, appointments, promotions and disciplinary and dismissal procedures. However, such demands are clearly unrealistic in the present political context, and indeed the fact that authorities such as the GLC are now attempting to exert greater influence over policing may itself be a factor in the government's determination to abolish the metropolitan tier of local government in London and the major metropolitan areas.

A further difficulty with the concept of local democratic accountability of the police[15] is the organizational/geographical level at which the majority of police operations are conducted. For example, in the Metropolitan Police area covering Greater London there are twenty-four police districts, most of which contain the area of one or more London boroughs (the smallest – and soon to be the only – unit of directly elected government in the capital). However, police operations in London are further subdivided into seventy-five local police divisions, and a similar organizational division of police activities below the level of elected local government exists in most large urban areas, with the country as a whole outside London containing a further 250 police divisions. A recent report on the Metropolitan Police has noted that

> it is the Chief Superintendent, in charge of each local division, assisted by a Superintendent, who decides how to deploy the officers under his command and what operations to mount. It appears that the Chief Superintendent has considerable autonomy. (GLC Police Committee, 1982, p. 28)

While the recent Policy Studies Institute Report on the Metropolitan Police has seriously called into question how far even these local police commanders exercise any effective super-vision over individual police officers and their day-to-day actions, noting that 'supervision tends to be "on paper" rather than by direct contact, and supervising officers . . . are not generally in a position to know much about the style or quality of work done by most of the officers under their command' (Smith *et al.*, 1983, vol. 4, p. 343). This again casts considerable doubt on the practical validity of the new administrative 'safeguards' provided in the Police and Criminal Evidence Bill, as their implementation will frequently depend in the first instance on the actions of these same local commanders. On the other hand, the Bill will confer on the divisional-based police superintendents very wide discretion in terms of being able to authorize on their own authority measures such as roadblocks, detention of suspects for up to thirty-six hours and the forcible taking of fingerprints and body samples, while it will require only an inspector (usually based at a local police station) to sanction police searches of an arrested person's premises. Even in those few instances under the Bill where the police will require prior permission from an external authority before exercising their exceptional new powers, as in the case of detention of suspects for up to four days and search of innocent persons' premises, this will come from local magistrates who, on the experience of the infamous Railton Road raids in Brixton in 1981[16] or the more recent search under warrant of journalist Duncan Campbell's premises, following his bicycle accident, may be expected readily to endorse police operational decisions. Thus while many of the 'safeguards' in the Bill rely on the doubtful supervision that local police commanders exercise over the lower ranks of the force, these same officers will have greatly enhanced their legal powers to control individual citizens and the community at large, and in this way the Bill will give new statutory backing to the autonomy of local police operational decisions regarding the deployment of officers and the types of operations to mount. Once enacted, therefore, the Bill will represent a further, legal barrier to any future plans to give local authorities or other elected bodies real and effective democratic control over the police.

The new legal powers now being conferred on local police commanders correspond directly with the emphasis being placed in police thinking and strategies – such as that currently advanced by Sir Kenneth Newman in London – on neighbourhood-level police operations and activities, especially those organized around the themes of 'crime prevention' and 'community policing'. It is worth recalling here that it was Newman, following his period as Chief Constable of the Royal Ulster Constabulary in the middle to late 1970s (where he developed 'one of the most sophisticated intelligence networks of any police force in Western Europe'[17]), who was responsible for reorienting the senior command course at the national Police Staff College at Bramshill towards the study of a 'multi-agency' approach to the problems of crime control and 'order management' in what was termed as inner-city 'ethnic flashpoints'.[18] This course concluded in July 1982 with a national conference attended not only by senior police officers drawn from throughout the country and from Chicago, West Berlin, Hong Kong and Barbados, but also senior Home Office officials, virtually the whole of the Department of the Environment's central Inner Cities Directorate (responsible for the urban programme), local government councillors and housing, planning and education officials, and sundry university-based local government experts and business consultants. This was followed in September 1982 by a further high-level seminar at Bramshill, headed this time by the Permanent Under-Secretary at the Home Office, Sir Brian Cubbon (himself closely associated with the Newman era in Northern Ireland as a senior civil servant at the Northern Ireland Office), on the theme of 'multi-agency' crime prevention involving the police, local government and other social agencies. An example of what such a co-ordinated or 'corporate' approach to 'crime prevention' might entail was given by a Department of Health and Social Security (DHSS) representative at the seminar:

The police, for example, can from their records plot the particular areas or estates from which offenders come. Similarly, information about children excluded or truanting from school can be presented systematically. Social services' caseloads can be plotted according to district. In fact it is often possible to determine those localities within a given area where action is most needed, and the nature of the information will often suggest the form that action might take and who might take it. (Home Office, 1982, p. 19)

After taking office as Metropolitan Police Commissioner in October 1982, Newman was quick to incorporate this new thinking on urban policing strategy into his policing plan for London and, at the same time, to redefine the objectives of policing in much wider terms. Thus in his first Annual Report as Metropolitan Commissioner Newman stressed that 'crime control is just one element of social control',[19] and in a newspaper interview he asserted that 'it would be better if we stopped talking about crime prevention and lifted the whole thing to a higher level of generality represented by the words "social control" '.[20] What this implies in practical terms is an attempt by Newman to project the police, through local commanders and new locally based initiatives such as consultative committees, neighbourhood watch schemes, crime prevention panels of local businessmen and other dignitaries, and closer police–local authority liaison focusing in particular on schools and housing and social services departments, into a position of much wider influence over the social and (in so far as it touches on this newly defined, extensive remit of policing) the political life of the community. Moreover, the Newman strategy cannot be regarded as a special and, therefore, purely London matter. Not only have Newman's plans received the enthusiastic backing of Home Office ministers and senior civil servants, but they are about to be recommended through a Home Office circular on crime prevention for implementation on a national scale. A draft of this circular sent out in July 1983 called (with little regard for traditional notions of the separation of powers) for 'the police, magistracy, and social and probation services and departments of education, housing and highways' to be drawn together for purposes of formulating local crime prevention strategies and specific programmes of 'multi-agency' co-operation around policing problems.[21]

It would be easy to dismiss the Home Office circular and even more Newman's 'corporate' policy plan for London as representing no more than the very belated discovery by the police and Home Office planners in this field of the types of 'corporate management' thinking that ran unchecked through local government during the late 1960s and early 1970s. Even more dangerous would be the belief that co-operation with the police on 'crime prevention' measures, for which there is a growing populist demand stemming from current conditions of economic and social disintegration, can in some way be separated off and isolated from the more coercive aspects of policing as represented in the provisions of the Police and Criminal Evidence Bill. In this regard it is important to note that the one common denominator in the various 'crime prevention' and 'community policing' programmes being instigated by the police is an increased (although frequently unstated) police emphasis on greater and wider surveillance and intelligence-gathering. At the centre of the new intelligence-gathering network now being created is the rediscovered 'bobby on the beat' whose function is to ensure a steady flow of information on 'sensitive' neighbourhoods and their residents to a 'collator' based at each local police station. In turn, he lodges this information on local police computers, from where it will be drawn for use in formulating local policing plans and informing specific police operations as well as passing it up through city-wide and national police computer networks. Under the Newman plan in London large numbers of officers are being redeployed back 'on the beat' and further being specifically tasked to promote and become involved with neighbourhood watch schemes, victim support groups, tenants' associations and inter-agency links with other service organizations and professionals. Of course, initiatives such as neighbourhood watch may serve marginally to supplement police manpower, especially in 'low-priority' outer urban areas or in terms of police public assistance functions, which Newman admits will need to be curtailed in order to concentrate resources on harsher and more intensive 'public order' and 'crime control' measures in the inner city. But these aspects cannot be isolated from the primary role of these programmes in improving police intelligence on society at large, for example, by recruiting 'community representatives' to patrol with the police in difficult areas to help identify local 'trouble-makers' or in organizing schools or local authority housing and social services departments to provide regular information on their clients and to help pick out potentially 'disruptive' elements in the community.

Again it may be argued that such schemes of co-operation and information exchange with the police do not represent a threat to individual civil liberties because they are geared, in the words of the draft Home Office circular, to 'the collection and collation of aggregate data' and '*not* information about identifiable individuals'.[22] However, this argument overlooks two crucial considerations. First, if data exchange arrangements with the police are entered into by local authorities or other agencies without having worked out in advance internal guidelines and procedures for protecting confidentiality, then the police may inadvertently but no less dangerously obtain access to individual details; and once such information has passed to the police, their very lack of accountability will ensure that there will be no safeguards as to how this information may be used. Indeed, such data, once in police hands, will be specifically excluded from the remit of the new data protection legislation. In this respect recent reports from the Children's Legal Centre of a computer system set up to be shared by the police and a local authority social services department in one English county, on which the police may gain access to social service clients' files and even hospital records, present an ominous warning to other authorities.[23] Equally even where a relationship with the police has been built up for general purposes, such as the involvement of police in schools for teaching civic responsibilities, this can be exploited for quite different purposes in the course of specific police operations. For example, in one recent case the police through a local 'community bobby' involved in schools liaison work requested and were given names and personal details of all black children attending a London school as part of an investigation of an incident of street robbery, and this led to the unjustified arrest and detention of one of the named children.[24]

A second important consideration is how far co-operation with the police in crime prevention and community policing programmes may endanger the *collective liberty* of the community or elements within it. Here it is vital to recognize that these programmes in no way constitute, as popular media representation and some police spokesmen would make out, an alternative to more coercive, 'fire-brigade' policing methods. Rather within the terms of the new policing strategy being advanced by Sir Kenneth Newman and the Home Office these locally based crime prevention and community policing initiatives are only one end of an operational continuum, designed to provide information and intelligence on which to base local and wider police operations geared directly towards 'crime control' and the maintenance of 'public order'. Thus the most important element of the Newman policing plan for London is the concept, drawn directly from his experience of anti-terrorist operations in Northern Ireland, of 'targeting' and his wider application of this concept to more common policing problems such as street robberies, burglaries and general social disorder and disruption in the community. More specifically, 'targeting' involves the *prior* identification of particular persons, groups, or geographical localities for a concentration of police resources and for special police operations involving such methods as large-scale stop and search, frequent roadblocks and raids on premises, and various surreptitious surveillance techniques. To effect this part of his plan Newman has not only established new Intelligence and Surveillance Units in each of the four areas into which the Metropolitan Police district is divided, but he has also refashioned the Instant Response Units set up after the 1981 'riots' into District Support Units and redefined their functions, almost precisely in line with the new powers in the Police and Criminal Evidence Bill, to include 'anti-burglary patrols, rowdyism patrols, searches, roadblocks, observations [and] execution of warrants'.[25] In other words, these units will serve as localized special squads, available to local police commanders to carry out special operations against particular sections of the community. Thus even if new programmes of multi-agency co-operation with the police are carefully designed and monitored to prevent their use in gathering intelligence on individuals, their open and explicit function will still be to provide data and assistance to the police in identifying areas and groups in the community as deserving of 'suspicion' and, therefore, open to the full application of new police powers and methods of control.

In an earlier analysis of a community policing experiment set up under the urban programme in one area of Birmingham this writer argued that this new approach to policing

> merges at the local level the coercive and consensual functions of government, enabling the police to wield a frightening mixture of repressive powers, on the one hand, and programmes of social intervention, on the other, as mutually reinforcing tools in their efforts to contain and control the political struggles of the black and working class communities. (Bridges, 1982–3, p. 183)

In the light of the Police and Criminal Evidence Bill and the development of urban policing strategy during the past two years it is clear that the only fault with the above formulation was the notion that it was solely the political liberties of the black and working-class communities that were under threat, whereas in fact these measures can be seen as fundamentally altering the relationship between the police and society as a whole, and in the process undermining the traditional basis of democratic policing in Britain. Certainly the idea of 'policing by consent', in which the police because of their limited formal powers and influence were placed in a position of having to seek the co-operation of the community in order to carry out their function, will soon have little relevance, for once the police have been given statutory powers to intervene and control the community, the need for any accommodation with the people will be eliminated. The point has been well made by Brian Hilliard of the *Police Review* in a recent television programme[26] on a neighbourhood policing experiment in Hackney, when he said:

> If the people of Hackney don't want neighbourhood policing, which means possibly the people of London don't want neighbourhood policing; if they refuse to give the police the assistance that the police need to fight the criminal, there can be no other result than the police become a continental type of force, a paramilitary body that is placed upon the community forcing it to obey the law.

In other words, rather than the police with their limited powers and thus a need to seek wider support in the community being placed continuously under popular, local democratic scrutiny, it is the community that is on trial before the police, and if they fail the test, then the Police and Criminal Evidence Bill will give the police all the legal authority they need to impose their will on the people. Equally the choice now facing the community and its local political leaders and institutions is whether to allow itself under this form of political duress to be drawn into ever-wider programmes of 'co-operation' with the police (and thereby sacrifice the individual and collective liberties of their fellow citizens) or to mount a campaign of political resistance against the albeit localized police state now being imposed on us.

NOTES: CHAPTER 14

This chapter is adapted from my two previous articles: 'Britain's new urban policy strategy: the Police and Criminal Evidence Bill in context', *Journal of Law and Society*, vol. 10, no. 1 (Summer 1983) (written with Tony Bunyan), and 'Policing the urban wastelands', *Race and Class*, vol. XXV, no. 2 (Autumn 1983): special issue, 'British racism: the road to 1984'.

1   Two other significant pieces of current legislation in this context are the Data Protection Bill and proposed changes to the Prevention of Terrorism Act.
2   See Scarman Report, 1981, para. 4.60.

3   The term is taken from Sivanandan, 1981.
4   For an excellent review of the literature on corporatism see Cawson, 1982. On corporatism in local government see Cockburn, 1977.
5   For a review of developments in policing during this period see Bunyan, 1982–3, pp. 161–9.
6   See *The Cranfield Papers*, 1979.
7   For a discussion of one such 'community policing' experiment in Handsworth (Birmingham) see Bridges, 1982–3, pp. 182–3.
8   For a discussion of police politicization during this period see Hall, 1979, and Kettle, 1980.
9   See Sim, 1982.
10 In fact the Scarman Report (1981) gave broad backing both to increases in police legal powers and to the methods and tactics employed in suppressing the 'riots' and in the general policing of 'high-crime', inner city areas. That a contrary view of the Scarman Report gained common currency was itself a product of police and media propaganda aimed at venting their anger over the wide publicity given to police critics during the Scarman Inquiry and elsewhere in the aftermath of the disturbances.
11 See Smith and Gray, 1983, vol. 4, pp. 320–3.
12 It is not possible here to analyse the complex provisions of the Bill regarding 'excluded' and 'special procedure' materials, although doubts have been raised as to their effectiveness in protecting some categories of confidential information. In any event, it may be expected that renewed efforts will be made to provide the police with access to such information through administrative or voluntary means, especially where this is held by other public bodies.
13 See the Metropolitan Police Commissioner's annual report, 1983, p. 3.
14 See GLC Police Committee, 1982.
15 Of course, one device for enhancing the significance of judicial, as opposed to administrative, control of the police would be tying any new safeguards to an exclusionary rule, under which violations of the rules and procedures laid down would make any evidence or confession subsequently obtained automatically inadmissible in court. It is not surprising that despite all the 'concessions' made on the Bill, the government and police spokesmen have steadfastly refused to contemplate any such exclusionary rule.
16 The raid, carried out as the Scarman Inquiry was sitting and in which eleven houses were forcibly entered at dawn and floors ripped up and furniture smashed in an unsuccessful search for firearms, was later the subject of a special Police Complaints Board report which found that the police had widely exceeded the authority of their warrants. However, in line with the above comments on administrative control of the police it is notable that this report was not made public until April 1983, some twenty months after the event, and specifically recommended that no disciplinary action be taken against individual officers.
17 See Taylor, 1980, as quoted in *Policing London*, no. 2, September 1983, p. 2.
18 See Police Staff College, 1982, Commandant's foreword.
19 Metropolitan Police Commissioner's annual report, 1983, p. 10.
20 *Financial Times*, 23 March 1983.
21 Draft Home Office circular, July 1983, para. 21.
22 ibid., para. 9; in the next sentence the draft circular goes on to say that it is '*not* intended to alter or extend in any way such arrangements as exist between agencies for exchange of confidential information' without specifying either the nature or extent of such arrangements.
23 *Childright*, November 1983, p. 6.

24   For details of this and similar cases, together with a review of developments in
      police interventions into schools see Webber, 1983, pp. 73–9.
25   Metropolitan Police Commissioner's annual report, 1983, appendix 31.
26   *The London Programme*, September 1983, as monitored by the Institute of
      Race Relations Media Research Project.

REFERENCES: CHAPTER 14

Bramshill Police Staff College (1982), 'The urban future: inner city conference',
    unpublished papers.
Bridges, L. (1982–3), 'Keeping the lid on: British urban social policy, 1975–81',
    Race and Class, vol. XXIII, no. 2–3 (Autumn–Winter), pp. 171–85.
Bunyan, T. (1982–3), 'The police against the people', *Race and Class*, vol. XXIII,
    no. 2–3 (Autumn–Winter), pp. 153–70.
Cawson, A. (1982), *Corporatism and Welfare* (London: Heinemann).
Cockburn, C. (1977), *The Local State* (London: Pluto Press).
Cranfield Papers (1979), *The Proceedings of the 1978 Cranfield Conference on the
    Prevention of Crime in Europe* (Cranfield: Cranfield Institute of Technology).
Criminal Law Revision Committee (1972), *Eleventh Report Evidence (General)*,
    Cmnd 4991 (London: HMSO).
Greater London Council Police Committee (1982), *A New Police Authority for
    London – a Consultative Paper on Democratic Control of the Police in London*
    (London: GLC Police Committee).
Hall, S. (1979), *Drifting into a Law and Order Society*, Human Rights Day Lecture
    (London: Cobden Trust).
Home Office (1982), *Crime Prevention: A Co-ordinated Approach* (London:
    HMSO).
Kettle, M. (1980), 'The politics of policing and the policing of politics', in P. Hain
    (ed.), *Policing the Police* (London: John Calder), Vol. 2, pp. 9–59.
Report of the Commissioner of Police for the Metropolis for the Year 1982, Cmnd
    8928 (London: HMSO).
Royal Commission on Criminal Procedure (1981), *Report*, Cmnd 8092 (London:
    HMSO).
Scarman Report (1981), *The Brixton Disorders, 10–12 April 1981*, Cmnd 8427
    (London: HMSO).
Sim, J. (1982), 'Scarman: the police counter attack', in M. Eve and D. Musson (eds),
    Socialist Register (London: Merlin Press), pp. 57–77.
Sivanandan, A. (ed.) (1981), 'From resistance to rebellion', in A. Sivanandan, *A
    Different Hunger* (London: Pluto Press), pp. 3–54.
Smith, D. J., and Gray, J. (1983), *Police and People in London* (London: Policy
    Studies Institute), Vol. 4.
Taylor, P. (1980), *Beating the Terrorists* (Harmondsworth: Penguin).
Webber, F. (1983), 'Teachers in uniform', *Race and Class*, vol. XXV, no. 2
    (Autumn), pp. 73–9.

III   Issues

15

Employment

JOHN MAWSON and DAVID MILLER

INTRODUCTION

The basis of postwar efforts to manage the spatial economy stems from an analysis made at the end of the Second World War of a dual problem of metropolitan congestion in the south-east and West Midlands and unemployment in the northern and western parts of the country. By lumping together these two (not necessarily related) problems, it was hoped to devise a strategy which would both restrict the further growth of large cities through land use planning controls and redirect surplus population and economic activity to the surrounding metropolitan hinterlands and underdeveloped regions. This was to be achieved through the application of floorspace controls in congested areas and through regional financial incentives and provision of infrastructure in the reception areas.

In terms of its initial objectives this dual strategy could be interpreted as a success. In all the major conurbations population and economic activity has decentralized to new and expanded towns, through both government action and free market move-ment, and research suggests that, as a result of regional economic policy, a large number of jobs have been created in the assisted areas (Tyler *et al.*, 1980, suggest 250,000 between 1960 and 1979). However, this approach has come under increasing scrutiny and criticism. Attention has focused on the arguments of local authorities, businessmen and trade union leaders, largely from traditionally prosperous areas in the south and Midlands, that the policy has had a restrictive impact on industrial growth and innovation, and that, while expensive, has failed to solve the problems of the assisted regions. While regional policy succeeded in diverting new industry to these areas, it failed to build up an economy capable of generating long-term economic growth. Moreover, the changing economic climate in the 1970s undermined many of the assumptions upon which the policy was based.

Faced with increasing national economic difficulties, the Labour government of 1974–9 and the subsequent Conservative governments reduced the level of expenditure on regional policy. Priorities for financial assistance from the Industry Acts shifted during the 1970s, from encouraging geographical mobility towards improving the efficiency and productivity of investment wherever it took place. With higher unemployment throughout the country, it became politically difficult to apply floorspace controls in the so-called prosperous areas and in December 1981 the government suspended the operation of industrial development certificate controls. Financial incentives and floorspace controls had become ineffective in a period when there was little mobile industry. These changes also reflected a recognition that disparities within regions are often greater than between them and led to the development of inner city policy and increasing local authority involvement in economic development. In 1979 following a review of regional economic policy the decision was taken to significantly reduce the coverage of assisted areas over a two-year period from 40 to 25 per cent of the working population, and in December 1983 the government produced a White Paper announcing its intention to introduce further changes in the system.[1]

Paralleling these changes in central government thinking during the 1970s, researchers, practitioners and local government politicians began to question the logic of traditional policies.[2] Research pointed to the diminishing significance of structural explanations of economic decline, that is, the domination of regional economies by declining basic industries.[3] Instead it was suggested that greater attention should be paid to factors such as poor management, shortages of development capital, inadequate infrastructure, low rates of new firm formation, and the absence of higher-level office activities and specialized financial, commercial and technical services. The policy implications of this type of analysis were to some extent recognized by regional planners in the 1970s. For example, the West Central Scotland Plan and the Northern Regional Strategy emphasized the need to improve the local economic environment and stimulate the indigenous sector rather than simply relying upon the movement of mobile industry to generate new jobs.[4] Underlying this approach were a number of objectives; in particular, the importance of improving a region's capacity to adapt its skills, attitudes, products, supporting institutions and infrastructure in response to changing economic circumstances.

It was recognized that this interpretation had significant organizational implications for the administration of policy. The nurturing of the indigenous, the small and the new required local knowledge and contacts in addition to selectivity in assistance. Selectivity meant not only variety in the instrument, but also discrimination in the industries, firms, areas and people which were helped in order to achieve local economic regeneration. It also implied the need to establish new agencies to facilitate such an approach.[5]

While such views were becoming increasingly fashionable in academic and professional circles during the 1970s, there was no comprehensive reassessment in central government. Rather the changes which were introduced in industrial and regional policy in this period reflected *ad hoc* responses to a range of national problems, specifically the need to improve the competitiveness of British industry, to reduce the overall level of public expenditure and to respond to the inner city crisis. In the regions themselves, faced with rising unemployment and an apparent failure on the part of central government to tackle their problems of economic malaise, new locally based initiatives began to emerge reflecting efforts to support existing industry and encourage new firm formation. Such initiatives were often undertaken by, or were the direct consequence of, actions taken by local authorities. By the turn of the decade civil servants were beginning to worry about the countervailing tendencies of these trends for nationally based urban and regional policy.

The following two sections of the chapter outline the emergence of these initiatives and the way in which central government in an *ad hoc* and uncoordinated manner was responding to changing national and regional economic problems.

THE INSTITUTIONAL RESPONSE TO CHANGING REGIONAL PROBLEMS

Regional Economic Policy

Until the mid-1970s the application of regional industrial policy rested on spatially differentiated industrial incentives combined with industrial location controls. The approach was always reactive, that is, both assistance and control applied to those manufacturing companies declaring their intention to move or expand their operations. The changing interpretation of the regional problem, the beginning of the slide into the recession exacerbated by the oil crises, the industrial strategy adopted by the Labour government in 1975 and the nationalist demands of the Celtic fringes created pressures for a more active, if not interventionist, form of regional policy.

The Industry Act 1975 set out a framework for regenerating British industry that recognized the need for more selectivity in the state's involvement in the economy and for direct investment by government in key sectors of industry. This approach was superimposed on the system of regional incentives which was retained as one dimension of economic policy contradicting to some extent the newly adopted sectoral approach. The centrepiece of the 1975 Act was the National Enterprise Board. More significant in the context of this chapter was the provision which set up the Scottish and Welsh Development Agencies. These agencies, which were originally intended to supplement the operations of the NEB, were charged with the task of restructuring the national economies of Scotland and Wales and given the powers and resources to do this in a far more sensitive way than was possible under a centrally operated policy. Their establishment was based on the underlying principles that a development agency ought to have the freedom to act outside the day-to-day political and bureaucratic constraints of government and to focus on the problems of the indigenously based industry sector rather than continue to rely on inward mobile investment.[6] The agencies have undertaken their role through a combination of powers to provide factor buildings and sites, derelict land clearance, advising small businesses, overseas promotion and through direct investment in companies.

Under the Conservatives they have been subject to much tighter financial control and encouraged to work in partnership with the private sector. In the case of the Scottish Development Agency (SDA) a further development has been the shift towards area-based investment programmes. Area projects, as they are known, are integrated urban renewal schemes with an industrial emphasis drawing together the SDA and regional and district councils.[7]

In the English regions regional economic policy has been managed in administrative and functional terms from Whitehall, with relatively limited autonomy given to the regional offices of the Department of Industry in handling selective financial assistance and other forms of industrial aid. However, a number of semi-autonomous government bodies have provided a more decentralized and specific focus for economic development, for example, the English Industrial Estates Corporation; in rural areas the Development Commission and its executive arm, the Council for Small Industries in Rural Areas (COSIRA); and the Department of Industry, Small Firms Service. There have also been a number of (English) regional agencies, the Industrial Development Associations (IDAs) concerned with industrial promotion, which have been jointly funded by central government and local authorities.

In recent years, however, support for these IDAs from some local authorities has been less than wholehearted. This is a reflection of the growing economic problems within the older, urban, industrial areas, and specifically a questioning of the relevance of industrial promotion strategies. In this context local authorities have begun to develop their own policies, focusing increasingly on indigenously based economic development rather than attracting inward investment.

Central Government Responses to Urban Problems: The Urban Programme

At a national level the economic and social problems posed by the decline of the urban areas took on increasing political significance towards the end of the 1970s. Following a review of inner city policy the urban programme, which had previously been the responsibility of the Home Office, was transferred to the Department of the Environment and reshaped to cover economic, industrial and environmental projects (see Chapter 5). The Inner Urban Areas Act 1978 proved to be an important stimulus to the development of local authority economic initiatives with designated district authorities given additional powers to declare industrial improvement areas and give a range of assistance to firms mainly for the provision, improvement and development of land and buildings.

However, from the outset there was a feeling among local authorities that the urban programme was more DoE policy than government policy. While there were some obvious contradictions between regional and inner city measures, it was also apparent that there was a lack of a corporate approach across central government departments. It was felt by some that 'the major economic department and agencies . . . are by no means totally committed to reversing the decline of the cities' (Lawless, 1981, p. 119).

More generally, local authorities have been angered by pressures from central government on partnership and programme authorities to cut expenditure on their main services, and pressure to spend money on the urban programme which has often involved projects seen as much less vital. Further, the initial conception of 'partnership' appears to have degenerated into the familiar pattern of local authorities proposing schemes and central government acting in judgement. Constraints both on the overall content of the programmes and on individual items within them have tightened under the Conservatives. There has been pressure to move away from social projects to economic and environmental projects, coupled with an emphasis on capital, as opposed to revenue schemes with a virtual embargo on schemes involving staff appointments. While the provision of additional funds and powers for local economic initiatives undoubtedly has stimulated this policy area in local government, some authorities have been unhappy about the extent and direction of control, particularly in regard to the 'capital' project bias as distinct from more employment and socially oriented schemes. However, at a time when local authorities have limited scope for action they have been forced to rely on the urban programme even though their priorities and analyses of need are sometimes at variance with those of central government and its agencies.

In 1981 the Secretary of State for the Environment introduced Enterprise Units into several DoE regional offices, in order to secure private sector involvement in the urban programme and greater co-ordination of the department's various economic initiatives. This development occurred at a time when a stream of new measures were being initiated: the legislation on enterprise zones, the idea of land registers, the introduction of urban development grants and the fostering of local enterprise agencies.

There are currently three such units in operation, in the north-west, the north-east and one covering both the East and West Midlands, based in Birmingham. Their work has been a mixture of exhortation, persuasion, the use of statutory powers where these have been available and efforts to 'bend' spending programmes to try to achieve the ends identified by ministers. To fulfil one of their main tasks, private sector involvement, the units have actively encouraged companies and business organizations to set up business advice centres in their areas and ensured that Chambers of Commerce in each of the partnership and programme authorities have been in agreement with the main thrust of the programmes before making urban programme payments. Underlying these efforts is the belief that the abilities required both to solve urban problems and to generate economic activity lie outside the structure of government and its bureaucracy.

This view was also implicit in the formation of the Urban Development Corporations to regenerate the decaying docklands of Merseyside and London, where some of the most complex problems of urban renewal are to be found. The aim was to mobilize private sector resources, reduce the bureaucracy involved in the land development process and, in the process, by-pass local authority planning policies. The objectives and general powers of UDCs are similar to those of the new towns and allow the corporations to bring land and buildings into effective use, to encourage the development of existing and new industry and commerce, to create an attractive environment, and to encourage people to live and work in the designated areas. In this regard there is an assumption that local authorities are too bureaucratic, slow to act and incapable of developing a satisfactory working relationship with the private sector. Central government has, therefore, seen fit to cut across local democratic institutions and control and co-ordinate policy implementation at the local level.

LOCAL AUTHORITY AND OTHER LOCAL ECONOMIC DEVELOPMENT AGENCIES AND INITIATIVES

The previous section has charted certain institutional responses by central government to changing urban and regional economic problems. These changes have to be seen within the wider context of rising unemployment, cuts in the levels of regional aid under both Conservative and Labour governments and the decision to significantly reduce the geographical coverage of assisted areas in 1979. As economic malaise spread throughout the country, even to previously prosperous regions, it is not surprising that a whole range of local economic and employment agencies and initiatives should develop in the policy vacuum left by central government. Such responses came from a wide range of organizations including trade unions, the business community, the voluntary sector, the unemployed themselves and, perhaps most important of all, local government.

In this role local government is uniquely well placed since it is the single public body whose concern resides with the interests of the local area. Although not possessing a clearly specified statutory remit to act in this policy field, local government has a significant range of functions and powers which directly and indirectly impact on the local economy. Local authorities are often the single largest employer in their area; they are major purchasers of goods and services in the local economy; through their education functions district authorities can directly influence the local labour market; they have statutory land use planning functions which can influence the type, scale and location of industrial and commercial development; and they are empowered to purchase land for industrial development, to clear derelict sites, to refurbish old factory buildings, to construct new factory units and in some cases declare industrial improvement areas. Local authorities can provide direct financial assistance to companies in the form of loans and grants as well as make available technical and business advice, and can engage in advertising campaigns to promote the advantages of their area.

The rapid expansion in local government activity in this field is apparent from the figures in Table 15.1, as is its significance in comparison with expenditure on regional economic policy. By 1981–2 the Department of the Environment estimated that total assistance by local authorities in England and Wales had risen to £218 million.

Table 15.1   *England and Wales Out-turn Prices (£m.)*

Local authority activities	1976–7	1977–8	1978–9
Local authority industrial estates and industrial development:			
capital	12	27	56
revenue	17	34	41
Advances and grants to industrial and commercial enterprises:			
capital	2	3	4
revenue	3	3	3
Government regional preferential assistance to industry			
Regional development grants	300	298	310
Selective financial assistance*	31	33	91
Factory building: EIEC	17	20	27
WDA	8	14	30
Calendar years	1976	1977	1978
Gross domestic fixed capital formation by industry (manufacturing sector)†	3,412	4,323	n.a.

* Figures for 'regional selective assistance' include payments to the Ford Motor Co. of £4·3m. in 1977–8 and £52m. in 1978–9.
† Figures for service sector not available; amounts include public sector investment.
n.a. = not available.
Sources: Regional Statistics, No. 15, 1980; *Burns Report*, 1980.

It is important, however, not to see local authority involvement purely in terms of direct economic development or employment-generating activity. There has also been a concern in recent years to facilitate inter-agency co-ordination and co-operation in the economic development tasks of the public sector and to forge links with the local business community and trade unions. One of the most significant developments has been the attempt to set up – sometimes in association with other interested parties – agencies to facilitate local economic development.

In this regard it is possible to identify three main types of organization: (1) local enterprise trusts and agencies; (2) local co-operative development agencies; and (3) local enterprise boards and economic development companies. While undertaking very different types of activity, such organizations have a number of features in common. They all seek to secure economic development through a locally based approach which builds on the skills, knowledge and commitment of individuals and organizations in the locality. They build on a 'shared awareness' of problems and a desire to work together for the common good of their area. Sometimes but not always the local authority has been the catalyst, facilitating their establishment. In certain areas there was a recognition by the local authority that there might be advantages in the agency distancing itself from the day-to-day bureaucratic procedures and constraints of local government and establishing a separate identity, perhaps, thereby achieving a closer empathy with the private sector. Through such a vehicle the scope for partnership between the public and private sector might be enhanced and hence the opportunity created for mobilizing additional resources to the task of economic regeneration.

It is useful to summarize the nature and character of each of the agencies in turn. Starting with enterprise trusts and agencies, these are business development organizations through which a number of firms in an area form a corporate identity with the objective of helping small businesses to start up and existing firms to prosper. These organizations are usually headed by a leading local businessman and backed up by the resources of sponsor firms giving advice on finance, management, marketing, legal procedures, accommodation and training.

The number of local enterprise agencies rapidly has multiplied since the late 1970s and recent estimates suggest that there are over 140 operating in different regions of the country.[8] Some of these organizations are based on local Chambers of Commerce. Undoubtedly the general philosophy behind enterprise trusts is that the private sector should provide the primary thrust since it has the experience and contacts. However, in some areas in the absence of private sector initiative the local authority has taken the lead and brought in private sector expertise to guide and run its own business advice centre.

Turning to the second type of organization, the co-operative development agency, it is important to bear in mind that there has been a rapid expansion in the number of co-operatives in the United Kingdom since the mid-1970s, which is due in some measure to the role of these bodies. Local government has played an important role in this context either by providing direct assistance to co-operatives in the form of advice, premises, or financial assistance, or indirectly by setting up co-operative development agencies in partnership with the local co-operative movement and other like-minded bodies. There are now over eighty co-operative development agencies in different regions of the country.

The third type of local development agency which has become increasingly prominent in recent years is the local authority development company or enterprise board. Local authorities have used the device of establishing development companies for a number of years to undertake those activities which are not within the local government legislation, that is, activities that could be regarded *ultra vires*. Originally local authorities used development companies primarily for land development purposes. By the end of the 1970s with increasing concern about local economic problems, the development aspect took on a specifically economic focus. The Manchester and Wigan development corporations, for example, were both established with the objective of providing infrastructure and land to secure commercial and industrial development.

The second stimulus to the growth of local authority development companies came with the imposition of central government capital expenditure controls in 1981. Local authorities were faced with the prospect of losing a substantial amount of capital resources unless they could find a means of undertaking expenditure prior to the imposition of controls. Some local authorities realized that by setting up separate, independent companies funds could be redirected and thus central government controls by-passed. This led to a significant increase in the number of local authority development companies in the 1980–1 period. A third phase of company formation came with the election of a number of more interventionist, Labour-controlled local authorities in 1981. They wanted to engage in direct intervention in industry through investment in local firms and it was felt that the legal position constrained the councils themselves from becoming directly involved in this type of activity. Establishing a company was again seen as a means for the local authority to become fully involved in the local economy.

As can be seen from Table 15.2, initial funding has usually been raised through section 137 of the Local Government Act and has varied from £600,000 to over £5 million. Additional funding has come directly from partnerships with private sector companies, banks, financial institutions and pension funds. In functional terms such organizations have been attractive to local authorities since they can develop business expertise and a management structure streamlined beyond the usual demands of local democratic accountability. Their separate legal identity and sometimes physical location from the town hall has meant that they are able to relate more easily to private businesses and financial institutions. While it is possible to identify certain common characteristics, there nevertheless remain fundamental differences in the style of operation and type of tasks undertaken. In addition, there are also differing political stances. The GLC and West Midlands enterprise boards, for example, reflect an overtly political perspective in their operations. Investments take into account the local authority's wider strategic policies and are encompassed within planning and investment agreements between the individual firms and the authority.

THE URBAN AND REGIONAL
ECONOMIC POLICY DEBATE

The previous two sections have shown that in recent years there has been a proliferation of economic development agencies undertaking a range of activities. Some have been central government-based, some locally based, while others have reflected a partnership between the public and private sectors. The emergence of some of these local institutions has undoubtedly caused disquiet in Whitehall and raises a whole series of questions about the future of urban and regional policy, including the extent to which central government should seek to control and regulate the activities of these organizations; the proper role of local government in economic development, and how far should central government seek to curtail its activities; should there be a role for public sector investment agencies at the regional and local levels; and how far central government needs to consider the question of co-ordination between its own regional and local agencies as well as the question of co-ordination with those of other bodies? Central government has been rather slow to come to grips with these issues.

Table 15.2 Funding of Local Authority Companies

Name of company	Parent authority	Year of registration	Initial funding (£m.)	Source of initial funding	Source(s) of continuing funding
Greater Manchester Economic Development Corporation Ltd	Greater Manchester CC and Metropolitan Districts	1979	5	Capital contribution from local authorities	
Wigan Metropolitan Development Co. Ltd	Wigan MBC	1980	2		
Oldham Economic Development Association Ltd	Oldham MBC	1980	0·77	Capital contribution from local authority	
Rochdale Economic Development Ltd	Rochdale MBC	1981	0·74		
Merseyside Economic Development Co. Ltd	Merseyside CC	1981	1·8		
Cheshire Economic Promotions Ltd	Cheshire CC	1981	2·0	Loan from county council	
Southwark Industrial & Development Co. Ltd	Southwark LBC	1981	1·04	Grant from local authority	
Greenwich Economic Development Co. Ltd	Greenwich LBC	1981	0·9	Capital contribution from local authority	
Swansea City Economic Development Co. Ltd	Swansea City Council	1981	0·66		
Kirklees Economic Development Ltd	Kirklees BC	1981	0·6		

Lancashire Enterprises Ltd	Lancashire CC	1982	2·1	Capital injection (section 137)	£2·55m. from Lancashire CC (capital grant), joint investments with district authorities and financial institutions
West Yorkshire Enterprise Board Ltd	West Yorkshire CC	1982	5·8	Grant from county council	
West Midlands Enterprise Board Ltd	West Midlands CC	1982	3·495	Grant from county council (section 137)	Grants from county council, joint investments with financial institutions and superannuation funds
Greater London Enterprise Board Ltd	GLC	1982			

Source: Compiled from various local authority documents.

The Development of Urban and Regional Economic Policy under the Conservatives

The review of regional economic policy undertaken in 1979 failed to reappraise the fundamental aims of the system. In particular, it left many questions unanswered about the relationship between the regional industrial policy of the DTI and the inner city policies of the DoE. In 1983 an inter-departmental committee of officials under a deputy secretary at the Treasury, Michael Quinlan, was asked to undertake a further review. At the same time, an inquiry was launched in the DoE to examine the inner city programme in the light of figures from the 1981 Census which indicated that high levels of unemployment were no longer confined to 'government-defined' inner city areas. Unfortunately when the government published its White Paper on Regional Policy in December 1983, there was little evidence of the wide-ranging discussions which had taken place in the Quinlan Committee. In the words of one distinguished observer,

> it is a tragic deterioration of a serious initiative to get regional policy right. Now it seems to be drifting towards ad hoc developments whereby the Secretary of State at the DTI gets better value for money . . . Government urban and regional policies are seriously inadequate. They are less cost effective and less co-ordinated than would be possible or is desirable. They need to be re-cast as soon as possible and re-cast together. (Manners, 1983, p. vi)

A further policy review of significance in the context of this discussion was that set up in May 1980 in response to pressure from local authority associations to clarify the position of local authority powers to aid industry, given that certain private Act powers would be coming up for renewal.[10] The inquiry which was headed by the chief planner at the DoE, Wilfred Burns, included representatives of the main local authority associations as well as the key government departments. It presented its evidence in July 1980 and there followed an eighteen-month delay while central government considered a response. It was rumoured that civil servants were surprised at the scale of local authority activity and this raised a whole series of difficult inter-departmental issues between DI, the DoE and the Treasury which proved difficult to resolve.

While the inquiry revealed substantial local authority activity, particularly in the field of infrastructure provision, the level of expenditure was relatively small in comparison with that on regional policy. The authorities themselves reported that they were constrained in their activities primarily because of difficulties with site development and the availability of resources. This problem had been made worse by new government capital expenditure controls. Private sector responses were: (1) critical of the use of financial incentives by local authorities; (2) argued that local authorities were seeking to outbid each other in the industrial promotion race; (3) stated that local authorities were not equipped to make commercial judgements; and (4) were concerned that the burden of the activities would fall on the rates.

Following the publication of the Burns Report the government proposed in its consultative paper a new general power for local authorities to assist independent firms employing up to twenty-five people subject to an annual limitation on their expenditure of the product of a half-penny rate. This would have replaced all local Act powers, and the use of section 137 of the Local Government Act 1972 (which enabled local authorities to spend up to a 2p rate product for the benefit of their areas) would no longer have been allowed, except for designated authorities under the inner urban areas act.

In practice the implementation of such legislation would have severely reduced the scope of local authority action in many parts of the country. However, following pressure in the House of Lords the government was forced to back down in the face of almost total hostility from the local authority associations and some of its own supporters. An amendment was drafted to the Local Government (Miscellaneous Provisions) Bill which effectively clarified the existing section 137 legislation as a general enabling power for the purposes of economic development.

However, of more significance in the context of this chapter were the statements made by the government in the consultative document about its view of local government involvement in economic development. They saw the contribution of local authorities as the proper exercise of statutory powers minimizing bureaucratic restrictions over businesses and avoiding unnecessarily heavy rate burdens. The government was at pains to point out that powers ought not to be used in wasteful industrial promotion. The primary role for local authorities was seen as 'assisting small firms which underpin the local economy and are relatively less mobile between different areas ... the location of larger mobile firms and plants is something which should be left to be determined by the interaction of market forces and the national regional incentives'. The government was also keen 'to encourage local authorities to use their new powers to assist industry and commerce directly, rather than set up special economic development agencies through which to channel assistance. Such agencies tend to develop into separate bureaucracies and hence to absorb some of the resources available' (see DoE, March 1982, p. 4).

Co-ordination of Central Government Policies
The Burns debate highlighted some of the major issues which need to be resolved in the development of a coherent approach to regional policy and regional and local agencies. One theme which arises time after time is the question of co-ordination: 'Too many agencies . . . competition . . . confusion . . . what is lacking is a body to co-ordinate initiatives' – these seem the key phrases of the moment. Goddard (1982) in a paper presented at the Civil Service college on 'Problems of co-ordination in industrial and environmental development' asked the question, what is the purpose of co-ordination? He said: 'co-ordination implies bringing policies into line not only with respect to one another but in relation to some common and higher objective. If such an objective does not exist then co-ordination becomes a "will of the wisp" concept, lacking any real substance'.[11] However, there is little point in central government arguing for greater co-ordination of regional and local agencies if it does not have a clear view of its own position. Unfortunately central government departments remain divided in their attitude and approach to this critical problem.

The experience of Michael Heseltine in Merseyside when he was Secretary of State for the Environment is instructive. It is widely known that the original ideas in his report after a trip to riot-torn Liverpool went far beyond the specific problems of Merseyside. They included: a new minister for inner cities; a major curtailment of the powers of metropolitan counties; a new central government directorate in each inner city to co-ordinate state spending and eliminate duplication and waste; and a new Whitehall committee to ensure that public spending was directly related to the assistance of private sector projects. With the exception of the last proposal, none proved acceptable. In practice they added up to: (1) a more active role for the DoE through integrated control over local government in inner city areas; and (2) an expanded role for DoE in economic development. Such proposals were resisted by the Department of Industry and the Treasury – 'because it is not clear how they could exercise control over it' (see *The Economist*, 6–14 August 1981).

What emerged in place of the original proposal was the appointment of the secretary of state as minister with special responsibility for Merseyside for one year, backed up by the taskforce. The aim appears to have been to bring together civil servants from various departments to ensure a more effective use of government money committed to the area and to secure through the authority of a Cabinet minister a 'community of purpose' out of people, companies and institutions.

Mr Heseltine undoubtedly secured some successes but there remained a number of fundamental problems. The failure to adopt a coherent view at the centre meant that there was 'an apparent reluctance to study the best overall deployment of public resources across Merseyside' (see McConaghy, 1982, p. 7). In 1981–2 local authorities were responsible for less than one-third of public expenditure in Merseyside. At the end of the day it is central government which is the main spender and controller of public sector agencies at the local level. Ironically while the Merseyside taskforce was exhorting local authorities to undertake various new activities, the DoE was cutting back their major municipal programmes via rate support grant.

The Heseltine approach was based on a series of *ad hoc* initiatives launched at the local level, many of which were dependent on the personal drive, commitment and intervention of the secretary of state. Laudable as it was, such an approach which has been repeated in different forms in other English regions cannot form the basis for a coherent long-term response to the economic and social problems of Britain's cities and regions. What is required is a fundamental rethink at the centre about the way public resources are allocated and policies formulated.

This point was clearly articulated by the ADC in their policy statement on employment creation:

> there are a number of serious impediments in the path of district councils who seek to tackle local economic, social and environmental problems comprehensively and in a corporate manner. One considerable handicap in practice is the inability of Central government to take an inter-departmental view of the local government services. This lack of corporate organisation within Central government results in a serious failure to understand and respond to the corporate approach locally. Central government could do much more to make the 'boundaries' between departments and policies, as they affect local authorities fewer and less rigid. Nowhere does this apply with more force than to policies of economic development and employment, where a greater corporate approach is needed

between the Departments of Environment, Industry and Employment. (Association of District Councils, 1981, p. 5)

Industrial Promotion and Advice

The question of co-ordination is not simply a matter of ensuring that there is a coherent view at the centre; it is also necessary to establish a satisfactory working relationship between agencies operating at the regional and local levels. This issue is of particular significance in regard to the question of industrial promotion.

Surveys undertaken for the Burns Report (1980) demonstrated that the great majority of local authorities were in different ways active in this field. Some were concerned with promotion of the area as a whole, others concentrated on individual sites and premises. It was recognized that there were dangers of overlap and duplication. This led the Burns Committee to argue that there was a need for more consultation among local authorities and between local government, regional and national bodies with a view to securing consistency of approach and value for money. This was a thoroughly sensible suggestion; however, the government went much further in its consultation paper when it sought to curtail the use of section 137 of the Local Government Act on the grounds that local authorities were using their powers wastefully in competition with one another and that they were deflecting mobile industry from government-designated assisted and inner city areas. Underlying the attempt to restrict assistance to firms of no more than twenty-five was undoubtedly the belief that this would prevent local authorities from distorting the government's 'fine-tuned' regional and inner city policy.

However, critics have pointed out that there is no evidence that local authority activities have seriously affected national policies, indeed a submission presented to the Burns Inquiry indicated that 'local authorities are focusing more on encouragement and creation of local industry than on attracting mobile industry'.[12] The irony is that it is the failure of central government's own regional and inner city policies based on outmoded assumptions about mobile industry and a precise demarcation of areas of economic decline that has forced local authorities outside these areas with high levels of unemployment to adopt indigenously based economic development strategies. Moreover, it is important to recognize that a very significant proportion of all expenditure on industrial promotion in the United Kingdom comes from government-funded agencies including the new towns expenditure by local authorities is small fry in comparison. Thus at the end of the day if sense is to be made of the industrial promotion problem, the lead has to come from central government.

LOCAL DISCRETION, FLEXIBILITY AND THE QUESTION OF FINANCE

The debate about industrial promotion highlights a further issue concerning the future development of urban and regional policy, namely, the extent to which central government should allow discretion and flexibility in the development of economic policies at the local level. The consultative paper seemed to accept that local authorities have a positive role to play and that they were the best judge of what was appropriate at the local level, yet the attempt to limit their economic development budget and to target assistance to small firms seemed to contrast with these assertions. Significantly the Association of British Chambers of Commerce argued in evidence to the Burns Inquiry that legislation should be flexible to cope with varying circumstances and pointed out that the economy cannot rely on small firms alone. They argued that too much emphasis on the sector was economically unsound. Monitoring in designated inner city areas has shown that jobs generated by small firms compensate for less than 10 per cent of overall job loss. Many local authorities see small-firm policies as just one component in their overall strategy and a number are placing increased emphasis on job retention in existing small- to medium-sized companies.

The attempt to restrict the scale and scope of local authority involvement in economic development seemed to reflect a further view of the government, namely, that local authorities are not adequately equipped to make financial judgements and cannot be relied upon to establish a successful relationship with the private sector. There is no hard evidence, however, to support such a view. Indeed, Mr Peter Walker of the Co-operative Bank, made the following observations at a 'Finance for industry' seminar in 1982:

Fears about L.A.s having the necessary commercial judgement to provide selective aid to industry are not necessarily shared by the banks . . . we have no evidence that L.A.s wish to use their powers in an irresponsible manner . . . Authorities such as West Midlands, Lancashire, South Yorkshire, Derbyshire, Sheffield and Newcastle have made it clear they wish to support only viable enterprises or those which appear to have good medium to long term prospects. (Walker, 1982, p. 11)

While the government was thwarted in its attempts to curtail local economic initiatives directly in the Local Government (Miscellaneous) Provisions Act 1982, its more recent efforts to control the general level of local government expenditure pose an equally if not more serious challenge to this policy area.

Local Government Finance and the Abolition of the Metropolitan Counties

Towards the end of the first period of Conservative government the issue of the reform of the rating system, local government expenditure and the role of the metropolitan counties loomed large in the thinking of the government. Such issues were, of course, not unrelated to the question of local authority economic initiatives. Much of the pressure for the reform of the rating system came from businessmen who objected to what they regarded as excessive rate rises in a period of economic recession. As the Burns Inquiry (1980) revealed, the business community felt that certain local councils were undertaking economically unsound and sometimes politically motivated employment initiatives, while at the same time putting viable companies out of business through rate increases. In this context the metropolitan counties, significantly all Labour-controlled and with unemployment rates above the national average, were often regarded as the major culprits.

Following its re-election in the summer of 1983 the government moved swiftly to tackle these problems. Having failed to come up with an alternative to the rating system, it introduced a White Paper indicating the government's intention to introduce a selective rate-capping procedure on high-spending local authorities backed up by general reserve powers.[13] In a separate White Paper, '*Streamlining the Cities*' (1983), it indicated its intention to abolish the metropolitan counties. Both measures have fundamental implications for the future development of local economic initiatives.

As far as the financing of local economic development is concerned this has already been badly affected by earlier efforts to curtail local government expenditure. There is no specific provision in the block grant schemes for expenditure on economic development, and it thus has to compete with other services for scarce resources. The capital control scheme introduced under the 1980 Act had a serious impact on the capital allocation of all local authority services but none more so than economic development.

The rate-capping legislation, and ominously the government's intention to give further consideration to the use of the 2p rate, is likely to place the local economic initiatives of those urban and largely Labour-controlled authorities in areas of economic decline under even greater pressure.

Turning to the question of local government reform, it is significant that the White Paper indicated that no specific arrangements needed to be made in respect of the loss of economic programmes of the metropolitan counties since it was argued that district councils already had the necessary powers. Irrespective of the merits of a second tier, the government's view that there is no requirement for a strategic economic development function in the major urban areas is somewhat short-sighted. The demand for major public investment opportunities cannot always be generated within the confines of a single local authority boundary. Similarly, economic problems and processes can spill over local authority boundaries.

In addition to carrying out their own economic initiatives and their involvement in partnerships and programmes, the metropolitan counties have been able to devote greater resources to research, lobbying and securing funds from the EEC than has often been possible in district authorities. They have also been innovative in developing new approaches to economic development. The 1976 Tyne and Wear private Act, for example, was influential in devising a number of concepts introduced in the inner city programme and Greater Manchester, West Midlands, West Yorkshire, Merseyside metropolitan counties and the GLC have introduced further innovations particularly enterprise boards and development companies.

CONCLUSION

This chapter has charted the institutional response to urban and regional problems in the past decade, in the context of the changing relationship between central and local government. The historical approach to tackling problems of area-based economic decline was one of transferring jobs via mobile industry policy to nationally designated 'assisted areas'. During the 1970s the traditional approach was undermined by changing macro-economic circumstances. Declining competitiveness of the national economy demanded a greater emphasis in the industrial aid system on improving productivity rather than encouraging industrial relocation. The IDC system was no longer effective with limited economic growth and politically unpopular with high unemployment spread throughout the country.

Under the Conservatives expenditure on regional policy and the geographical coverage of the assisted areas was reduced. The traditional approach was also undermined by the changing interpretation of regional problems with higher and more widespread unemployment and new policy prescriptions which suggested a greater focus on assisting indigenous industry and improving the local economic environment.

Despite the changing context there was no fundamental review of regional policies by central government. However, there were a number of *ad hoc* developments in response to the changing situation reflecting the requirements for a more decentralized and locally based approach. In Scotland and Wales, for example, regional development agencies were established, focusing their policies on indigenous economic development. In the English regions the Development Commission, English Industrial Estates Corporation and the DTI's Small Firms Advice Service came to play an increasingly important role. The development of the urban programme provided another example of the emergence of a more locally based approach to economic development, encouraging local authority initiatives in partnership with central government. While these developments were taking place at central government level, in the policy vacuum left by the reduction of assisted areas local authority and other locally based initiatives emerged as a counter to rising unemployment and economic decline. These initiatives grew in scale and momentum, while many in central government remained unaware of their existence or significance.

Set against the trend to a more locally based approach to economic development, a number of centralizing and regulating tendencies are discernible. While extra finance was being made available to designated districts for local economic initiatives, the very same authorities were suffering the effects of reductions in rate support grant. And while fostering local economic initiatives, central government sought to control them through 'partnership' structures. A lack of confidence in the ability of local government to tackle the complex problems of urban renewal and economic decline was reflected in the manner in which central government attempted to regulate the activities of the partnership and programme authorities and in the decision to establish Urban Development Corporations. Central government seemed to hold the view that the public sector could not go it alone in urban regeneration, and furthermore that local government was too bureaucratic and lacked the expertise to undertake local economic initiatives. Central government has, therefore, sought wherever possible both to encourage and manage the relationship between local government and the private sector.

By the early 1980s the proliferation of economic development agencies and organizations, both within central government and at the local level, began to pose questions about duplication and overlap of activities and demonstrated a lack of co-ordination and overall direction in public policy. The response from central government was a series of direct and indirect attempts to review the various aspects of this policy field. The reviews of regional policy in 1979 and 1983–4, the DoE's examination of inner city policy in 1983, the Burns Inquiry (1980) into local authority economic initiatives, and the various proposals for the reform of local government and its financing, reflected a failure to come to grips with this complex problem.

The Burns debate highlighted a series of important questions about the role of local authority economic initiatives. The attempt to curtail powers and resources in order to fit them within the context of an outmoded regional policy reflected a lack of knowledge of development on the ground and was, therefore, doomed to failure, voted out by the government's own supporters in the House of Lords. The Quinlan review (1982), which raised complex issues concerning the relationship between DoE and DTI policies, proved too difficult for Whitehall to handle and the subsequent White Paper did not consider in any detail the increasingly important role played by local authorities in economic development. This attitude was also reflected in *Streamlining the Cities* (1983), with no recognition given to the major contribution played by the metropolitan counties in economic regeneration and an ominous reference to a further review of the use of section 137 of the Local Government Act 1972.

At a time of rising unemployment and further planned reduction of expenditure on regional policy it is not surprising that local authorities should view these developments with concern. Given the nature of present problems, it is only at the local level that many of the tasks of economic regeneration can be effectively implemented. Local government has the political will and, in many respects, the information and capacity to regenerate the local economy, but it does not have the resources. What is required is the development of a better relationship between the centre and the regions, which allows central government to develop broad overall strategies and control over the general level of expenditure and yet, at the same time, gives local government and other local agencies the means to develop and implement policies tailored to the needs of specific localities.

NOTES: CHAPTER 15

1   See Department of Trade and Industry, 1983.
2   See Firn, 1980; Segal, 1979.
3   Fothergill and Gudgin, 1979.
4   See Northern Region Strategy Team, 1977.
5   Mawson, 1981.
6   Cunningham, 1978.
7   Wannop, 1984.
8   Commission of the European Economic Communities, 1983.
9   ibid.
10   Burns Report, 1980.
11   Goddard, 1982.
12   Convention of Scottish Local Authorities, 1980, p. 9.
13   Department of the Environment, 1983b.

REFERENCES: CHAPTER 15

Association of District Councils (1981), *Economic Development by District Councils. Paper 3, Business Enterprise Agencies*, Report of the Industrial Land and Development Working Party (London: ADC).

Burns Report (1980), *Review of Local Authority Assistance to Industry and Commerce* (London: Department of the Environment).

Cambridge Economic Policy Review (1980), 'Regional policy for the 1980s', *Cambridge Economic Policy Review*, vol. 60, no. 2, pp. 36–46.

Commission of the European Economic Communities (1983), *Community Action to Combat Unemployment. The Contribution of Local Employment Initiatives*, COM (83) 622 Final (Brussels: EEC).

Convention of Scottish Local Authorities (1980), *Evidence to the Inquiry into Local Authority Assistance to Industry and Commerce (Burns Inquiry)* (Edinburgh: COSLA).

Cunningham, E. B. (1978), 'Regional policy and the role of a development agency', paper presented to PTRC Summer Annual Meeting, University of Warwick, 10–13 July 1978.

Department of the Environment (DoE) (1982), *Local Authority Assistance to Industry and Commerce*, consultation paper (London: DoE), March.

DoE (1983a), *Streamlining the Cities: Government Proposals for Re-organizing Local Government in Greater London and the Metropolitan Counties*, Cmnd 9063 (London: HMSO).

DoE (1983b), *Rates: Proposals for Rate Limitation and Reform of the Rating System*, Cmnd 9008 (London: HMSO).

Department of Trade and Industry (1983), *Regional Industrial Development*, Cmnd 9111 (London: HMSO), December.

The Economist (1981), 'Heseltine worries colleagues with his ghetto plans for them', *The Economist*, 6–14 August, pp. 19–20.

J. Firn (1980), 'Economic policies for the conurbation', in G. Cameron (ed.), *The Future of the British Conurbations* (London: Longman), pp. 252–76.

Fothergill, B., and Gudgin, G. (1979), *Regional Employment Change: A Subregional Explanation*, Progress in Planning series (Oxford: Pergamon).

Goddard, J. B. (1982), 'A possible framework for co-ordination in the regions', paper presented at Problems of Co-ordination in Industrial and Environmental Development Seminar, Civil Service College, Sunningdale, 20–21 December.

Lawless, P. (1981), *Britain's Inner Cities: Problems and Policies* (London and New York: Harper & Row).

McConaghy, D. (1982), 'Consultations or conflict?', *Plannernews* (August), pp. 7–8.

Manners, G. (1983), *Report of an Inquiry into Regional Problems in the United Kingdom* (Norwich: Regional Studies Association/Geo Books).

Mawson, J. (1981), 'Changing directions in regional policy and the implications for local government', *Local Government Studies*, vol. 7, no. 2 (March–April), pp. 68–74.

Northern Regional Strategy Team (1977), *Strategic Plan for the Northern Region. Main Report* (Newcastle upon Tyne: NRST).

Segal, N. S. (1979), 'The limits and means of self-reliant regional economic growth', in D. Maclennan and J. B. Parr, *Regional Policy, Past Experiences and New Directions* (London: Martin Robertson), pp. 211–24.

Tyler, P., Moore, B., and Rhodes, J. (1980), 'New developments in the evaluation of regional policy', paper presented to SSRC Urban and Regional Economics Seminar, Birmingham University, April.

Walker, P. (1982), Report of a talk at the Finance for Industry Seminar, in *Industry, Commerce and Development: Official Journal of the Association of Industrial Development Officers*, vol. 1 (July–August), pp. 11–12.

Wannop, V. (1984), 'Strategic planning and the area development projects of the Scottish Development Agency', *Regional Studies*, vol. 18, no. 1 (February).

16

Racial Disadvantage

KEN YOUNG

Exploring central–local relations in the field of race is fraught with difficulty, not the least is that there is no discrete policy sector of race. Rather racial and ethnic issues arise within many diverse policy sectors including, crucially, education, housing and employment. Accordingly, race-related initiatives are the property of no single government department. Indeed, even the lead role of the Home Office is shrouded in ambiguity: while the Home Secretary has 'the leading Ministerial role in relation to race relations and racial disadvantage and thus a responsibility for shaping the climate and setting the direction in this field', nevertheless 'individual Departments must remain responsible for their own policies and programmes'.[1]

This plurality of institutions is compounded by a plurality of goals, ranging from 'good race (i.e. inter-group) relations' through multi-culturalism to 'equality of opportunity' and racial equality. Yet these goals are not themselves unambiguous; the last is frequently seen as antithetical to the first as when the government warns that 'measures to combat racial disadvantage may be counterproductive if they foster resentment in other sections of the community'.[2]

Moreover, while these and other objectives have been articulated at different times by diverse central and local policy-makers, the means chosen for their pursuit have more often been covert than overt, more often passive than active and more often inexplicit than explicit. 'Doing good by stealth' is a frequently quoted characterization of central departments' activities; even 'doing good by doing little' has in the past been seen as an appropriate way to proceed.[3] The policy positions of central departments and local authorities, and in particular the not uncommon 'policy not to have a policy', are a manifestation of the *culture of inexplicitness* which deprecates any differentiation of people in terms of their ethnic or racial origins and so renders race issues and race policy initiatives undiscussable.[4]

This combination of factors – the plurality of institutions and goals, compounded by inexplicitness – served to shape central–local relations in respect of race throughout the 1960s and 1970s. They continued to prevail at least until 1981, notwithstanding the apparent espousal of ethnic pluralism during Roy Jenkins's second period at the Home Office, the publication of the Labour government's White Paper and the subsequent Race Relations Act 1976. Indeed, when PSI accepted a Home Office brief to investigate 'policy implementation in the field of racial disadvantage' during 1979–81, it was quickly found that the question was misconceived; there was very little central 'policy' whose local implementation could be studied. As a senior civil servant remarked during the early spring of 1980, race issues were 'rather on the back burner'. Yet the aptness of this metaphor – back burner issues can boil over – was well established a few weeks later by the eruption of violence in the St Paul's area of Bristol.[5]

The impact of the riots has been considerable. Indeed, central–local relations in respect of race fall into two distinct periods: that before the disorders of 1981, and that which followed. Although the response of government in the last two years has not been entirely consistent, still less strategic, many new developments have taken place each of which, however modest in itself, adds its weight to the cumulative impact of change. Race is no longer a back-burner issue. The Scarman Report, the report of the House of Commons Home Affairs Committee and our own study for the Home Office were all published in the summer and autumn of 1981[6]. All three to some degree, and in the terms appropriate to their authorship, commended the Department of the Environment for its active and comparatively energetic approach to tackling deprivation through the urban programme.

Experienced Whitehall-watchers will have enjoyed the subsequent spectacle of the former Secretary of State for the Environment grasping the opportunity to extend his department's territory to the apparent discomfiture of the Home Office. Michael Heseltine's Merseyside initiative generated several important new developments in urban policy.[7] More generally, Sir George Young – Heseltine's parliamentary under-secretary – was designated as the minister with specific responsibilities for race-related matters within the DoE, upstaging for a while the formal and continuing responsibilities of Home Office ministers. The urban programme once again proved its flexibility as an instrument of policy; with some steering and signalling from Sir George, a significant upturn in 'black benefit' projects occurred, despite the recently emphasized thrust of the urban programme as a measure of economic regeneration.[8]

The introduction of the civil service ethnic monitoring experiment to ascertain the ethnic composition of the government's own workforce and its subsequent extension may well prove important, not least for its possible effects on an issue the discussion of which is often overweighted with symbolism.[9] The Secretary of State for Employment's acceptance of the CRE's Code of Practice and its prompt approval by Parliament is also significant. Moreover, the acceptance of the Code which came into force in 1984 signals the beginning of an intense campaign by the Commission for Racial Equaity (CRE) to secure its adoption in employment practices, not least those of local authorities.[10]

The Commission has itself proved to be a centre of development and change, partly in response to the further report from the Home Affairs Committee.[11] The new chairman, Peter Newsam, is held in high regard in many local authorities. Nevertheless, the Commission's relations with them are never likely to be comfortable: local government people have in the past been quick to dismiss the Commission and local authorities have an inbuilt disposition to reject comparisons and to resist 'outside pressure'.[12]

One body which has traditionally been concerned to exert pressure for development and change in the education field is Her Majesty's Inspectorate (HMI); Sheila Browne, the retiring Chief Inspector, has been succeeded by Eric Bolton, who has been long identified with the provision of more appropriate multi-ethnic, multi-cultural education.

These recent developments, taken together with a large number of specific and unspectacular ministerial initiatives, demonstrate a new commitment to look constructively at the specific problems faced by black Britons. As a result, issues of opportunity and equity are beginning to achieve salience within the central–local government relationship. Space does not permit a full review of the ways in which this is happening; a more selective and focused approach is called for. Accordingly, this chapter reviews, first, the broad approach of government to the goal of *tackling racial disadvantage*. Secondly, it mentions some of the factors which appear to bear upon local authority responses to race issues. Finally, a *control/capacity analysis* is proposed as a tool for understanding the nature and limits of effective intervention in this highly charged area of racial discrimination and disadvantage.

CENTRAL GOVERNMENT AND RACIAL DISADVANTAGE

Not all of the various goals which have been enunciated in respect of race are engaged by the processes of central–local relations. For example, securing good inter-group relations or 'racial harmony' has been seen historically as a primary concern of Community Relations Councils (CRCs) rather than local authorities, although the latter also have to pay regard to good race relations under the 1976 Act.[13] The goals of those authorities which have chosen to celebrate *multi-ethnicity* and its consequent cultural, religious and linguistic diversity lie well beyond the boundaries of what is seen as feasible central encouragement, but by the same token no particular obstructions are placed in their path by central government. Tackling racial *discrimination* in local authority activities is generally seen from Whitehall as something for the local authorities themselves to take on within the framework of the law; it is left to the CRE to seek its enforcement, to make the necessary exhortations and thus to draw the fire of opposition. These very broad goals are somewhat peripheral to central–local government relations. For the purposes of this discussion the range of central government concern is encompassed by the aim of tackling *racial disadvantage*.

Racial disadvantage is currently defined in terms of disproportionate deprivation, wherein many members of the ethnic minority communities

> experience the deprivations of the poorer sector section of the white community, but to a greater extent. This is due to a variety of factors: newness, cultural differences, demographic factors (for example, the younger age structure of the ethnic minority population with young people in general suffering disproportionately during the recession) and racial discrimination (which is difficult to prove but remains a factor). (House of Commons Home Affairs Committee, 1982, p. 4)

The term racial disadvantage gained popular currency in the mid-1970s with the publication of Smith's *Racial Disadvantage in Britain* (1977). The House of Commons Home Affairs Committee turned its attention to this issue in its 1981 report on *Racial Disadvantage*.[14] The theme was taken up by a specially convened (and indeed unique) joint working party of civil servants from the relevant Whitehall departments and the three local authority associations; their report, *Local Authorities and Racial Disadvantage*, was published in 1983 and is an important milestone in the changing approach to race matters.[15] The latest (October 1983) publication in the DoE Inner Cities Directorate series on the urban programme is actually entitled *Tackling Racial Disadvantage*. This is not to say that the concept of racial disadvantage has been properly thought through, for in particular it evades the important question of how far the experience of *discrimination* should be counted an important component of *disadvantage*. The too-ready and sometimes glib use of the term racial disadvantage tends to deflect attention from the discriminatory practices which to some extent sustain it. If racial disadvantage refers to a disproportionately low level of possession, by minority ethnic groups, of a range of life-chance attributes, then exclusionary practices – 'institutional discrimination' – undoubtedly play a part in producing such disproportionality. So far, governments have failed to consider whether a more promising route to the eradication of 'disproportionate' disadvantage among Asian and Afro-Caribbean people might lie in taking positive steps to eliminate discrimination, both direct and indirect, against them. The Commission for Racial Equality is the sole official body to urge changed practices and it is hardly surprising that, in the absence of corresponding pressures from government, it is seen by many public sector people as engaged in special pleading.

Moreover, closer inspection of racial disadvantage as a current policy concern of the Department of the Environment suggests that it amounts to little more than a rediscovery of race within the longer-standing concern for urban deprivation. Central and local initiatives alike have followed the timeworn pattern of directing resources towards specific small-area concentrations of deprivation (area-targeting) combined with some limited resources directed to the needs of particular locally based ethnic minority organisations (group-targeting). The organic nature of policy change in bureaucracies is such that much of what is now done is an extrapolation of past practice.

The substance of the Department of the Environment's attack on racial disadvantage is therefore redolent of earlier, equally particularistic approaches to urban deprivation, and reflects the centrality of the urban programme in the department's range of policy tools. For DoE ministers, the urban programme is an unusually flexible instrument of policy, relatively easily retargeted from year to year, and (subject to the authority within the Cabinet of the secretary of state) relatively elastic in its expenditure limits.

The urban programme is rightly seen as having a significance far in excess of what the global sums would imply, in particular, for its direction of resources through voluntary sector projects to the minority communities themselves; moreover, more than 40 per cent of Britain's black population live in partnership and programme areas. None the less, the government's emphasis on the urban programme runs the risk, common to all supplementary schemes and bodies, of operating at the margin of mainstream practice and resource allocation.

Central government has generally been less concerned with such mainstream practices as the provision of services, its role here being limited by the extent to which local authorities as service delivery agencies are themselves willing to recognize and respond to ethnic diversity. Consider, for example, the housing needs of extended Asian families in relation to the patterns of housing provision maintained by local housing authorities; the dietary, dress and religious requirements of, for example, the Muslim communities in relation to the practices of many schools; or the restricted availability of a wide range of services and benefits to communities to whom English is a second language. The diversity of needs is now gradually becoming recognized among the service professionals, and the last few years have seen a flurry of reports which embody the first stages of a process of professional self-questioning, prompted and encouraged in most cases by the CRE.[16]

Among the means by which local authorities can adapt their service provision to an ethnically diverse clientele is through the appointment of specialist staff to work with the ethnic minority communities and to advise on the adjustment of service provision; and foremost among the ways in which such developments can be facilitated and encouraged is the operation, by the Home Office, of the scheme of grant aid available under section 11 of the Local Government Act 1966. Here again there have been recent developments of major importance to central–local relations.

Section 11 empowers the Home Secretary to make payments in respect of the salaries of staff appointed by those local authorities which have to make 'special provision in the exercise of their functions in consequence of the presence within their areas of substantial numbers of immigrants from the Commonwealth whose language or customs differ from those of the rest of the community'.[17] A subsequent circular defined the limits of this 'additional burden' as encompassing 'a person, adult or child, born in another country of the Commonwealth, who has been ordinarily resident in the United Kingdom for less than ten years and the child of such a person'. Local authorities' own eligibility for grant aid was judged in the first instance by the incidence of immigrant children on their school rolls.[18]

The failings of section 11 have long been recognized, particularly as regards the restrictiveness of the Commonwealth origin and ten-year residence criteria and the inappropriateness of assessing eligibility on the basis of a school population. Faced with trenchant criticism by the House of Commons Home Affairs Committee, the government announced in 1982 that certain elements of the scheme would be revised within the limits of the existing statute, fresh legislation having been ruled out.[19]

The details of the section 11 scheme and its recent revision cannot be excluded from any consideration of recent central–local relations, for it is an eloquent example of how the 1981 riots, having established the existence of a grievance, prompted more far-reaching reforms than would otherwise have occurred. The primary issue for this discussion is the extent to which the current administration of the scheme reinforces the widespread moves among local authorities to review their provision and to revise their decision-making structures the better to meet the needs of their multi-racial areas. Here as with the urban programme, government practice has shifted notably since the riots of 1981, and as a result section 11 expenditure has risen progressively from £40 million in 1978–9 to around £90 million in 1983–4.

Two points need to be made about the revision of section 11. The first concerns the wide range of staff appointments which can benefit from section 11 entitlement. Throughout most of its life section 11 has been used to support additional teaching staff in schools, and still the greater proportion of expenditure is made by LEAs for this purpose. The growth in expenditure is, however, also attributable in part to the quickening uptake of grant opportunities in local authority departments outside education. Notable examples would be in planning, social services and housing departments, in the appointment of personnel officers with equal-opportunity responsibilities or – most significantly perhaps – in the rapid spread of race relations advisers and units, where the officials concerned are often expected to change institutional practices, and where their support staff may also be funded by section 11 grant. There are indications that the Home Office is concerned to bring the possibilities of exploiting this scheme, itself uniquely free from cash limits, to the attention of local authorities and to take a flexible and sympathetic approach to helping them to meet locally defined needs.

The second point is that, as a *quid pro quo* for the liberalization of section 11, the new arrangements provide for a review of all existing posts and a (renewable) limit of three years on new posts. The review process, the details of which were announced in a circular letter of 30 August 1983, is of the greatest importance to central–local relations with regard to race.[20] The Home Office has asked local authorities to review and report on whether existing posts meet the criteria announced in circular 97/1982, wherein the post must 'meet the needs of Commonwealth immigrants', needs which 'are either different in kind from, or are the same but proportionately greater than, those of the rest of the community'. The post must 'represent special provision by the local authority', and the post holder must be readily identified. Moreover, in scrutinizing individual posts in the light of these criteria local authorities 'will need to consider their existing Section 11 provision in the light of *their general strategy for meeting the needs* of the Commonwealth immigrants in their areas and in the light of consultation with the intended beneficiaries of the provision' (emphasis added). Reports will be expected to include a statement of the objectives of the posts or schemes, and to indicate to what extent these objectives are being met. Home Office officials will then review these reports, visiting some local authorities and discussing their provision with them.

Civil servants are not much given to hyperbole, and the recent remark by one of them that these changes in section 11 constitute 'a quiet revolution' may be a fair assessment. The review requirements, coupled with the encouragement of new types of post, promises to shift the emphasis within the pattern of local provision. Without a doubt, many LEAs will find it difficult to justify their section 11 teaching provision without some redeployment; the review calls for a degree of explicitness about provision *for* minority ethnic pupils that will not come easily to them. The original assumption that section 11 was to be seen as resource supplementation to those carrying the 'burden' occasioned by the very presence of Commonwealth immigrants can no longer be sustained. Having ruled out the legislative replacement of section 11, the government has gone about as far as is feasible within these statutory constraints. The continued reference to 'Commonwealth immigrants' is irksome to many, but the substance of the changes has been generally welcomed. Thus the Home Office has succeeded in sharpening this important policy tool; it remains to be seen how energetically it will use it.

These changes of emphasis by the central departments signify a more explicit approach to tackling racial disadvantage. However, as the Labour government acknowledged in 1976, it is at the local level where ultimately the future of race relations will be determined. How, then, do these initiatives at the national level engage with the policy processes of the local authorities themselves?

LOCAL AUTHORITIES AND THE REDISCOVERY OF RACE

While the Department of the Environment, the Home Office and the CRE may appear to be initiating change by adopting a promotional role, their endeavours can do no more than capitalize on locally generated processes of change, facilitating, encouraging, and disseminating the fruits of experience elsewhere. The dynamic in policy development remains a local quality.[21] That this process of change is driven from the periphery, not the centre, is in part due to adaptations in professional practice arising in the field, much change being practitioner-led. In part it is because the desires and demands of particular minority groups differ as between localities and are increasingly expressed in local politics. In part it is because some councils have defined black minority ethnic interests as an important constituency, even where local groups are neither vocal nor attempting to exert much influence. Many local politicians and officers now find themselves driven in unexpected directions by this recent rediscovery of race.

In July 1982 I published an article setting out the then existing pattern of local activity as it appeared to me.[22] I characterized local authorities in four groups: the *pioneers*, those who were at the frontier of equal opportunity: the *learners*, those with a commitment to change and considerable uncertainty as to what to do; the *waverers*, those whose concern was expressed among leading members and officers but where the risks of change seemed too high; and the *resisters*, those who repeatedly claimed to 'have no problems here'. This grouping was intended to make the point that the DoE (and other agencies) should adopt a *differentiated* approach to the promotion of change. It may, however, be thought to imply a continuum, a curve of learning, with authorities steadily moving 'up the line' towards the adoption of policies appropriate to a multi-racial society.

If this (unintended) implication was misleading in 1982, it is all the more so today. The election of a number of left-inclined Labour councils confirms that there is no single route to equality of opportunity; nor, perhaps, is there any irreversible direction. Attempts by Labour groups to monopolize the issue of racial equality can be divisive (in the sense that they may discourage other authorities of different complexion), and fragile (in the sense that they diminish the chances of continuous development of policy and practice under another regime). Further, the ambitions which are expressed in some recent declarations of policy are lacking in substance: symbolic, declamatory and rhetorical. There is little evidence of any appreciation of the timescale and intractability of the types of fundamental organizational change which the Race Relations Act 1976 calls for.

Even today, there is little recognition of the force of the statutory responsibility which local authorities have under section 71 of the Race Relations Act 1976. Section 71 states that:

> it shall be the duty of every local authority to make appropriate arrangements with a view to securing that their various functions are carried out with due regard to the need
> (a) to eliminate unlawful racial discrimination, and
> (b) to promote equality of opportunity, and good relations, between persons of different racial groups.

The interpretation of section 71 is a crucial aspect of local authority responses on race.

The history of section 71 is itself indicative of the general reluctance on the part of government to impose such an obligation on local authorities. The clause was introduced by a Labour backbencher at the committee stage of the Bill and was resisted by the government, only to be reinstated in amended form under crossfire from the House of Lords and the local authority associations.[23] The government view at the time was that such a declaratory provision, backed by neither sanctions nor resources, could only create cynicism and disenchantment. The subsequent circular which brought the Act into force in 1977 did nothing to explain the potential significance of section 71, merely noting that 'its effect will clearly differ from area to area'.[24] Perhaps more important, in view of the obligation to eliminate unlawful discrimination (which may be seen as both a highly technical and a potent obligation), is the absence of any attempt to explain the Act's prohibitions on discrimination to the local authorities; the Home Office *Guide to the Race Relations Act 1976* was distributed, on request, to a handful of authorities.

The response of local authorities to the growing recognition of Britain as a multi-ethnic society has been muted to some degree by widespread ignorance of the law, particularly as regards understanding of the nature of unlawful *indirect* racial discrimination.

Indirect discrimination arises from the maintenance of practices which, while they may have no discriminatory intent, have the *effect* of disproportionately excluding members of particular ethnic and racial groups from full access to jobs or other benefits.[25] In another paper Naomi Connelly and I argue that this 'effects test' requirement, inherent in the prohibition of indirect discrimination, requires local authorities to undertake comprehensive and continuing reviews of their operations.[26] Only a few authorities are engaged on such reviews; widespread ignorance of the law, and the failure to place section 71 within the broader context of the anti-discrimination provisions of the Act, together with a general resistance to racial explicitness, have blunted the impact of section 71.

Like central pressure from Whitehall and the CRE, the provisions of the Act have had little direct effect on the practices of local authorities. It is perhaps more surprising that local pressures from black groups have not proved more effective. The disorders of 1981 certainly had the effect of raising the salience of race issues in many authorities. But the overall impression is of the debate over local authorities' responsibilities taking place *in camera*, characteristically in the form of private struggles between groups of officers – sometimes even between officers and members – to establish what can and should be done in this sensitive and potentially explosive area.

The key issue in these struggles has often proved to be the role of the local authority as an employer. Because employment is a corporate issue, it can be raised with potent effect by officials of one department seeking to promote change in another. It is also well suited to the purposes of a group of members attempting to secure a place for race issues on the policy agenda: employment practices are more nearly within the control of elected members than most service-delivery matters. Employment also has a very real significance for minority groups in the community, first, because it is widely felt that services provided by black staff may well be provided with more awareness of the sensitivity to the needs of black consumers; and secondly, because access to local authority employment may be of vital importance in those declining inner city areas where the local authority is often the largest single employer.

The resolution of these local conflicts will determine the outcome of the drive to tackle racial discrimination and disadvantage and to promote equality of opportunity. The three major central contributions to local authority operations – urban programme funding, section 11 grants and the interventions of the

CRE – are likely to have significance only for those authorities where there is some prior recognition of the need to adjust practice and provision to correspond with the realities of a multi-racial society. The pace and direction of policy development will continue to be locally determined; a 'centralist' position emphasizing increased controls by Whitehall departments is virtually untenable. But this is not to say that central departments have no option but to adopt a passive stance. In the following section I hope to show that there are other feasible options in this novel and disputatious area of public policy.

CONTROL, CAPACITY AND CONFLICT

The previous sections of this chapter argued, first, that concern for questions of racial discrimination and disadvantage is highly diffuse, and can be located within no single set of institutions; and secondly, that the ambiguities of national policy are compounded by uncertainty and ambivalence among local decision-makers. To date, central governments have neither given a strong lead on race questions nor achieved much success with their limited initiatives. It is appropriate at this point to approach central–local relations with respect to race in a more analytic fashion, to determine whether a clarification of the nature of the interaction might yield useful insights as to how much-needed change in local policy and practice might be achieved; what follows is, then, both analytic and prescriptive.

The public discussion of central–local relations in the early 1980s is bedevilled by a polarization into the centralist and localist camps. This polarization seeks to deny two obvious truths: first, that all complex societies embody a high degree of pluralism (if only the inherent pluralism of complexity); and secondly, that national governments rightly seek to influence local affairs on issues which they deem to lie within the national interest. To deny that there are such interests over and above the maintenance of a system of 'local democracy' is nonsense; so too is the contrary belief that increasing central controls will necessarily bring the results that governments seek.

In an earlier essay on this topic I set out what I take to be the most basic formulation of the problem of achieving national goals through the agency of autonomous local bodies.[27] I emphasize two dimensions of the central–local relationship: that of *control* and that of *values*; or to generalize the point the *organizational and appreciative contexts of decision*. The organizational context comprises the powers, incentives, controls, routines and channels of influence which characterize the relationship between central departments and local authorities. The appreciative context comprises the field of beliefs, images, values and perceptions within which that relationship as it pertains to a particular set of policy issues, is embedded. We can, for the sake of argument, characterize the organizational context in simple dichotomous terms as one of autonomy or dependence, acknowledging that in real life most situations fall on a continuum between these two poles. We can similarly characterize the appreciative context as one of value consensus or value conflict. Figure 16.1 sets out what I take to be the four possible ideal types of local policy outcome which emerge under these conditions.

Figure 16.1   *The Local Outcomes of Central Policies*

	High	Assimilation	Implementation
Appreciative context (shared values)			
	Low	Variation	Evasion
		Low	High

Organizational context (control)

Where a policy sector is characterized by local autonomy and value conflict, the local outcome of central policy will be one of *variation* in provision. If under these conditions of divergent appreciations central control and regulation is intensified, local energies are likely to be devoted to *evasion*. Where central and local policy-makers share a common appreciation of the issues under conditions of local autonomy, we may speak of the (mutual) *assimilation* of the issues and of a congruence between centrally preferred and locally produced outcomes. *Implementation* can only strictly be said to occur under conditions of (partial or relative) dependence and shared appreciations.

I argued in *National Interests and Local Government* (1983, p. 8) that 'the fate of central policies rest heavily upon the appreciative context of their application; centralization under conditions of value conflict is a recipe for costly exercises in evasion and control'. This model is intended to be of general applicability, and it is not difficult to place a wide range of central policy issues into the respective outcome categories. Each will have its own sector-specific characteristics, and its analysis on these two dimensions helps reveal the type of influence strategy which a central department might adopt.

It remains now to consider where policies to tackle racial disadvantage fall within this matrix. It is convenient to restrict our consideration to the three race-specific aspects of central–local relations: the Home Office section 11 programmes; the 'ethnic element' in the urban programme; and the role of the CRE. The most cursory analysis of the resource dependencies inherent in these channels of central–local interaction reveals that local policy-making on race issues is characterized by virtual autonomy.

In respect of the urban programme the Department of the Environment can only exhort local authorities to consult local black communities, and itself decline to fund unsuitable projects; it can do little to cause local authorities to steer urban programme funds towards black community organizations. With section 11 programmes, the Home Office has had even less discretion: those local authorities which care to apply for funding either qualify under the rules governing the scheme or they do not; the area of central discretion is very small. That the Home Office has now taken steps to ensure that grant recipients *actually* comply with the intentions of the statute and the subsequent circulars at first sight hardly represents a major increase in central control. Moreover, the Home Office may *advise* local authorities to consult ethnic-minority organizations but it cannot require it; such a condition would require statutory amendment. The significance of this initiative is that it combines a closer administrative control over local provision with a persuasive redefinition and reinterpretation of the purpose of the statute from which that power is derived.

Virtually the sole control-related resources of the Commission are its investigative powers and its general duty to ensure compliance with the anti-discrimination provisions of the Act. The former are of necessarily restricted utility; the Commission can only investigate selectively and must select its targets with an eye both to the likelihood of finding discriminatory practices and the possibility of a beneficial 'ripple effect' leading to changes in the practices of other similar bodies.[28]

Turning to the appreciative context of race policies, the two central departments are at least within communicable distance of a sizeable number of local authorities; indeed, their emphasis upon *tackling racial disadvantage* ensures that there can be some common ground with local authorities as need-meeting agencies. Provided, that is, local authorities are willing to recognize the particular circumstances of minority ethnic groups. To do so, however, requires them first to accept a degree of explicitness about race in policy discourse, an explicitness which as Kirp (1979) has shown is uncharacteristic of British culture. Thus proposals to tackle racial disadvantage fall on stony ground in those authorities where a 'colour-blind' approach to race is maintained. The value conflict between even the mildest of governmental initiatives on race and the prevailing climate in those authorities is absolute. Yet many of them receive substantial sums of section 11 money for their teaching staff. The Home Office proposal that they should justify their expenditure in relation to a strategy for tackling racial disadvantage is, then, a new departure; it seeks to move the local definition of the race issue on to new ground and thereby bring about a shift in the *appreciative context* of race policy in favour of a positive and explicit approach.

The CRE concern is a little different. While it contributes to discussion on the revision of the urban programme and the section 11 scheme, its primary objective is to eliminate discriminatory practices. Yet the core of the 1976 Act is the new prohibition on *indirect* discrimination, a concept which is particularly difficult to communicate. Because unlawful indirect discrimination (as defined under the Act) is concerned with disproportionality – specifically, unjustifiable disproportionate exclusion – the Commission seems, to the unsympathetic listener, to be engaged in 'special pleading' on behalf of particular groups in the population. And its case is likely to be least well received in the area where as a matter of distributive justice it perhaps matters most: local authority employment.

The dilemma for the central institutions – the Home Office, the Department of the Environment and the Commission for Racial Equality – is, then: should they attempt to enhance their existing powers, or should they aim for a closer congruence between central and local appreciations of race issues? The implication of the argument so far is that the latter is the most promising option. What we think of as 'implementation failures' are rarely attributable to the lack of legal and administrative powers; and on this analysis more forceful central control would be subverted by widespread evasion.

It is, of course, true that ministers and civil servants often see the choices facing them as lying between further intervention on the one hand, and passivity on the other. The third possibility, of working on the appreciative context, is likely to be unrecognized, or seen as limited to the persuasive (or unpersuasive) medium of speech-making and exhortation. These stark choices overlook the potential for the most creative form of relationship between central and local government, wherein the centre takes as its goal the enhancement of local authorities' *capacity to cope*.[29] But what constitutes that capacity, and what would a capacity-building strategy look like?

In sketching out a reply to this question it is necessary first to reiterate that the dynamic element in policy development is locally situated, and lies within the local authorities' own decision-making processes. *A capacity strategy is one which seeks to shape the conditions of local choice, whereas a control strategy seeks to pre-empt or determine the choice itself.*

'Capacity', moreover, is always capacity with respect to an area of operation, and in the case of race issues it can be identified as the possession of a number of quite specific abilities. These include: a degree of sensitivity to the rapidly changing complex of factors which determine the life-chances of people in the black communities; the ability to identify and assess their needs; having in post specialist staff where these are necessary to the sensitive and equitable delivery of services; having in operation decision-making processes that ensure that the ethnic dimension of new and existing policies is considered; having sufficient control over the recruitment system to eliminate direct and indirect discriminatory practices; being able to present a credible favourable image to minority communities, so ensuring that there is no reluctance to approach the local authority; and, above all, having the capability to review and assess the effects of the local authorities' operations upon distinct minority communities. The centrality of these abilities to the appreciative context of race policy will be apparent; all depend upon the prior recognition of the need to make explicit provision, and devise procedures, for a society which is characterized by the pluralisms of ethnicity, faith, language and culture.

A capacity-building strategy is not, however, one which simply seeks to establish new perceptions in abstraction from concrete issues of local authority performance. Rather it aims to promote development and change of the sort that *embodies* that different perception. The requirement that local authorities consider, review and report on their section 11 provision is an excellent example of an administrative action that draws in its wake a host of awkward questions and thus serves to destabilize long-standing assumptions about colour blindness.

The three keys to such a strategy are organization development, skill development and the dissemination of good practice. The first two are closely related, in that they presuppose a major training effort both to help local authorities to recognize and adapt to the organizational implications of tackling racial discrimination and disadvantage, and to help individual officers in key positions to fulfil their responsibilities in a more effective manner.

The responsibility for promoting organization development in this area surely lies with the Department of the Environment, the Local Government Training Board and the major training institutions at Birmingham and Bristol universities. The constraint under which they labour – that there is little real experience from which to evolve lessons for organization development – is a real one at this time. Identifying just *what*, in concrete terms, a local authority should do, and *how* it should manage its operations to ensure appropriate responses to a turbulent and complex political environment, is actually beyond the present abilities of *any* of the several agencies involved in this field. It is vital, then that current developments be carefully monitored and transferable lessons drawn from them. This is unlikely to occur without commitment – and commensurate funding – from the centre.

The development of personal and inter-personal skills through the training of individuals also depends for its success on complementary programmes of organization development. Yet this responsibility is diffused among a large number of professional bodies and educational institutions most of whom have given scant attention to training for a multi-racial society. 'Race relations training' in the past has accordingly placed too heavy an emphasis on the (sometimes counterproductive) provision of 'cross-cultural' information to individuals and has largely ignored the point that effective training must be transferable into the performance of a role.[30] That transfer can only be achieved if training is situated in the organizational and environmental realities of the everyday world of the practitioner. That is to say, the target of new initiatives should be the organization, its culture and the norms it prescribes for the performance of roles rather than the individual, his or her personality, beliefs and images. A capacity-building strategy must, then, tackle organization and skills development as two interdependent parts of a single initiative; it will require the careful concertation of the activities of several agencies.

The third key to the promotion of local development and

change, the dissemination of good practice and the provision of information and advice, can be of critical importance. A capacity-enhancing strategy would place a major emphasis on facilitating change through this medium. From what has already been said about the Commission for Racial Equality's promotional and enforcement roles it will be apparent that it can play a part, although a limited one, in this respect. A more satisfactory solution would be for the local authority associations, in conjunction with other interested parties, to arrange for the establishment of a special-purpose clearing-house or information exchange covering all aspects of policy and practice as they arise in local authority operations in multi-racial areas. The initial development work for such a national facility has now been funded by the Department of the Environment, the Home Office and the Local Government Training Board, and a new organization, the Local Authorities Race Relations Information Exchange (LARRIE), was expected to commence operations in September 1984.

Such a strategy of promoting local development by discussion, questioning, training support and the provision of advice is very much the package suggested to the DoE in the earlier PSI publication, *Policy and Practice in the Multi-racial City.*[31] The present chapter has sought to provide a rationale for such an approach, and to contrast it with the shift towards greater central control which on my analysis would, if it came about, prove self-defeating. The renegotiation of the ground rules for section 11 provision, the limited encouragement for training initiatives given by the Department of the Environment, the general support given to the local authority associations/Whitehall departments' paper on racial disadvantage and the funding of development work for a race relations clearing-house are all encouraging signs that central departments are moving, in an *ad hoc* and incremental fashion, towards a capacity-building approach. If these initiatives are successful, it will be a development of great significance both for race relations and for a more fruitful partnership between central departments and local authorities.

NOTES: CHAPTER 16

I am grateful to my colleague Naomi Connelly for her comments on a draft of this chapter.
1   See House of Commons Home Affairs Committee, 1982, p. 7.
2   ibid., pp. 5–6; here the government echo the warning delivered by the Home Affairs Committee in their report.

3 See Kirp, 1979.
4 For further discussion of Kirp's concept of racial inexplicitness see Young, 1983a, pp. 297–9.
5 See Young and Connelly, 1981, chs 8–9.
6 See Scarman Report, 1981; House of Commons Home Affairs Committee, 1981b; Young and Connelly, 1981.
7 House of Commons Environment Committee, 1983.
8 House of Commons, *Debates*, 7 July 1982, cols 149–50.
9 For the origins of this initiative see Civil Service Department, 1978.
10 Under section 47 of the Race Relations Act 1976 the Commission may prepare and publish a draft Code of Employment Practice which gives practical guidance in this field and which may, after Parliamentary approval, be taken into account in industrial tribunals.
11 House of Commons Home Affairs Committee, 1981a.
12 Young and Connelly, 1984, ch. 8.
13 See Commission for Racial Equality, 1980; Barker, 1975; Hill and Issacharoff, 1971.
14 House of Commons Home Affairs Committee, 1981b.
15 That the Department of the Environment would initiate discussion with the local authority associations was indicated in the government's reply to the Select Committee report; the joint working party was subsequently established under the chairmanship of Michael Bichard, chief executive of the London Borough of Brent. Their report, *Local Authorities and Racial Disadvantage*, has been circulated to all local authorities and has itself helped to trigger such further developments as a Local Government Training Board initiative in this field.
16 See, for example, Commission for Racial Equality/Royal Town Planning Institute, 1983.
17 Local Government Act 1966, section 11.
18 Home Office, 1967.
18 The Home Affairs Committee report of 1981 observed that 'there is no single aspect of Section 11 payments that has escaped criticism': see House of Commons Home Affairs Committee, 1981b, para. 49. The previous Labour government issued a consultation paper, *Proposals for Replacing Section 11 of the Local Government Act 1966*, in 1978; the subsequent Ethnic Groups (Grants) Bill fell with that government in 1979 and a subsequent Liberal attempt to reintroduce it in the House of Lords was defeated.
20 Home Office, 1983.
21 Such was the essence of the argument put forward in Young and Connelly, 1981, pp. 156–72. The suggestion that this argument represents a 'centralist' viewpoint can hardly be sustained by a reading of those pages; yet this assertion is surprisingly made by Stewart and Whitting, 1982, p. 58.
22 See Young, 1982.
23 See Nixon and Cohen, 1978.
24 Home Office, 1977.
25 Race Relations Act 1976, section 1(i)(b); see also Lustgarten, 1980, pp. 43–64.
26 See Young and Connelly, 1984, pp. 16–17.
27 See Young, 1983a, pp. 6–10.
28 See Sanders, 1983, pp. 79–81.
29 See especially Young, 1983a; Fox, 1983.
30 See Peppard, 1980; Newby, 1982.
31 Young and Connelly, 1981, pp. 164–72; Young, 1982, pp. 54–70.

REFERENCES: CHAPTER 16

Baker, A. (1975), *Strategy and Style in Local Community Relations* (London: Runnymede Trust).

Civil Service Department (1978), *Application of Race Relations Policy in the Civil Service* (London: HMSO).

Commission for Racial Equality (1980), *The Nature and Funding of Local Race Relations Work: Community Relations Councils* (London: CRE).

Commission for Racial Equality/Royal Town Planning Institute (1983), *Planning for a Multi-Racial Britain* (London: CRE).

Fox, Derek (1983), 'Central control and local capacity in the housing field', in K. Young (ed.), *National Interests and Local Government* (London: Heinemann), pp. 82–100.

Hill, M., and Issacharoff, R. (1971), *Community Action and Race Relations* (London: Oxford University Press).

Home Office (1967), *Commonwealth Immigrants*, Circular 15/1967 (London: HMSO).

Home Office (1977), *Race Relations Act 1976*, Circular 103/77 (London: HMSO).

Home Office (1983), *Section 11 of the Local Government Act 1966: Review of Posts*, Circular 94/1983 (London: HMSO).

House of Commons Environment Committee (1983), *The Problems of the Management of Urban Renewal: The Government's Initiative on Merseyside, 1981–2. Third Report, Session 1982–3* (London: HMSO).

House of Commons Home Affairs Committee (1981a), *Commission for Racial Equality. First Report, Session 1981–2* (London: HMSO).

House of Commons Home Affairs Committee (1981b), *Racial Disadvantage. Fifth Report, Session 1980–81* (London: HMSO).

House of Commons Home Affairs Committee (1982), *Racial Disadvantage: The Government Reply to the Fifth Report from the Home Affairs Committee, Session 1980–81*, Cmnd 8476 (London: HMSO).

Kirp, David (1979), *Doing Good by Doing Little: Race and Schooling in Britain* (Berkeley, Calif.: University of California Press).

Lustgarten, L. (1980), *Legal Control of Racial Discrimination* (London: Macmillan).

Newby, Tony (1982), 'Training and race relations: 3, attitude change', *Training Officer*, vol. 18, no. 9 (September), pp. 227–30.

Nixon, J., and Cohen, G. (eds) (1978), 'Race relations: dimensions of equal opportunity', in *Yearbook of Social Policy in Britain, 1977* (London: Routledge & Kegan Paul), pp. 162–79.

Peppard, Nadine (1980), 'Towards effective race relations training', *New Community*, vol. 8, no. 1–2 (Spring–Summer), pp. 99–106.

Sanders, Peter (1983), 'Anti-discrimination law enforcement in Britain', in N. Glazer and K. Young (eds), *Ethnic Pluralism and Public Policy* (London: Heinemann), pp. 75–82.

Scarman Report (1981), *The Brixton Disorders, 10–12 April 1981*, Cmnd 8427 (London: HMSO).

Smith, David J. (1977), *Racial Disadvantage in Britain* (Harmondsworth: Penguin).

Stewart, J. M., and Whitting, G. (1982), *Ethnic Minorities and the Urban Programme* (Bristol: Bristol University School for Advanced Urban Studies).

Young, K. (1982), 'An agenda for Sir George: local authorities and the promotion of racial equality', *Policy Studies*, vol. 3, no. 1 (July), pp. 54–70.

Young, K. (1983a), 'Beyond centralism', in K. Young (ed.), *National Interests and Local Government* (London: Heinemann), pp. 1–10.

Young, K. (1983b), 'Ethnic pluralism and the policy agenda in Britain', in N. Glazer and K. Young (eds), *Ethnic Pluralism and Public Policy* (London: Heinemann), pp. 287–300.

Young, K., and Connelly, Naomi (1981), *Policy and Practice in the Multi-racial City* (London: Policy Studies Institute).

Young, K., and Connelly, Naomi (1984), 'After the Act: policy review for local authorities under the Race Relations Act 1976', *Local Government Studies*, vol. 10, no. 1 (January), pp. 13–25.

Conclusion: Implications for Policy and Institutions

GEORGE JONES

POLICY, INSTITUTIONS AND POLITICS

The cutting edge of the terms 'policy and 'institution' is in danger of being blunted by recent attempts at definition and qualification. 'Policy' can be explained as the products of government, everything it does, or indeed chooses not to do.[1] This description is so broad as to exclude very little, which makes it not a very helpful notion in analysis; far more useful is restricting it to explicit expressions of governmental intention. These statements can be discovered in a variety of places, statutes, White Papers and ministerial announcements for central government, and council and committee resolutions and reports for local government.

However, such public manifestations of governmental aims are, it is frequently pointed out, often very general, vague, ambiguous and indeed contradictory; and frequently leave to the implementors considerable discretion to inject their own objectives and apply their own methods, which may frustrate the achievement of government's plans. Policy-making, in this view, is seen as emanating more from the bottom up than from the top down, and can lead to policy being in practice whatever happens.[2] If policy is to be a useful analytical concept, it needs to be focused more precisely; encompassing so much, it dissolves into vague generality. It should describe the openly stated intentions of government: whether they are in fact attained is another matter.

'Institution' is another term much devalued of late. It is noted that the plethora of institutional reorganizations of the 1960s and 1970s in both central and local government changed behaviour hardly at all. More important than formal structures, it is argued, are informal processes. Studies of decision-making, of what actually occurred, often reveal that those formally endowed with institutional authority, ministers and councillors, mainly ratify at a late stage what had elsewhere been earlier determined by parties, officials, specialist advisers, interest groups, a tangle of administrative organizations, a ruling elite, or some dominant economic class or fraction of it. These entities also ensure that the implementation of policy is shaped more to their wishes than to the intentions of those formally in charge of the institution.

The role of institutions should not be so denigrated. They indicate whom society thinks should be making authoritative and binding collective decisions. They reveal the values and norms of society about the legitimate location of government power. By thus representing what society intends, institutions embody the pressures that shape the behaviour of those who work within them, and of those who seek to influence them. Such actors have to conform to formal arrangements or be liable to condemnation.

Institutions give structure to the processes of governmental decision-making. They group particular clusters of personnel together for particular tasks, and can thus shape how problems are perceived and what range of possible solutions is explored, whether broad or narrow, depending on the expertise and experience of the people involved. They provide a range of incentives and constraints on the behaviour of those who work within them, a set of routines to adopt, a repertoire of instruments to deploy and timescales to obey. They also confer authority on the decisions finally reached.

Institutions and their formal procedures contain channels of influence that determine how open their policy system is to the environment. Some outside individuals and groups will have easier access than others. Some will have more access to a specific stage of the policy process than to others. Different groups will thus have differential influence over policy formulation, resource allocation and policy application. These varying amounts of influence will be shaped by the access afforded by the structures of the institution. Institutions, then, are significant in determining who will be involved in policy-making, how and with what effect.

The allocation of functions between institutions reflects society's priorities on policy, and the distribution of formal authority within institutions reflects prescriptions about who should be in control – and held responsible and accountable. Institutions reveal both what society regards as the main policy sectors requiring attention and those to whom it gives the task of tackling them. They reflect the legitimate distribution of governmental authority, and thus provide clear points to praise or blame. They also provide a yardstick against which to measure performance, for if the operations of institutions do not match what is laid down, in both process and substance, then the deviation should alert society and elicit examination, and corrective action. Institutions, then, provide a basis for structuring the complexity of policy-making. If they are played down or neglected in analysis, description becomes a shapeless mass; whatever happens is accepted as legitimate, or else particular observers intrude their personal visions of what should happen when assessing what in fact takes place. Institutions are the significant templates both for practitioners and those seeking to influence them, and for analysts intent on understanding their activities. Institutional change is, therefore, important. It is worth attempting to design appropriate institutions for specific tasks since they constitute elements of permanence, stability and legitimacy.

Policy is made and applied through institutions that serve political objectives. Legitimate authority is conferred on elected representatives and those accountable to them, ministers and MPs in central government, councillors in local government. The job of officials is to serve these political masters, to advise them and to carry out their wishes, within the law. Policy-making, therefore, is suffused with politics. Councillors and ministers hope for re-election, and thus have to assess the consequences of policy proposals on their chances of re-election. This need to attract public support, and not to alienate actual or potential support, is prominent in the considerations of those who lead the institutions of public policy-making. To these political pressures can be added the politics of the institution itself, and the officials who become committed to it and its perspectives and seek to win support within and without the institution for what is seen as the interests of the institutions, which may also coincide with their own convenience and ambition. These two types of political process, of politicians concerned with support and of officials also concerned with support, constantly interact and explain why policy is so often expressed in terms of such generality, vagueness and ambiguity, together with incompatibilities hard to operationalize.

The political dimension is never absent from policy-making in central and local government, and in the relationships between them. Each is rooted in election, enjoying the legitimacy that flows from a mandate. Each has its own voters with interests to promote and is formed from parties with interests that have to be looked after. The relationship between central and local government, then, is politically highly charged. Tension arises as each strives to advance the interests of its backers, often against each other.

Politics is so pervasive, liable to strike anywhere at any time on any aspect of policy, that power can be said to lie with the specialists in politics, namely, the ministers and councillors. They may listen closely to a variety of internal and outside pressures, but ultimately they take the critical governmental decisions and are held accountable for them; they are responsive to external pressures of various kinds but finally are responsible for the eventual authoritative decisions. Their advisers too, who may make many decisions themselves, act within the constraints of what political masters will find acceptable. Politics, then, is most often dominant over bureaucracy.

In any consideration of the relationships between central and local government it is, therefore, important to focus attention on the policies of institutions, to be aware of their political nature and to hold accountable for their policies those formally endowed with authority over the institutions.

These general reflections shape the recommendations made in this chapter for the reconstruction of the relationships between central and local government, and for the revitalization of local government. Policy is regarded as the explicit expression of governmental intention; and governments should be encouraged to be explicit about their policies, so that accountability can be ensured. Performance needs to be judged against objectives to make democratic control a reality. Both central and local government should have clear policy responsibilities: confusion and ambiguity should be reduced, so that the main responsibility for policy is located *somewhere*. One major policy responsibility of central government is the design of the structure of relationships between central and local government. It should seek to promote local accountability, and so should declare it as an explicit national strategy, creating institutions and procedures to sustain not undermine that objective.

Because they embody values and help shape behaviour, these institutions and procedures should be designed to support local accountability and the wide discretion to be enjoyed by local government. They should be constructed to eliminate central government intrusion in matters that should be the responsibility of local authorities.

Within the institutions the focus of attention must be on the elected representatives. Their role should be acknowledged as prominent in order to ensure that democratic accountability and popular control are strengthened. This concentration on the politicians, then, is also to encourage their involvement in the policy process. As the specialists in the politics of policy they should be at the forefront of determining policy. Institutions and procedures must not allow non-elected participants among officials and civil servants, professionals and trade unions to usurp the responsibilities of the elected members, nor should the latter avoid their accountability by allowing the others to carry the blame. Accountability and responsibility for policy should be clearly placed in the hands of the elected representatives.

Before presenting the recommendations that follow from this approach, it is first necessary to make the case for local government and local responsibility.

THE CASE FOR LOCAL GOVERNMENT

Governmental institutions embody the values and norms of society, thus local government institutionalizes certain values which society finds desirable.[3] First, local government reflects a commitment to pluralism, to a diffusion of power in society, since many local authorities can provide a check and counterweight to central government. A dispersal of governmental authority can avoid an overconcentration of power in the central place, with the concomitant dangers of arbitrary and unresponsive action. If power is focused and placed in one location, bureaucracy and professionalization will tend to prevail in the policy process since elected representatives of the people will find it difficult to control the large organizations. The centre will become overloaded: it will be distracted into essentially local issues and away from national concerns. It will neglect its role of setting the broad, national strategy and objectives by absorption into local matters.

Secondly, local government promotes democracy. It offers more opportunities for the people to participate in government, both as elected representatives and as citizens and group members seeking to influence the policy process of government. Bureaucracy is brought more closely and directly under the control and direction of the people and their representatives in local authorities than in the only alternative forms of government, central departments and nominated or appointed boards. Government, through local government, is made more accessible and visible to the public, more comprehensible and more open to criticism. Its services are more immediately shaped in response to the wishes of the local community since the people's views can be the more effectively injected into the policy process. The decision-makers themselves are closer to the people whose lives they affect and to the environment they shape; policy-makers deal not with generalities and abstractions, but with an immediate reality.

Central decision-makers lack this local awareness and knowledge. Government acquires a more 'human face', reducing the possibility of citizens becoming alienated from the polity: the civic spirit, social cohesion and loyalty to the political system are more encouraged by the network of local attachments inherent in local government than in a remote national structure.

Thirdly, local government promotes effectiveness in service - delivery since it will be provided in ways sensitive to local conditions and circumstances. It can avoid the danger, then, of imposed central provision inappropriate to a specific locality. Central policy is likely to be determined by somewhat general, abstract and rigid formulations of problems and solutions. It will embody national targets and standards and be based on formulas – such as the grant-related expenditure assessment calculated from over sixty factors. Central computers are no substitute in the assessment of local needs for the amassed wisdom of that far more effective 'computer', the collective brain of many local authorities. Further, the one central solution – so easily perpetrated – is likely to go wrong somewhere, and yet is not able to be quickly adapted. With local government, the risk of perpetuating error is less likely since the indicators of failure may be picked up and policy speedily changed. The immediate challenge makes its impact more directly on government.

Through many local authorities society may experiment in search of fresh solutions to old and new problems. Society can learn from a diversity of attempts at different patterns of provision. Such potential for innovation and creativity is more likely to produce the best solutions than any quest by the centre for the single national standard and answer.

Local government is able to explore community problems with a perspective that encompasses the community, whereas the centre tackles social problems through a functional perspective that thinks in terms of single services. It lacks the corporate, community vision of local government and cannot devise that mix of services most appropriate to local needs and priorities. Centralization reduces the capacity of society to learn how to handle social problems since many possible answers, or combinations of solutions, are sifted out as they mount the hierarchy of national bureaucratic departments and boards.

Local government facilitates the solution of social problems by disaggregating them such that they become more manageable. The centre can become too congested with factors and variables to cope, overwhelmed by the pressures of a variety of groups into indecision and paralysis. Local policy-making involves more people from different places, with different experience, association, background and political persuasion, than can be accommodated by the central policy process. Through local government the potential of the people can be tapped more effectively.

Fourthly, local government promotes the wiser use of resources. The centre, organized functionally, sees only one aspect of policy, but local government can take a local, community-wide view. It can tailor individual services to local needs, desires and conditions, determine priorities between them and relate this mixture to resources available. It is able to match services more closely to requirements than does the remote centre, and thus achieve a better use of resources, avoiding the waste of imposed national standards irrelevant to specific localities. True economy demands the fitting of local needs to local resources; local government, more aware of the impact of services and their costs locally, is more likely than central government to promote this true economy.

Local government is also to be valued for offering a way to solve two major problems facing government today. First, as central government intervenes more in society it has become more dependent on others for the attainment of its objectives, both to accept the interventions and to carry them out. Frictions and tensions build up in the complex network of interdependencies. Mutual frustrations fester, as no one can achieve their goal. The reaction by the centre is usually to seek further centralization, in the hope that the quest for control will finally deliver to it the capacity to impose its solutions. But the consequent overload and the further intensification of hostile responses leads more often to policy failure. The solution to this problem is a radical change of strategy – to decentralize, so that policy problems are more manageable and the web of interdependencies is diminished.

Secondly, the growth of government has led to an increase in taxation to finance its interventions. With centralization, people cannot see so easily the connection between the taxes they pay and the services they receive. The gap between benefits and taxation widens. The result is that people turn against taxation and government, and the notion of public provision. The concept of collective services to promote a view of a good community is eroded as citizens increasingly focus on their private concerns. What is immediate, tangible and offers a direct reward is valued: the willingness-to-pay principle is the only criterion by which to judge anything. With local government, the citizen can see more clearly the linkage between taxes paid and services received, both to him personally and to the local community around him. He is, therefore, more likely to support collective community provision and eschew self-seeking individualism. A community spirit is more likely to be encouraged by local rather than central government. This defence of the locality goes against the twin trends of current government policy towards local government. On the one hand, it has embarked on strengthening 'hierarchy'. It is clearly increasing central controls over local government. The powers of ministers in many fields – financial and in specific policies – have expanded at the expense of local government discretion. Central responsibility is being substituted for local responsibility. On the other hand, it is seeking to strengthen 'markets'. It encourages privatization and seeks to give consumers, as individuals, groups and firms, more influence over local government's decisions – as in education, housing and the social services, and in direct labour operations such as housebuilding and maintenance, street-cleaning and refuse collection. Local authorities have to provide considerable information on their activities, so that performance and value for money can be assessed by the citizens. Defenders of the government's approach see no inconsistency in promoting 'hierarchy' and 'markets'. Indeed they would argue that hierarchical control is sought in order to force local authorities to be more open to market pressures.[4] Once it is achieved, control might be relaxed. Real decentralization to the individual consumer can be achieved only by first centralizing to destroy the power of local government.

However, a central government genuinely intent on promoting local accountability to citizens would seek first to improve the electoral process, and to devise a local financial system that ensured the bulk of local finances came from local taxpayers and voters, not from a central grant or taxes that do not bear directly on local voters. A government that genuinely believed in local accountability would also allow the elected representatives of the community to decide on what they thought was an appropriate balance for their community between public and private provision. Centralization, whether to enhance 'hierarchy' or 'markets', is still centralization, eroding local democratic accountability.

The local authority feels squeezed: ground between the centre pressing from above and some 'consumers' from below. Local elected members are trapped by these pressures, and by an additional, formidable pressure coming from their own work-forces in the unions and professions. The space for action to promote their view of what is good for the local community is restricted. Indeed, they feel that they have no scope to meet the wishes of anyone locally since the centre is setting their levels of expenditure and taxation. They are becoming agents of the centre. The shift to 'markets' is to be condemned as a centralist imposition. It may be right in some services in some areas, but the best people to make the choice are those in the localities. The centre should set the framework in which local authorities can make an informed choice in full appreciation of the costs involved. The danger of uniformly forcing 'markets' everywhere is that it weakens the concept of local government as a set of elected representatives seeking to promote the welfare of the community and accountable for a wide range of community services to local voters who provide the bulk of the finance for those services.

Local democratic self-government is undermined by centralization both into hierarchy and into markets. Emphasis on the centre makes it the target for those seeking particular expenditure and taxation decisions in particular areas. Local accountability is replaced by central accountability. The emphasis on 'markets' makes dominant the 'willingness-to-pay' principle, eradicating a sense of community standards – minimum, common, or at the highest possible levels. Community government is replaced by fragmented consumerism, in which the richest consumers and groups achieve the services they want, consigning the rest to charity or the barest of public provision. The whole community is likely to be better served by community government than by an imposed hierarchy and imposed markets.

LESSONS FOR THE FUTURE

Having set out the case for local government, this chapter now draws lessons for policy, institutions and procedures, based on the desirability of having a clear allocation of policy responsibilities, institutions and procedures that promote local accountability and a concentration on the involvement of elected representatives in the policy process. It also seeks to remedy the failings of present arrangements as revealed by the history of central–local relations since the 1970s,[5] and described in the Introduction.

The first, and major lesson from this sorry saga is the one emphasized in the Layfield Report (1976) of the need to clarify responsibility. The main responsibility for local government expenditure and taxation decisions must be located more clearly either with central or with local government. The present confusions and ambiguities constitute a system of joint irresponsibility. 'Partnership' is merely rhetoric for a set of arrangements enabling each side to pass the buck to the other. The centre can increase its power while claiming that it is encouraging local accountability, and local authorities can blame any failures or shortcomings on the centre while grabbing credit for any success. The choice has to be made, between more explicit central and local responsibility.

If the latter is the desired objective, then it is important for the centre to signify its commitment to a decentralized system of government. It should be prepared to resist the pressures to intervene in local responsibilities, and concentrate its attention on its own responsibilities. Therefore, it must limit the scope of its surveys and plans for public expenditure to its own expenditure, and exclude local government expenditure. It must not presume to set obligatory targets for the expenditures of individual local authorities, or of local government in general, as long as the expenditure is financed from local taxation. It should control borrowing by local government and its own grant. Grant should not be used to penalize or reward particular local authorities, or to subsidize particular classes of local taxpayers. Nor should it embody any central government assessment of what local authorities need to spend since to attempt to do so would assume that the centre is able to understand the varied conditions and needs of local areas. The rationale for local government is that local authorities are the best judges of what their local areas need. Grant should be limited to the objective task of equalizing the taxable capacity, the resources, of local areas at whatever level the government thinks desirable. In this way grant will no longer be a device used by the centre to undermine local government.

The centre should also indicate its support for the value of local diversity in governmental decision-making by reducing the dependence of local government on grants. A high grant level sets up pressures that encourage the centre to intervene in how grant is spent, and it helps undermine local accountability since local expenditure decisions become more influenced by the grant from the centre than by a local appreciation of local needs, resources and priorities. To replace the lost grant a new local tax is required. The only one that promotes local accountability by bearing directly and perceptibly on local voters is a local income tax. A central government genuinely committed to sustain local democracy must introduce this new source of revenue for local government. Domestic rates should remain a local government tax since they too bear directly on some, but not all, voters. They require not abolition, but supplementation by local income tax, and reform to make them more understandable and fairer – by a move from rental to capital valuation. Non-domestic rates should not be a local government tax because they weaken local accountability. These reforms would ensure that most local expenditure would be financed by local taxation levied on local voters, so that if local authorities wanted to spend more, they would have to levy more taxation; if they wanted to have less taxation, they would have to cut expenditure; and in this way their decisions to spend would be closely linked to their decisions on taxing, promoting local responsibility and accountability, while the centre would focus on its task of managing the national economy and performing its national roles.

One major national role is to be responsible for the overall system of government. The reforms so far suggested would reflect central support for pluralistic decentralization. Further, they should reinforce local accountability – ensuring that the local electoral system enables the views of local communities to be fairly represented in the local councils, and that voters and councillors are provided with full information about their authority's performance.

The most difficult problem to be faced is resisting the pressures to intervene in local responsibility to protect or promote a specific interest or cause. Such pressures will emanate from a variety of groups, both central and local, from professional bodies, parties and MPs, anxious citizens and indeed from councillors and officials from the local authorities themselves, seeking central support for particular causes. One way to bolster a central commitment to local accountability, and to buttress its intention not to intervene in local responsibilities, would be the institution of a charter of local government and a Royal Commission on central and local government relations. The former, modelled on the recent European Charter for Local Self-Government, might contain a set of principles that would govern central–local relations and a series of authorizations and prohibitions, providing a yardstick against which to measure both legislative proposals and the actions of central and local government. The responsibility for ensuring that the charter's provisions were adhered to, and for reporting any breaches, should be laid upon a standing Royal Commission on central and local government relations. Its reports, and the provision of the charter, would not override any statute, but their existence would ensure that proposed legislation or administrative action that had implications for the centre–local relationship were examined and explicitly commented on. Parliament and the public would be made more aware of the consequences of such proposals. Central government would, moreover, know that intrusion into the responsibilities of local government, or any erosion of local accountability, would be reported on, and it would have to provide a justification for its measures. Such a charter would not in any way weaken parliamentary sovereignty. What is required is a simple Act providing the charter with the force of law, unless Parliament were expressly to state otherwise by further statute. Thus any breach of the charter's provisions would require the explicit approval of Parliament – hardly likely to be given without the government at the least having to run the gauntlet of rebuke from Parliament and the country generally.

The standing Royal Commission might eventually evolve into a Commission for Local Government, overseeing a range of functions that impinge on central–local relations. It might, then, become the body responsible for the audit of local government, both of the legality of its expenditure and its cost effectiveness, or of the value for money, replacing the Audit Commission; it might become the body to which the Commission for Local Administration, the local ombudsmen, report, thus replacing the representative body. In addition, it might assume the responsibility for training, replacing the Local Government Training Board, and for research – which at present nobody sponsors. It might come to act as the secretariat for a consultative council on local government finance, providing authoritative statistics on local government. Finally, it might have a remit for disseminating good practice and bright ideas among local authorities. The objective of all these reforms would be improved policy formulation, and implementation and communication throughout local government; and avoiding a take-over by central departments, the establishment of a body answerable only to the local authority associations seen as biased and at times ineffective because of internal divisions, or retaining the present fragmented set of separate bodies overlapping, duplicating and at times omitting some crucial tasks. An independent standing Royal Commission, composed of those with experience of different areas of the public service and of the private sector, together with experts at various levels, would provide an authoritative forum able to demolish myths and untruths about local government and to defend it against attack, while supporting it with a range of services. However, before undertaking these tasks it must be firmly established, to monitor the relationships between central and local government and to ensure that the provisions of the charter are adhered to.

A DEFINITION OF RESPONSIBILITIES

The assumption of the recommendations in this chapter is that the government reverse the centralization of power in its own hands, and promotes decentralization to the local authorities who would enjoy wide autonomy and be accountable to their local electorates. This enhanced role for local government is advocated both as a means of promoting local democracy and accepting the primacy of political control over the bureaucracy and of the need to provide public services responsive to local wishes as a means of solving society's problems. Uniform standards from a single central government source are unlikely to be the answer to the apparently intractable social and environmental problems of the future. A diversity of approaches, through the experiments of innovative local authorities, is more likely to ameliorate the ills of society than nationally imposed instructions.

Opposition to this approach will come from those who believe that the centre possesses a greater democratic legitimacy and superior knowledge and expertise than local government. Those who hold such a view will campaign for an explicit national government responsibility, for local government to be clearly an agent of central government.

Opposition will also come from those who call for partnership between central and local government,[6] who regard central–local government relationships as a complex web of interdependencies. Each needs the other to help achieve its objectives. Any attempt to separate their respective responsibilities into distinct packages is doomed to failure by the ties of mutual dependence in modern society, and by the advantages each enjoys when responsibilities are blurred, in manoeuvring, bargaining, escaping blame and claiming the credit. A sophisticated version of this partnership model would assert that the role of the centre is to set strategic national objectives and leave administering these national policies to local government discretion. The centre should not seek to manage and deliver local services itself, but enhance the capacity of local authorities for innovatory provision. Central and local government should seek to understand each other, through better communication, perhaps joint training of staff, frequent staff transfers and secondments, and through concertative and corporative bodies on which central and local government can work together as partners in handling problems and devising policies.

Such a model has an appeal, especially when set against present confrontational relationships but it suffers from some serious defects. First, the establishment of forums in which both central and local government can come together may have value in helping each better to understand the other better and in enabling one to put its views to the other, that is, as chambers of discussion and debate; but they are useless if not dangerous as centres for governmental decision. Such collective bodies, entailing the sharing of responsibility, tend to operate as ways of evading responsibility, thus perpetuating the present damaging ambiguity. Or else they become a means through which the junior partner puts in its bid for resources from the senior, while the latter uses the body as a platform to announce its unilateral decisions. A significant disadvantage of such forums or joint bodies is that those who constitute them regard their prime loyalty as being to the institution they represent. As if ambassadors, they seek to promote the interests of those they speak for – the constituent entities with their own separate perspectives and views of what should be done. Confrontation will become a feature of the forum, policy a compromise or paralysed. The evolution of the Consultative Council on Local Government Finance, of the inner city partnerships and of some other of the policy-planning systems illustrates the drawbacks of joint bodies in taking governmental decisions. Responsibility should be clearly pinned somewhere, in either central or local government.

The second defect of this partnership model is that it devalues the role of local government as the implementor of a centrally set strategy. It in effect assumes that strategy and implementation can and should be separately ascribed to distinctive institutions. It reproduces the old division of central government policy and local government administration, allowing local authorities scope to make discretionary responses to the centre's policy – interpreting, adapting, elaborating, assimilating, inverting, or ignoring, but not themselves making the policy. This view of the role of local government is too narrow – regarding it as virtually decentralized administration albeit enjoying some discretion or interpretative space. However, local authorities are endowed by Parliament with considerable power to make policy. They have long been able to make their own decisions on expenditure, and have been given taxation powers to finance that expenditure. Parliament has also established that the channels of accountability for these policy, expenditure and taxation decisions should run not to ministers, nor to Parliament and its committees, but to the local electorate. Apart from the House of Commons, local authorities are the only elected bodies in this country; their policy-making roles arise from the legitimacy flowing from elections and local taxes that finance their expenditure. They have a positive, initiating part to play in policy-making and are not just reactive interpreters of central impulses. The role of central government is to promote the national interest. Given the problems that the country faces now and in the future, it is vitally in the national interest for central government to encourage the maximum possible decentralization to local authorities. Such a commitment to the virtues of pluralistic government will enable society as a whole to learn from a diversity of attempts to tackle social and environmental problems. It is an important national interest to create and sustain a viable and stable framework in which local authorities can operate. They should be granted autonomy to experiment, a legal competence to provide services to their communities, as long as the powers are not expressly forbidden them by statute, and a wide multi-functional competence, so that they can device the most appropriate balance of provision to meet the needs of their local communities.

It is in the national interest that local accountability should flourish: the centre should ensure that no obstacles impede the representativeness of councils and that local decision-makers, officials, councillors and voters are aware of the real costs of the expenditure they choose to incur. It is in the national interest too for central government to support local government, to facilitate its activities, to enhance its capacity to handle problems and to stimulate its innovations. And further, it is in the national interest for the centre to consult widely with local government so as to increase its understanding, and from time to time to set in statute clear national goals and strategies – but not to seek to manage, control, or direct the provision of local services. It can seek to influence local government, exposing problems, setting up possible solutions, provoking a national debate and shaping a climate of opinion; but it is not in the national interest for central government to take over what should be local government's responsibilities. If it withdraws from them to focus on its national responsibilities, the centre may well find that it will be more effective. Less overburdened and distracted, less frustrated by entanglements with local government issues and less intent on control over local affairs, it may find that it has more control over national affairs.

NOTES: CONCLUSION

1   See Burch and Wood, 1982, p. 12.
2   See recent work from the School for Advanced Urban Studies, for example, Barrett and Fudge, 1981.

3   See Jones and Stewart, 1983, especially ch. 1.
4   See Bulpitt, 1982, pp. 139–76, and 1983, pp. 200–33.
5   Jones and Stewart, 1983, ch. 15.
6   A good account of such a view appears in Young, 1983, ch. 1.

REFERENCES: CONCLUSION

Barrett, S., and Fudge, C. (1981), *Policy and Action* (London: Methuen).

Bulpitt, Jim (1982), 'Conservatism, unionism and the problem of territorial management', in Peter Madgwick and Richard Rose (eds), *The Territorial Dimension in United Kingdom Politics* (London: Macmillan).

Bulpitt, Jim (1983), *Territory and Power in the United Kingdom* (Manchester: Manchester University Press).

Burch, M., and Wood, B. (1982), *Public Policy in Britain* (Oxford: Martin Robertson).

Jones, George, and Stewart, John (1983), *The Case for Local Government* (London: Allen & Unwin).

Layfield Report (1976), *Local Government Finance: Report of the Committee of Inquiry*, Cmnd 6453 (London: HMSO).

Young, K. (1983), 'Introduction: beyond centralism', in K. Young (ed.), *National Interests and Local Government* (London: Heinemann).

Index

Index